Disney FAVORITES

Simple Sheet Music + Audio Play-Along

To access audio visit:
www.halleonard.com/mylibrary

Enter Code
1541-2752-1196-3174

ISBN 978-1-5400-3594-3

Visit Hal Leonard Online at
www.halleonard.com

Contact us:
Hal Leonard
7777 West Bluemound Road
Milwaukee, WI 53213
Email: info@halleonard.com

In Europe, contact:
Hal Leonard Europe Limited
42 Wigmore Street
Marylebone, London, W1U 2RN
Email: info@halleonardeurope.com

In Australia, contact:
Hal Leonard Australia Pty. Ltd.
4 Lentara Court
Cheltenham, Victoria, 3192 Australia
Email: info@halleonard.com.au

CONTENTS

Welcome to the ***INSTANT Piano Songs*** series!

This unique, flexible collection allows you to play with either one hand or two. Three playing options are available—all of which sound great with the online backing tracks:

1. **Play only the melody with your right hand.**
2. **Add basic chords in your left hand, which are notated for you.**
3. **Use suggested rhythm patterns for the left-hand chords.**

Letter names appear inside the notes in both hands to assist you, and there are no key signatures to worry about. If a **sharp** ♯ or **flat** ♭ is needed, it is shown beside the note each time, even within the same measure.

If two notes are connected by a **tie** ‿, hold the first note for the combined number of beats. (The second note does not show a letter name since it is not re-struck.)

Sometimes the melody needs to be played an octave higher to avoid overlapping with the left-hand chords. (If your starting note is C, the next C to the right is one octave higher.) If you are using only your right hand, however, you can disregard this instruction in the music.

The backing tracks are designed to enhance the piano arrangements, regardless of how you choose to play them. Each track includes two measures of count-off clicks at the beginning. If the recording is too fast or too slow, use the online ***PLAYBACK+*** player to adjust it to a more comfortable tempo (speed).

Optional left-hand rhythm patterns are provided for when you are ready to move beyond the basic chords. The patterns are based on the three notes of the basic chords and appear as small, gray notes in the first line of each song. Feel free to use the suggested pattern throughout the song, or create your own. Sample rhythm patterns are shown below. (Of course, you can always play just the basic chords if you wish!)

Have fun! Whether you play with one hand or two, you'll sound great!

Sample Rhythm Patterns

4/4 Meter

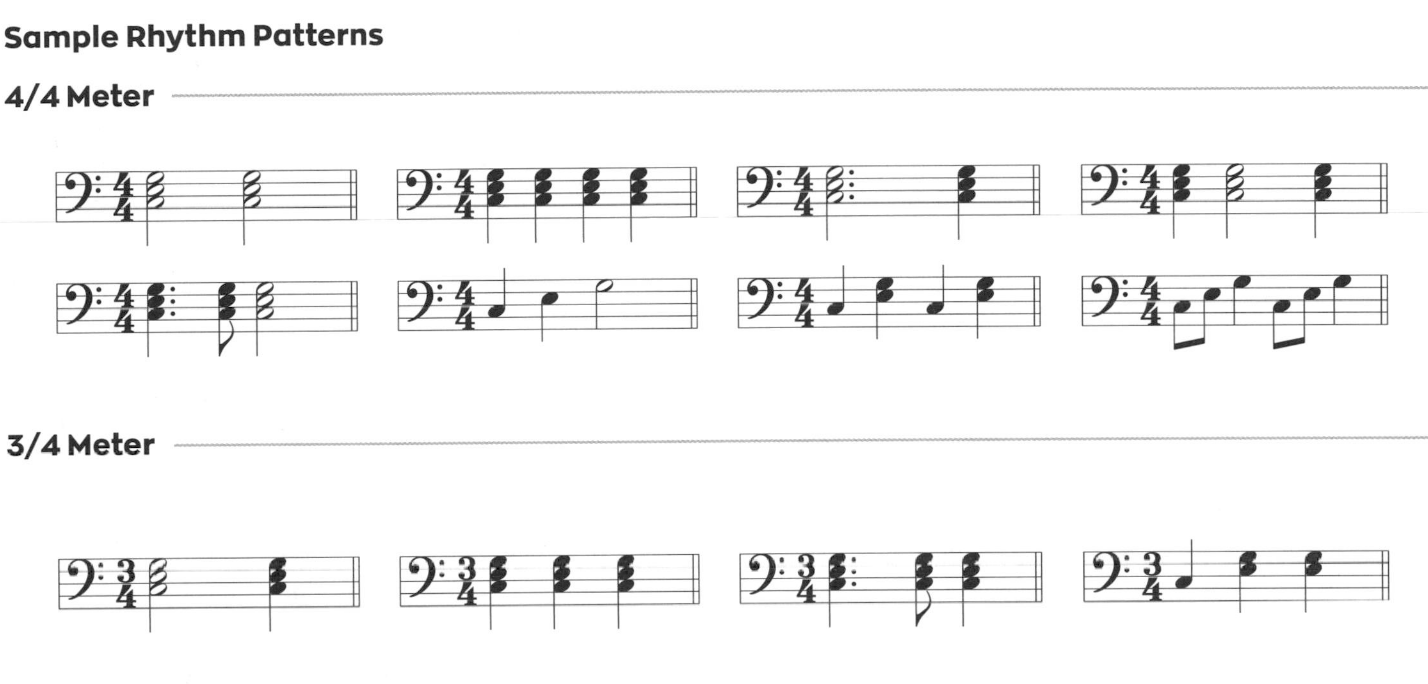

3/4 Meter

6/8 Meter

Also Available

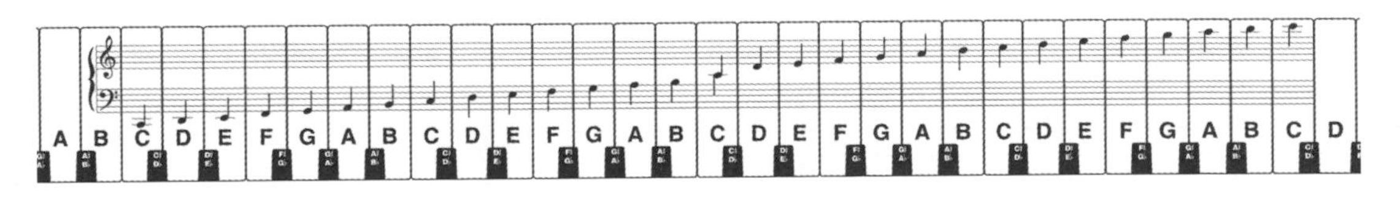

Hal Leonard Student Keyboard Guide HL00296039

Key Stickers HL00100016

The Ballad of Davy Crockett

from DAVY CROCKETT

Words by Tom Blackburn
Music by George Bruns

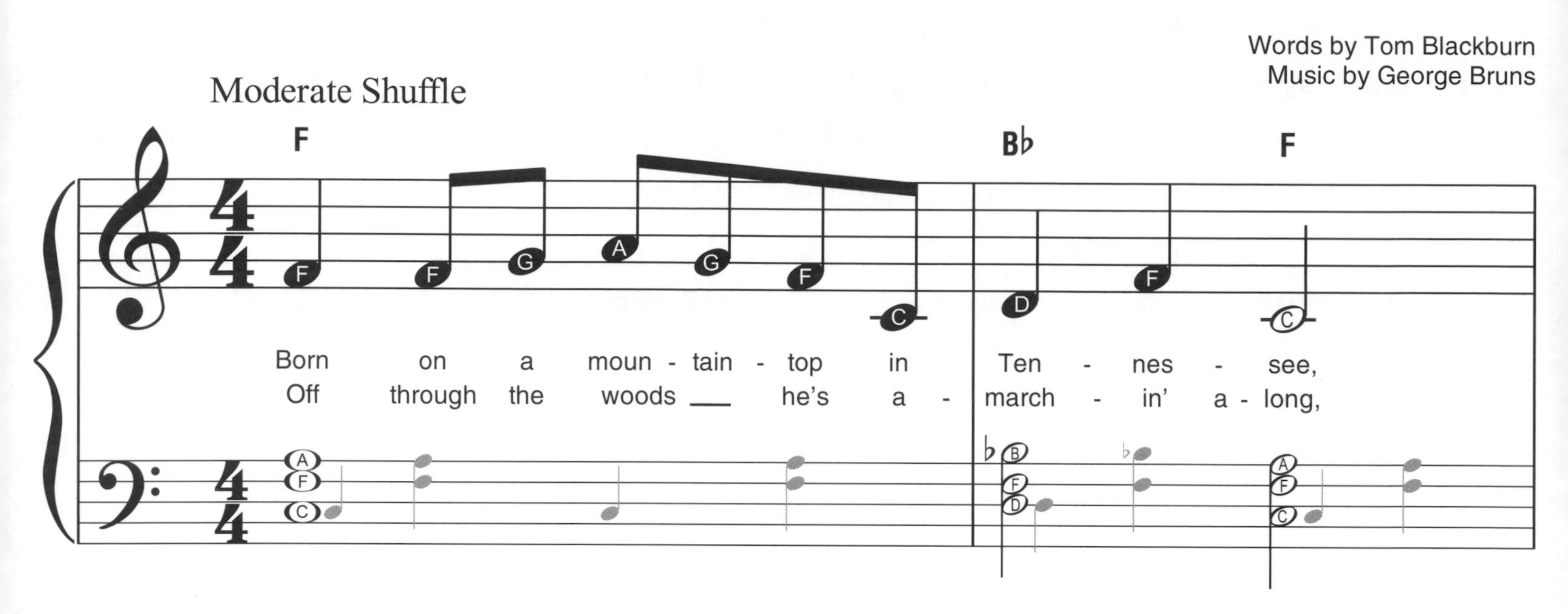

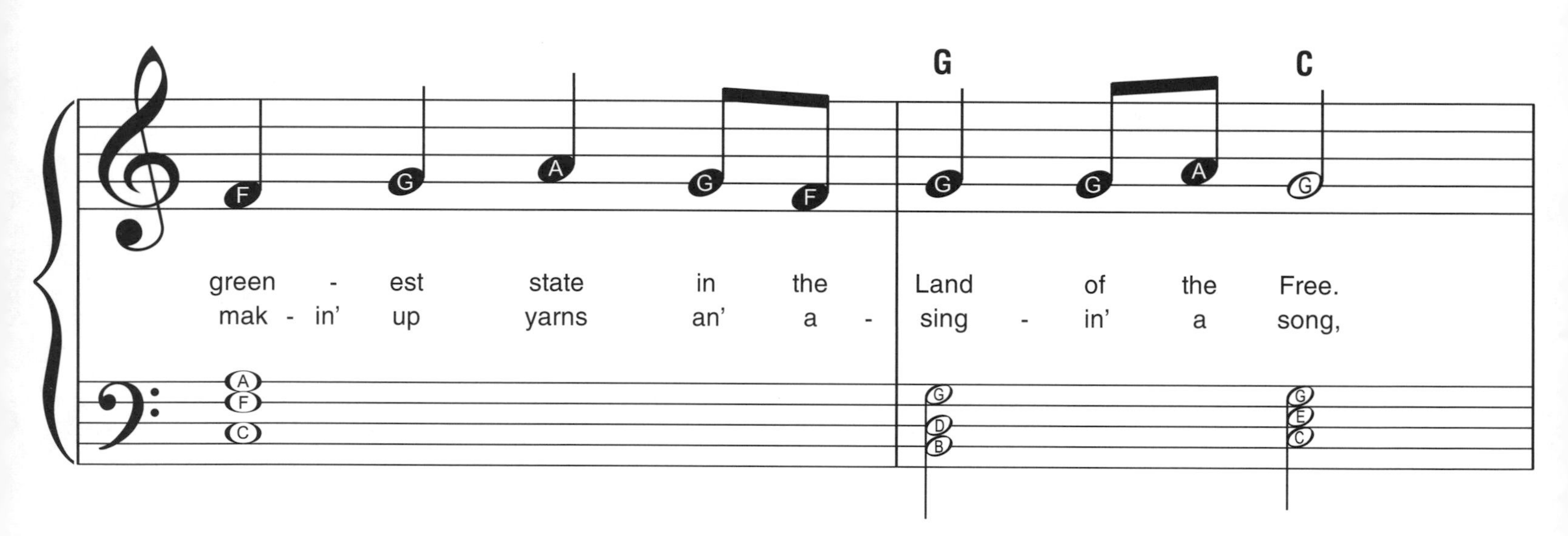

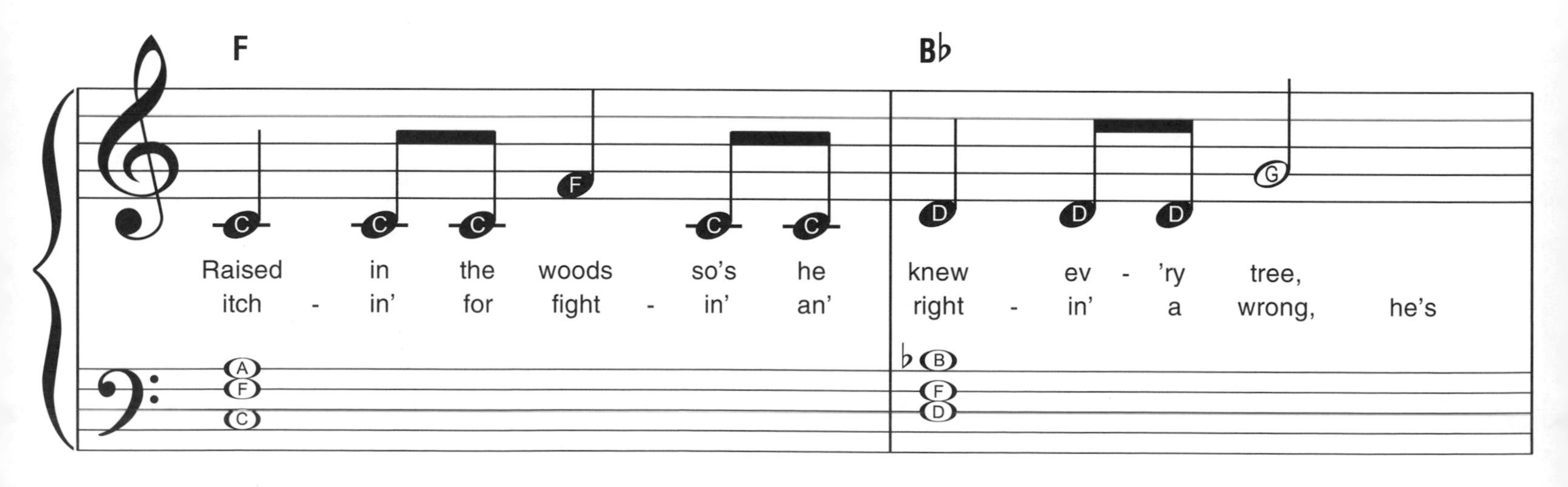

C
F
E
E
E
E
D
C
C
D
E
F
kilt him a b'ar when he was on - ly three.
ring - y as a b'ar an' twict as strong.
G
E
C
G
E
C
A
F
C

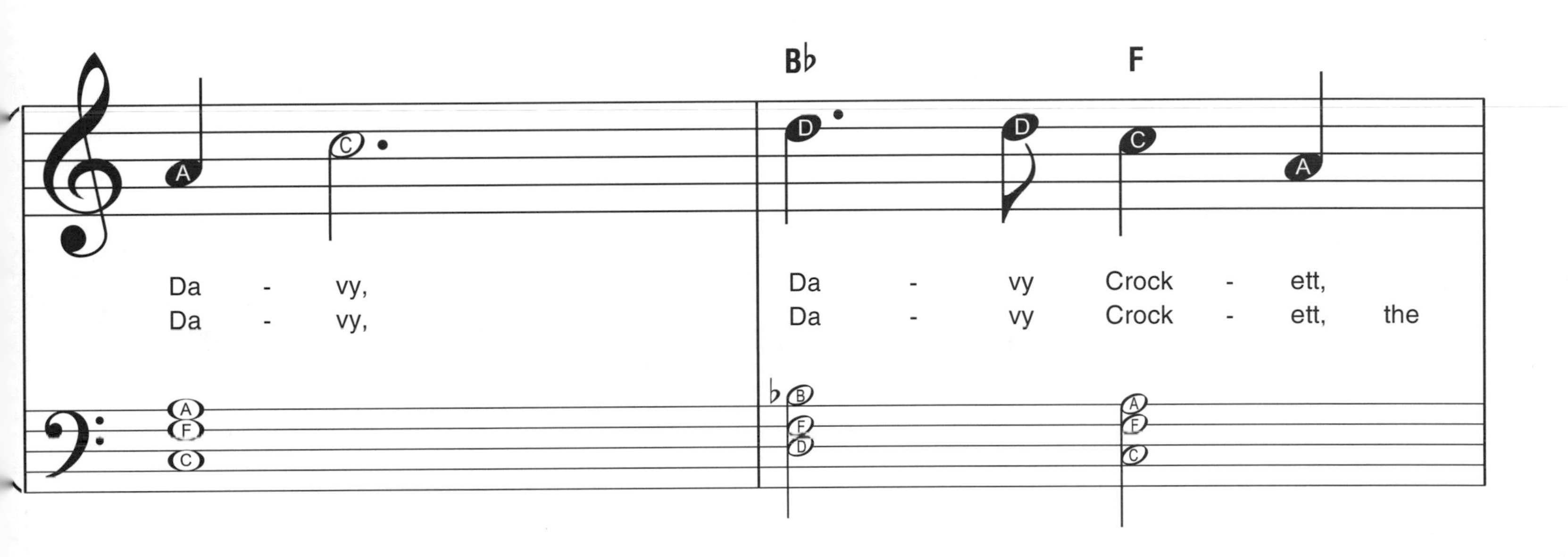
B♭
F
A
C
D
D
C
A
Da - vy, Da - vy Crock - ett,
Da - vy, Da - vy Crock - ett, the
A
F
C
B
F
D
A
F
C

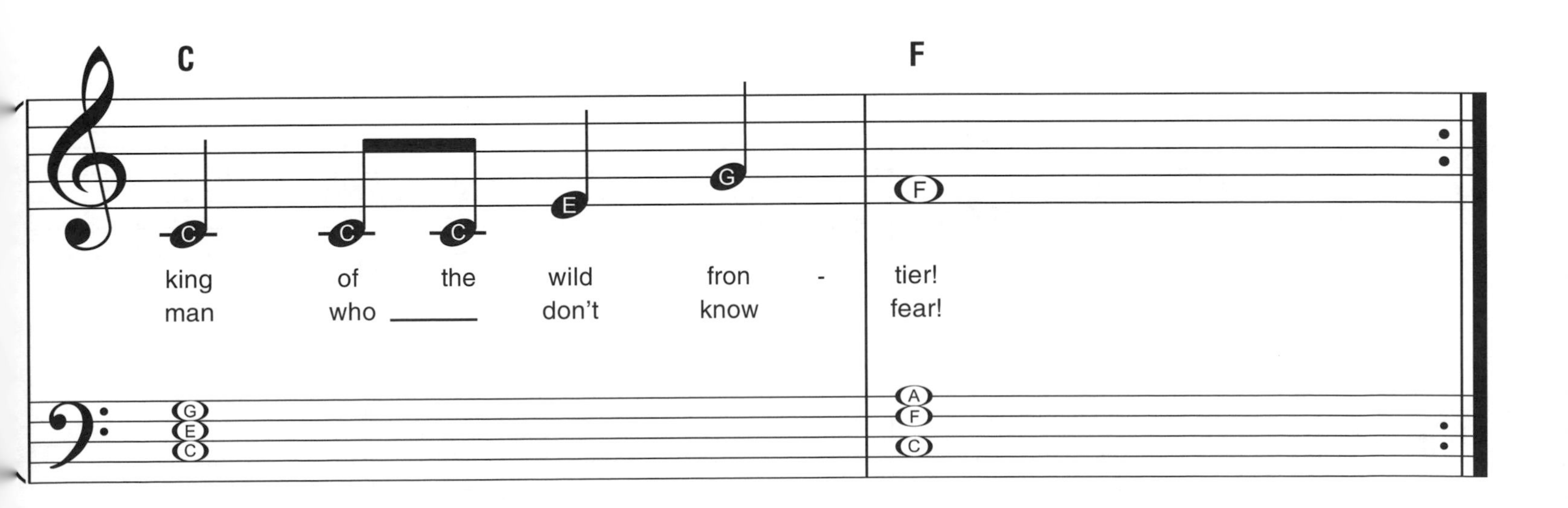
C
F
C
C
C
E
G
F
king of the wild fron - tier!
man who don't know fear!
G
E
C
A
F
C

The Bare Necessities
from THE JUNGLE BOOK

Words and Music by
Terry Gilkyson

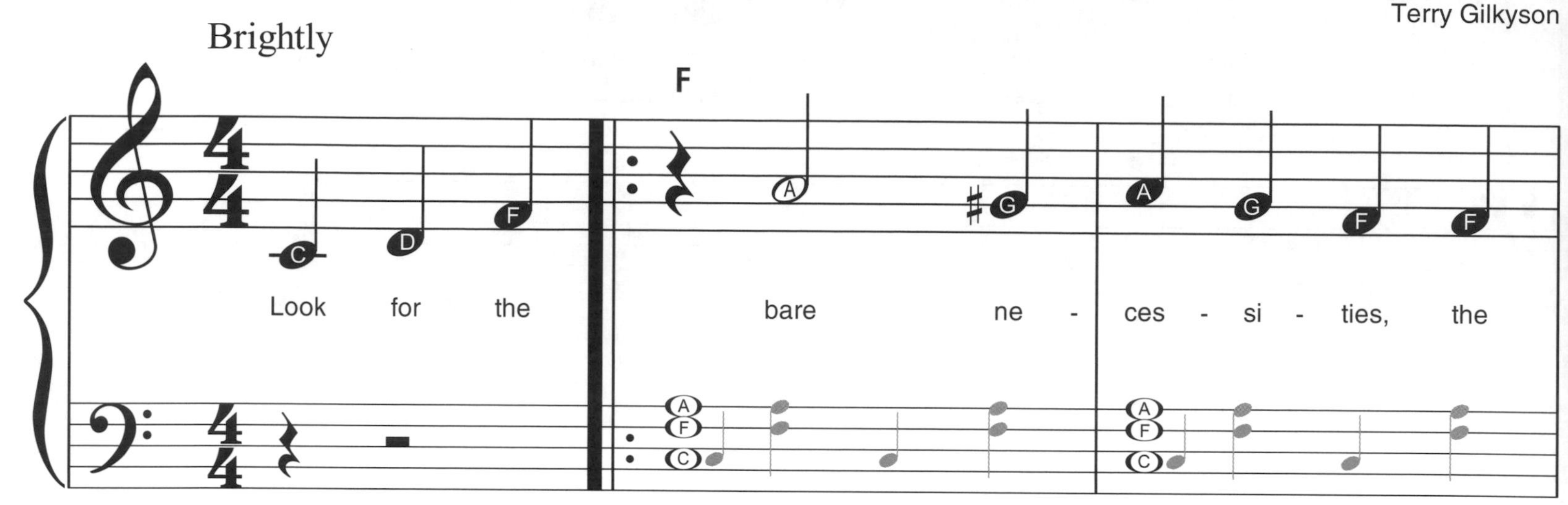

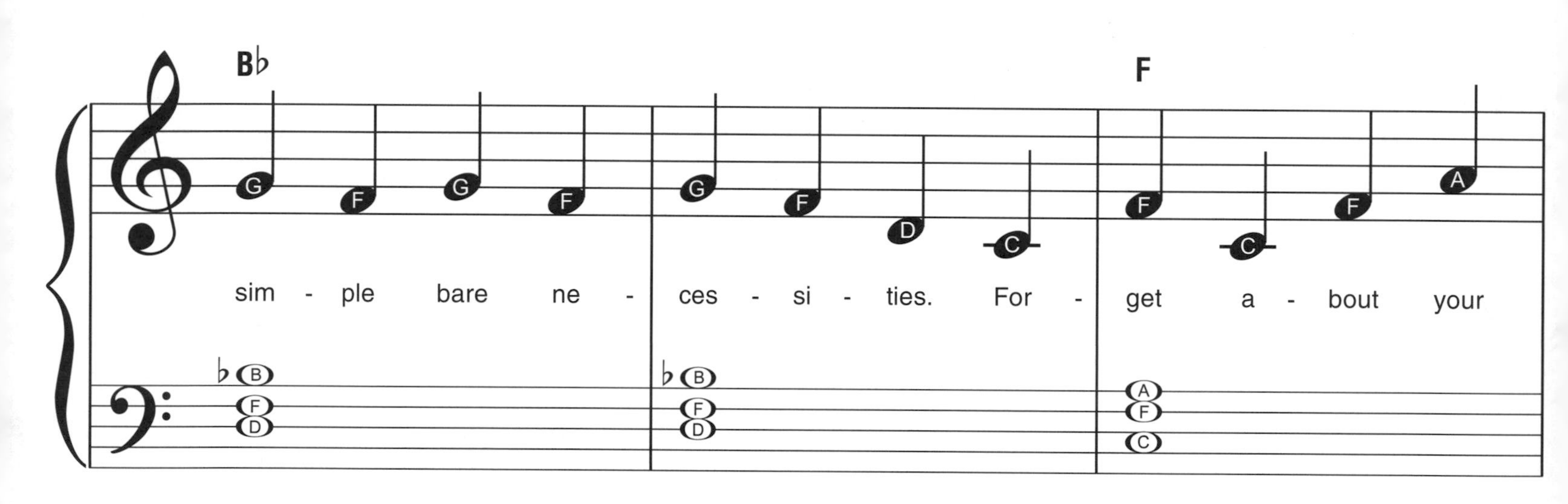

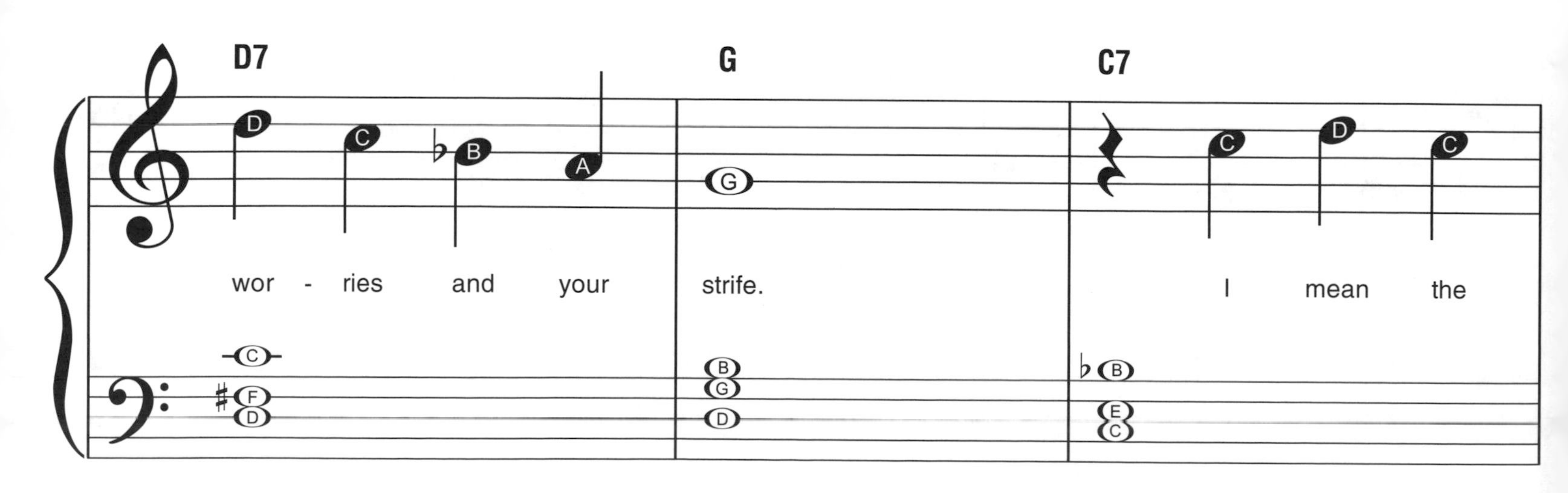

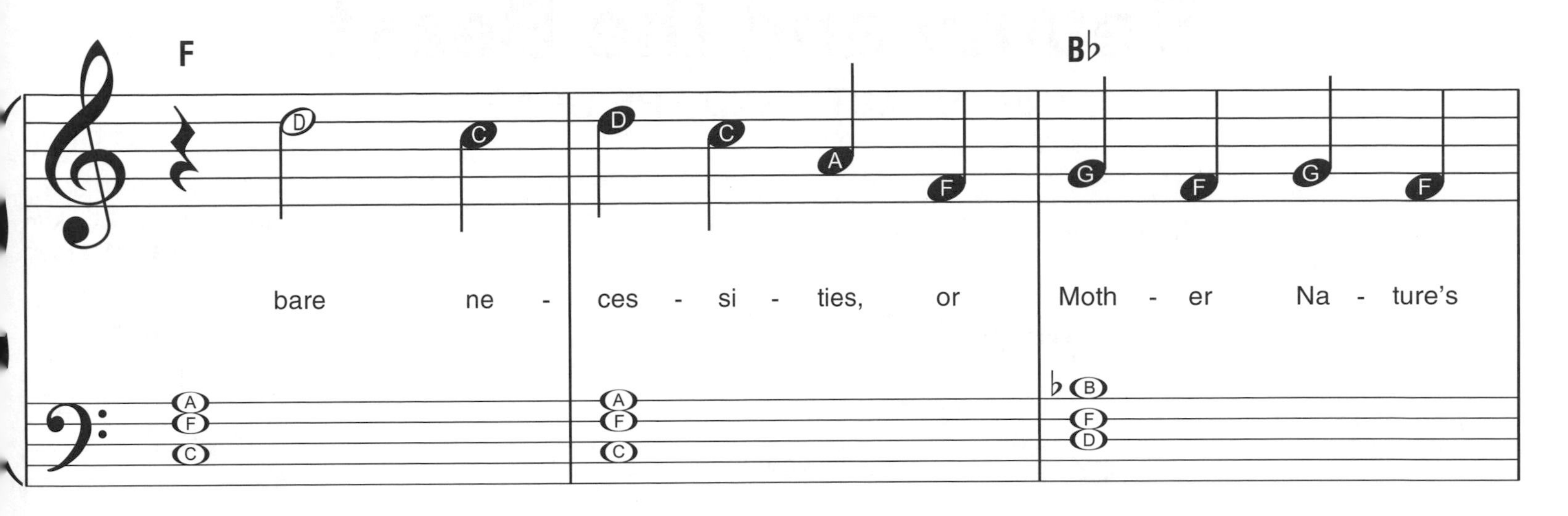
F
B♭
bare ne - ces - si - ties, or Moth - er Na - ture's

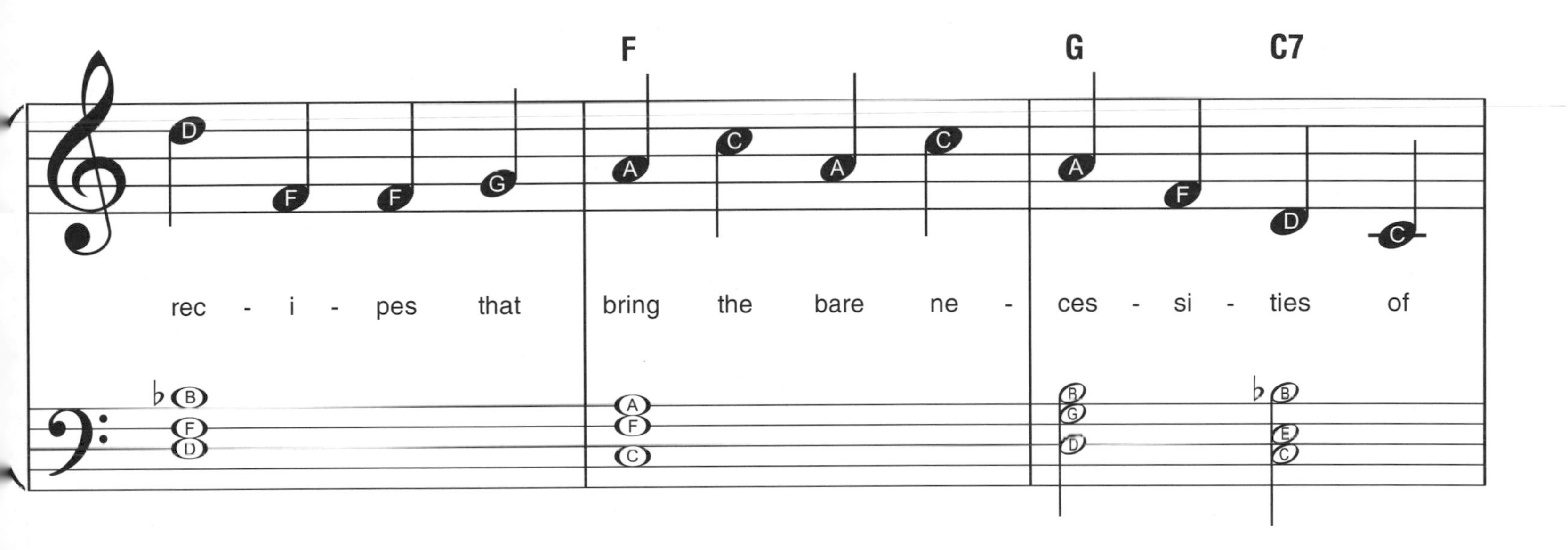
F
G
C7
rec - i - pes that bring the bare ne - ces - si - ties of

1.
F
2.
F
life. Look for the life.

Beauty and the Beast

from BEAUTY AND THE BEAST

Music by Alan Menken
Lyrics by Howard Ashman

Moderately slow

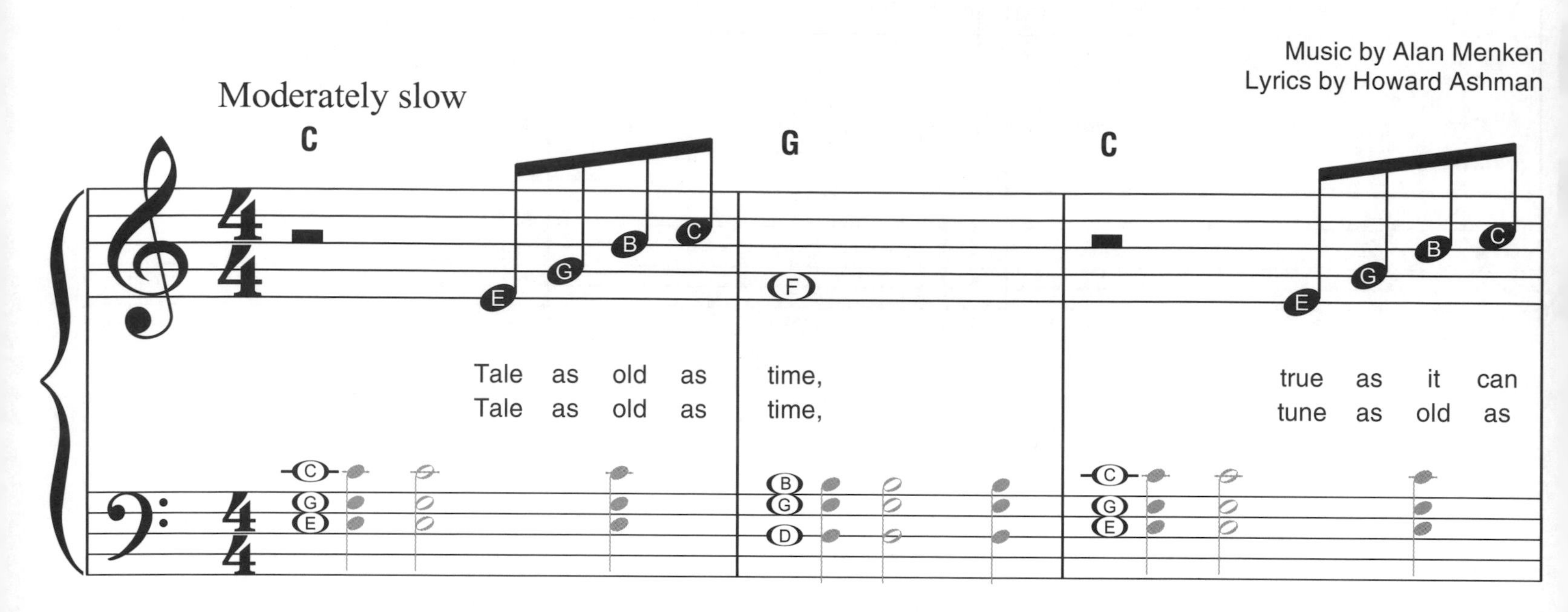

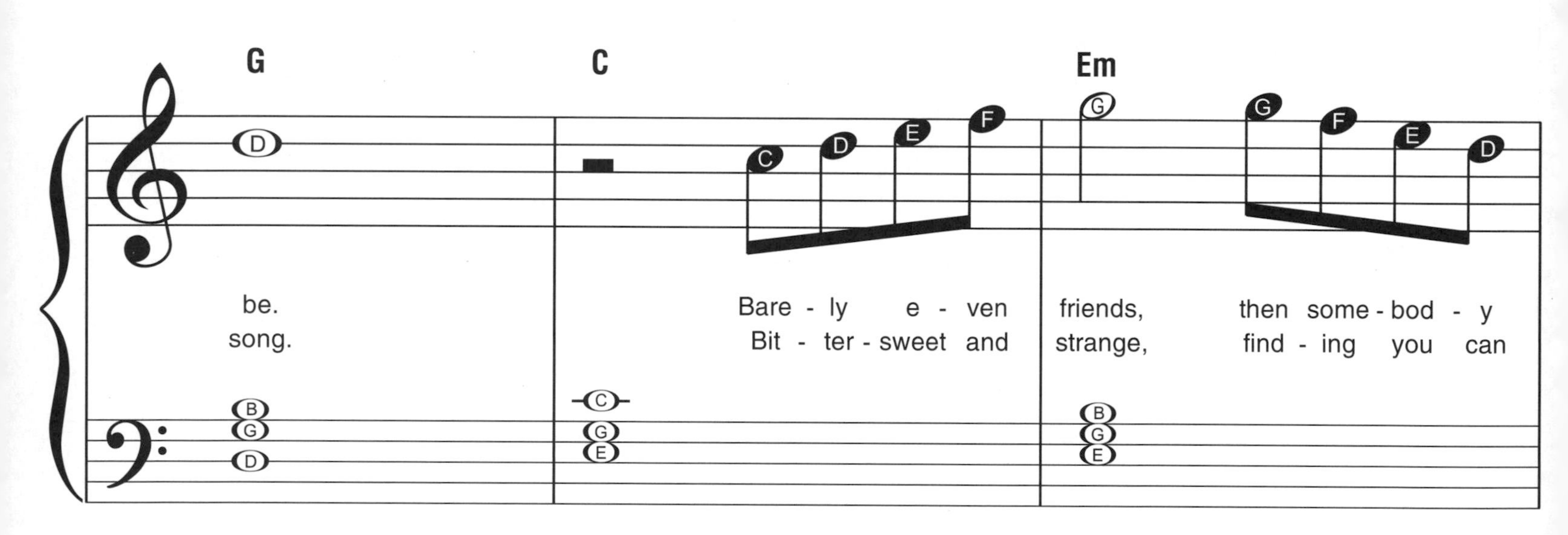

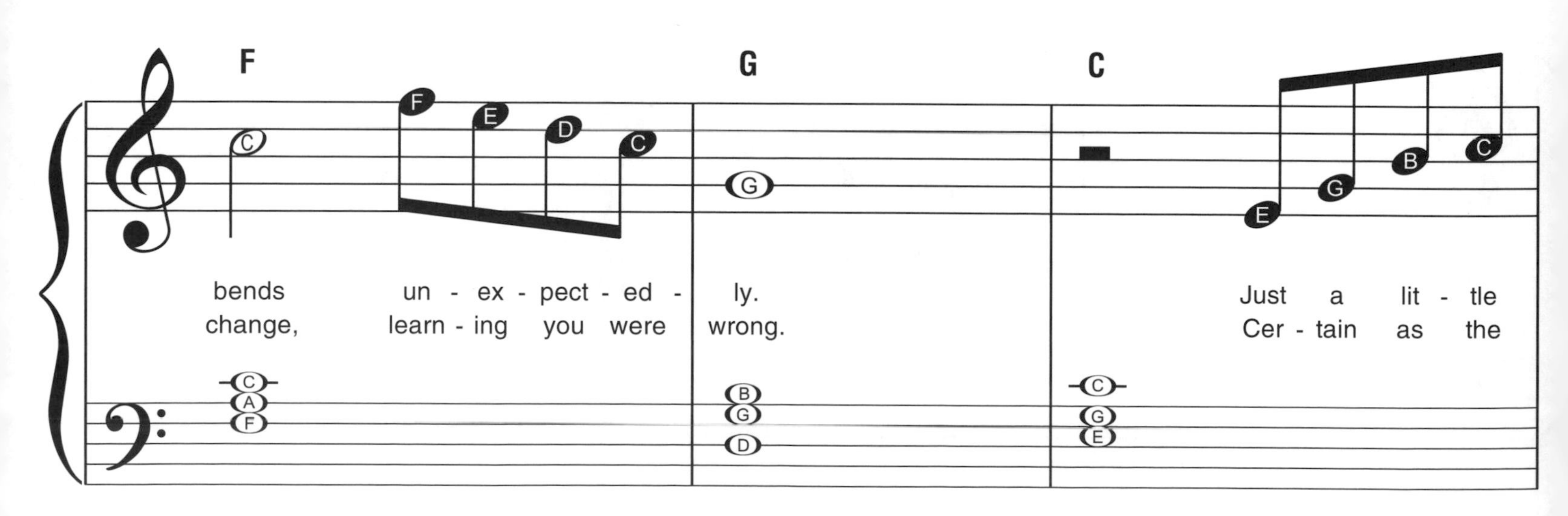

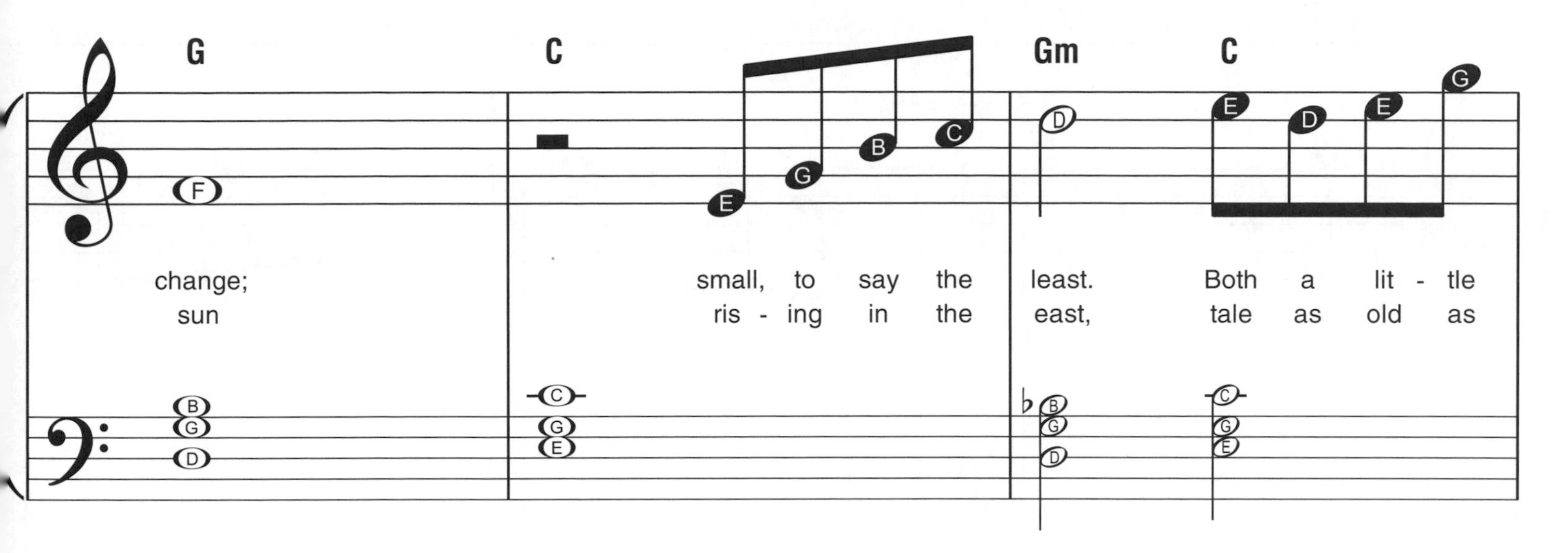
G C Gm C
change; small, to say the least. Both a lit - tle
sun ris - ing in the east, tale as old as

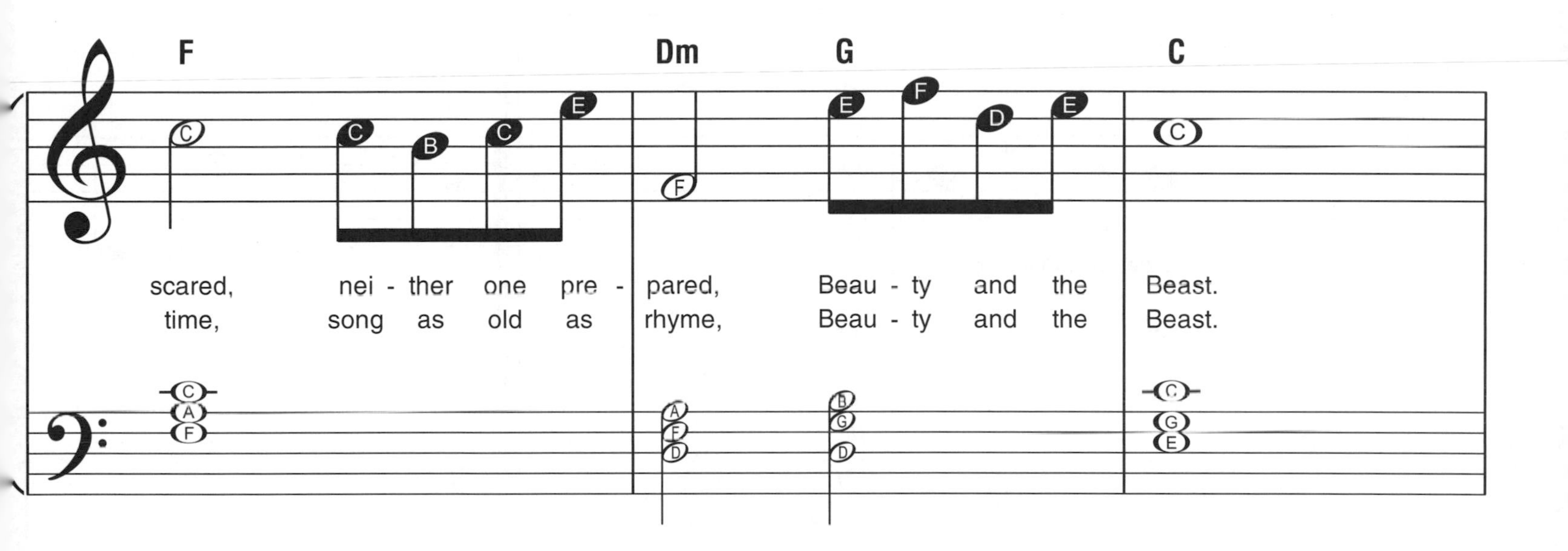
F Dm G C
scared, nei - ther one pre - pared, Beau - ty and the Beast.
time, song as old as rhyme, Beau - ty and the Beast.

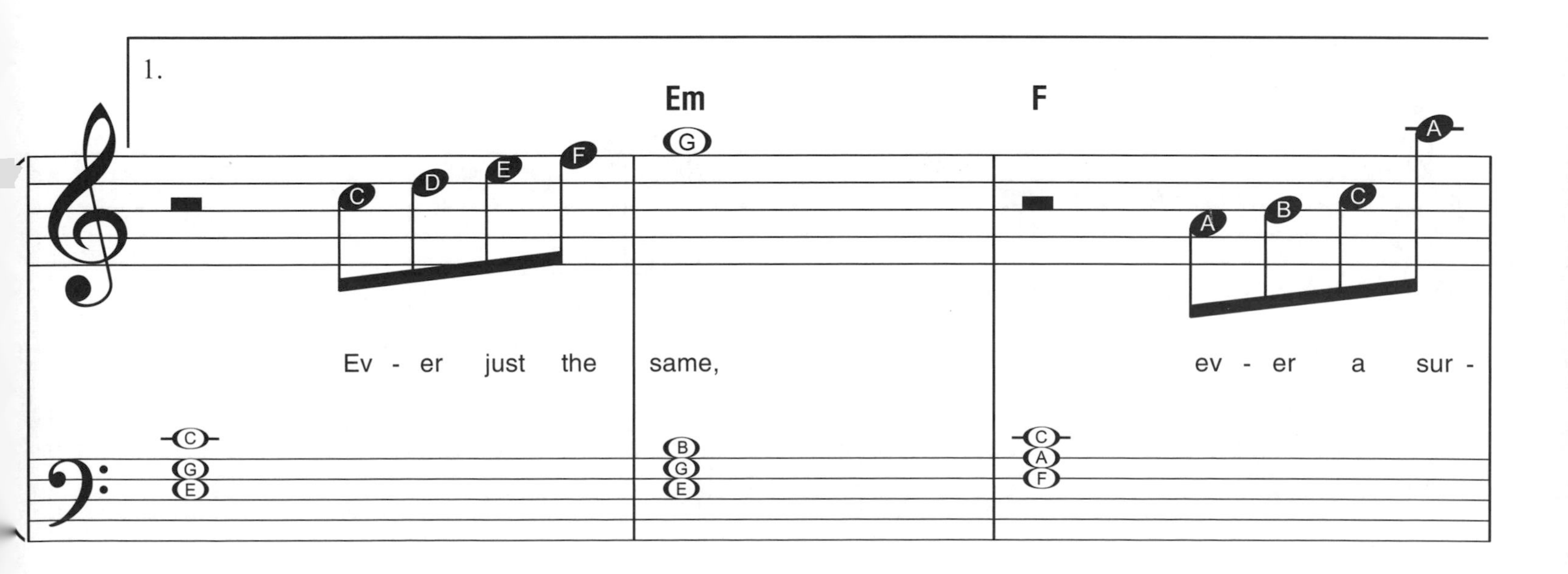
1.
Em F
Ev - er just the same, ev - er a sur -

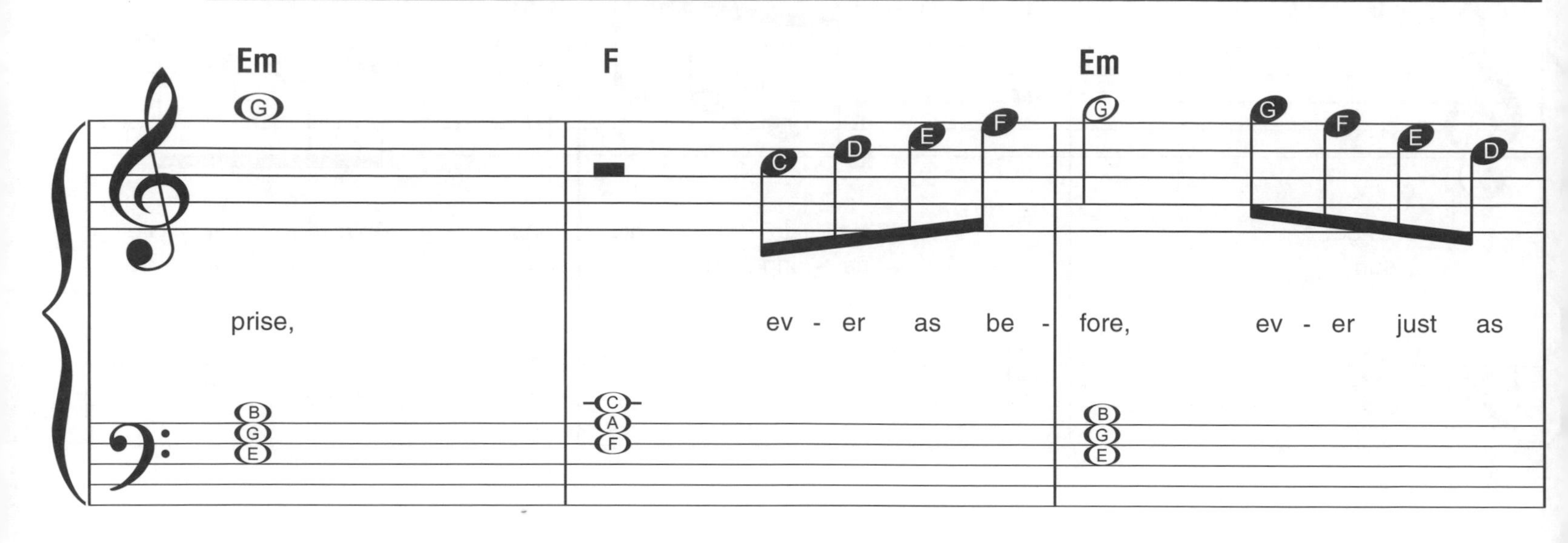
Em
F
Em
prise, ev - er as be - fore, ev - er just as

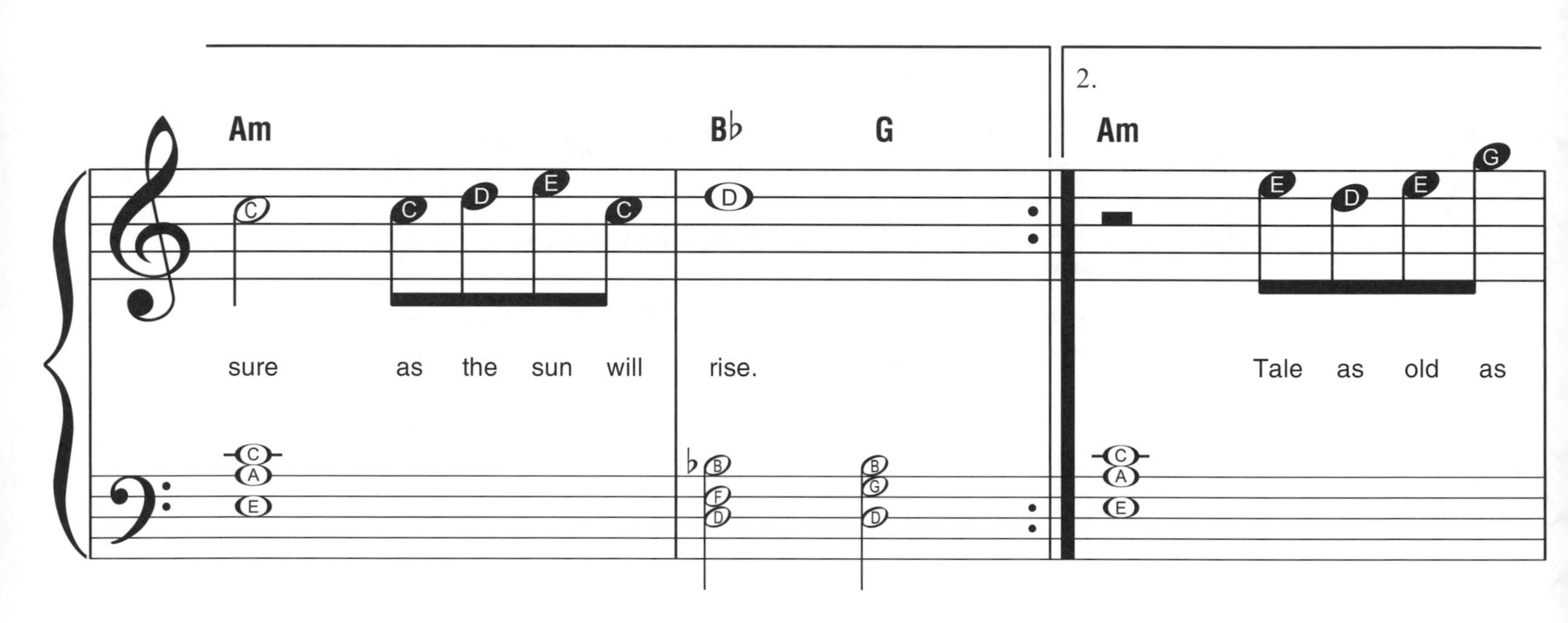
Am
B♭
G
2.
Am
sure as the sun will rise.
Tale as old as

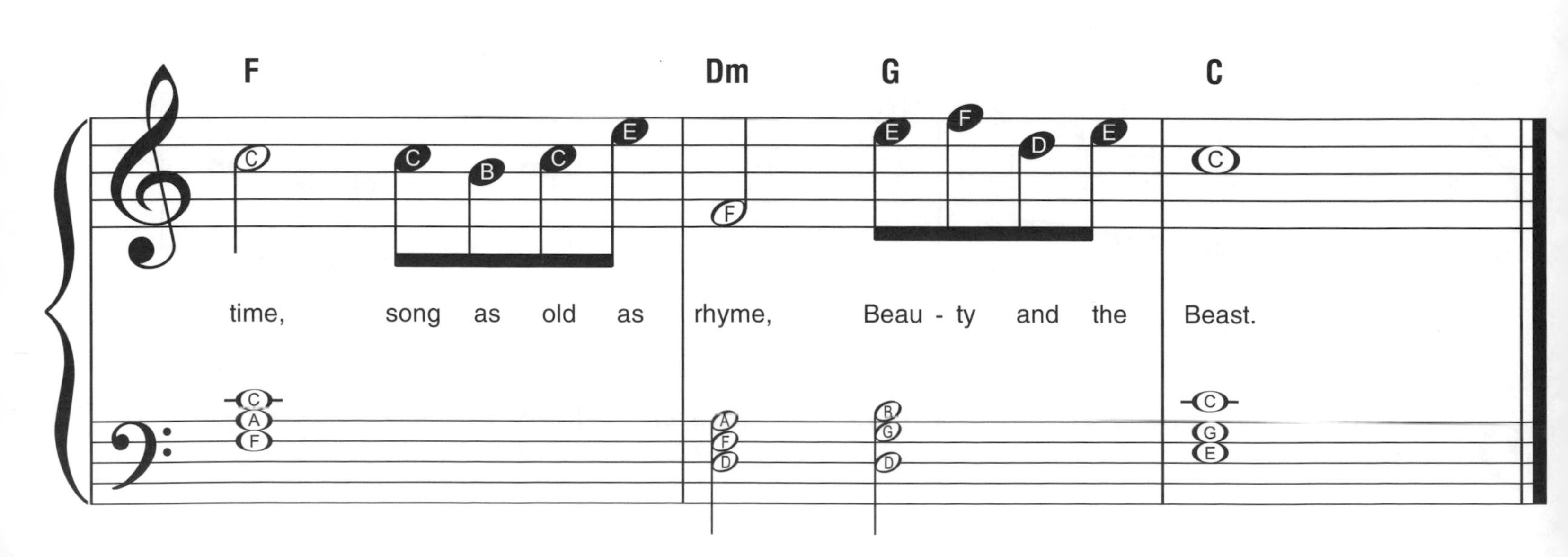
F
Dm
G
C
time, song as old as rhyme, Beau - ty and the Beast.

Bibbidi-Bobbidi-Boo

(The Magic Song)

from CINDERELLA

Words by Jerry Livingston
Music by Mack David and Al Hoffman

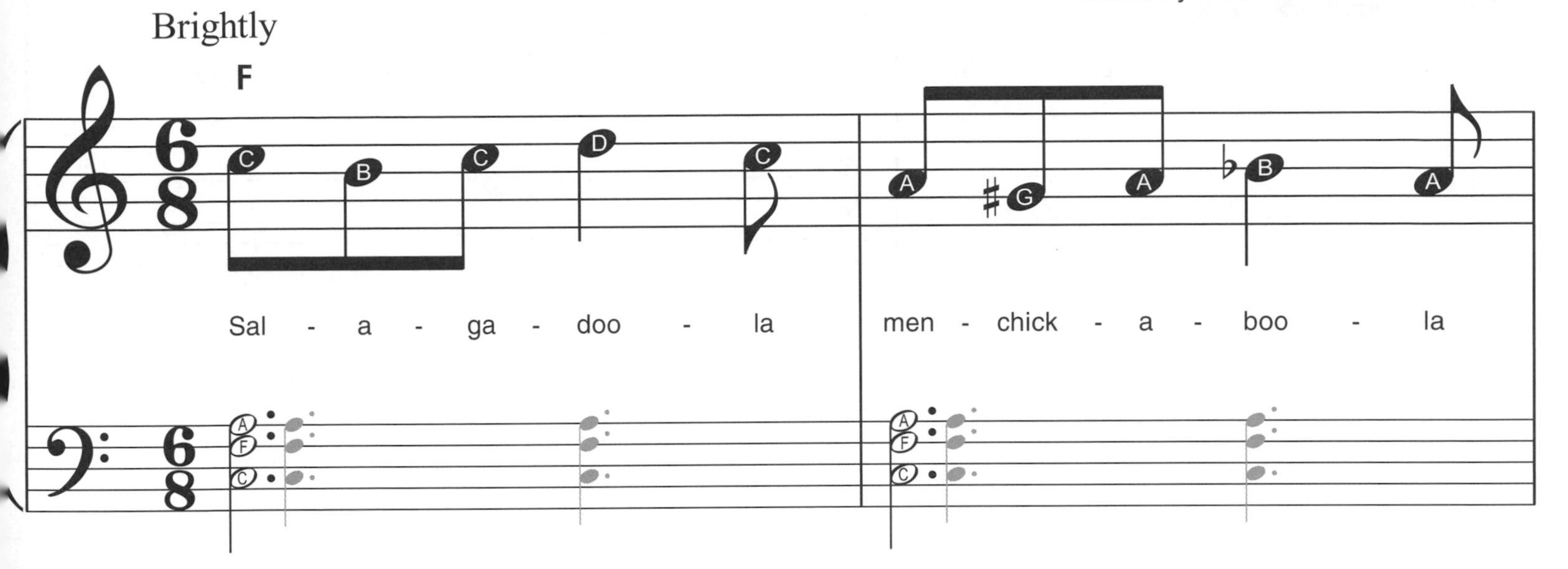

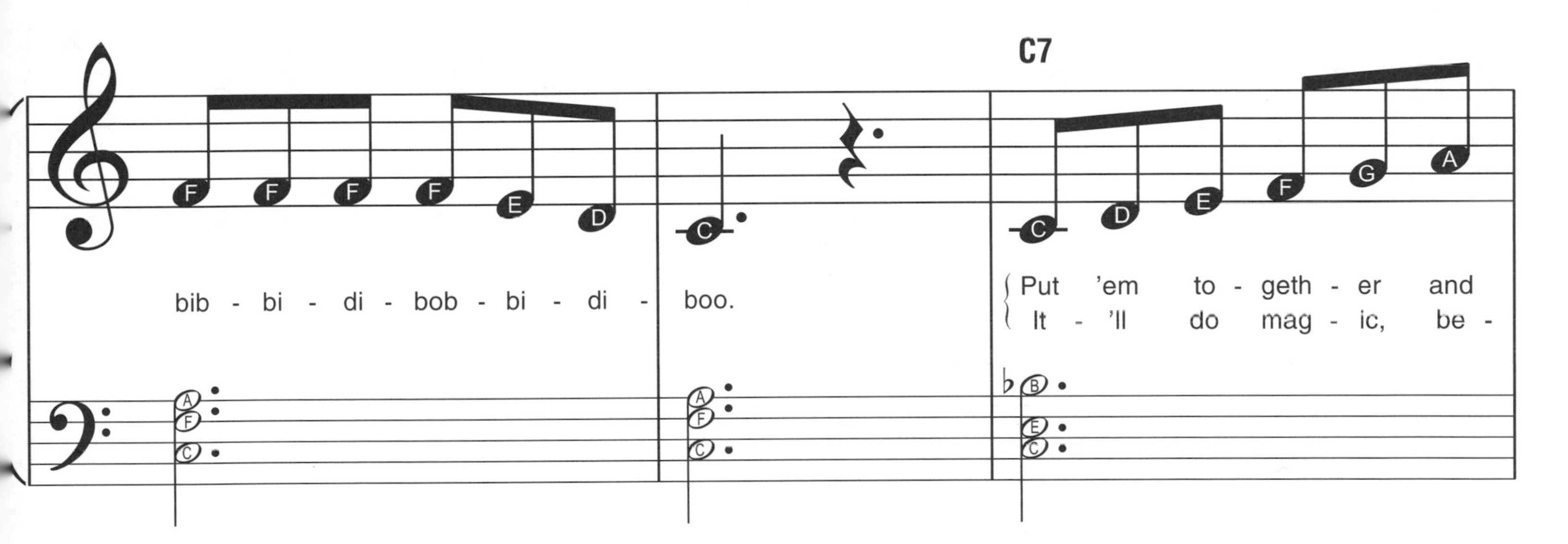

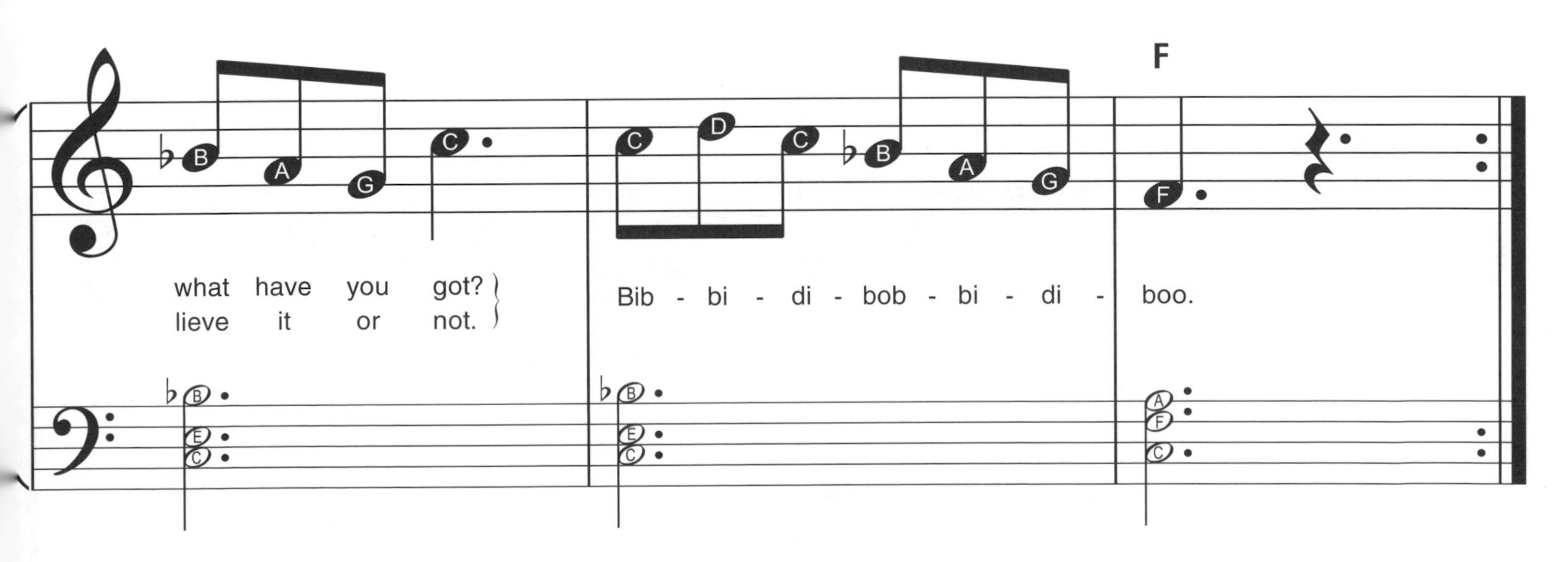

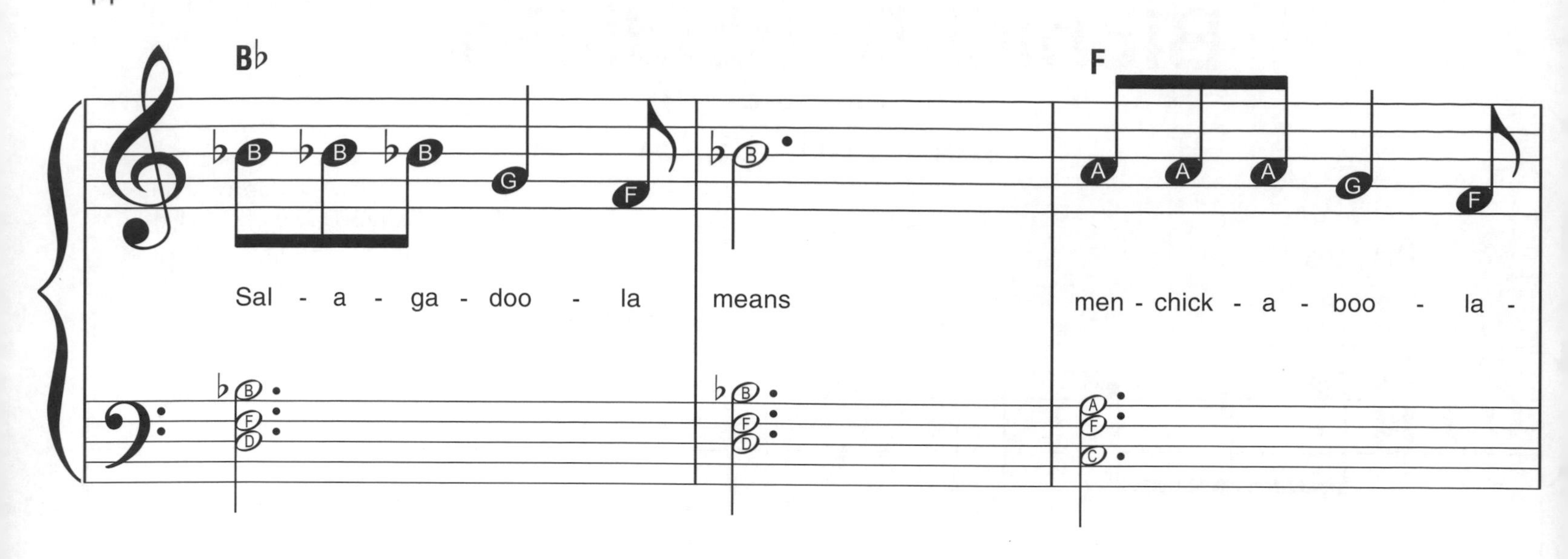
B♭
F
Sal - a - ga - doo - la
means
men - chick - a - boo - la -

G
roo, but the
thing - a - ma - bob that
does the job is

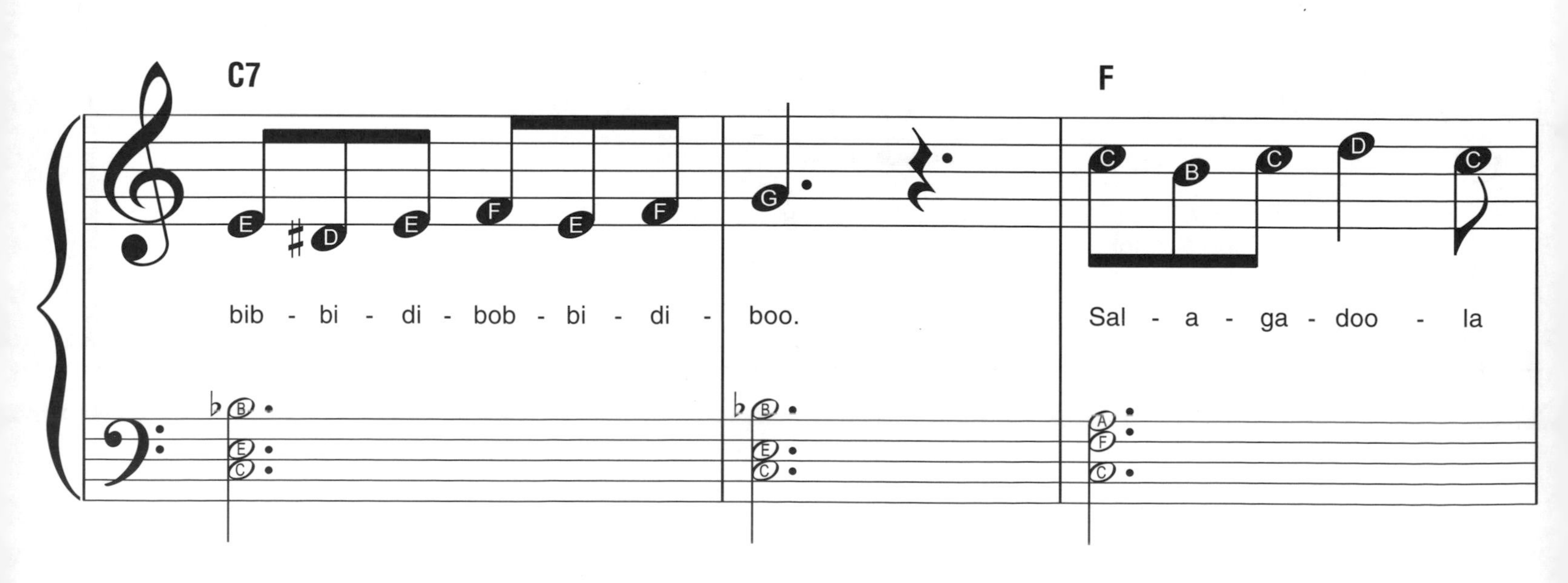
C7
F
bib - bi - di - bob - bi - di -
boo.
Sal - a - ga - doo - la

A
G
A
B
A
F
F
F
F
E
D
C
men - chick - a - boo - la
bib - bi - di - bob - bi - di - boo.
A
F
C

C7
C
D
E
F
G
A
B
A
G
C
C
D
C
B
A
G
Put 'em to - geth - er and
what have you got?
Bib - bi - di - bob - bi - di,
B
E
C
B
F
C

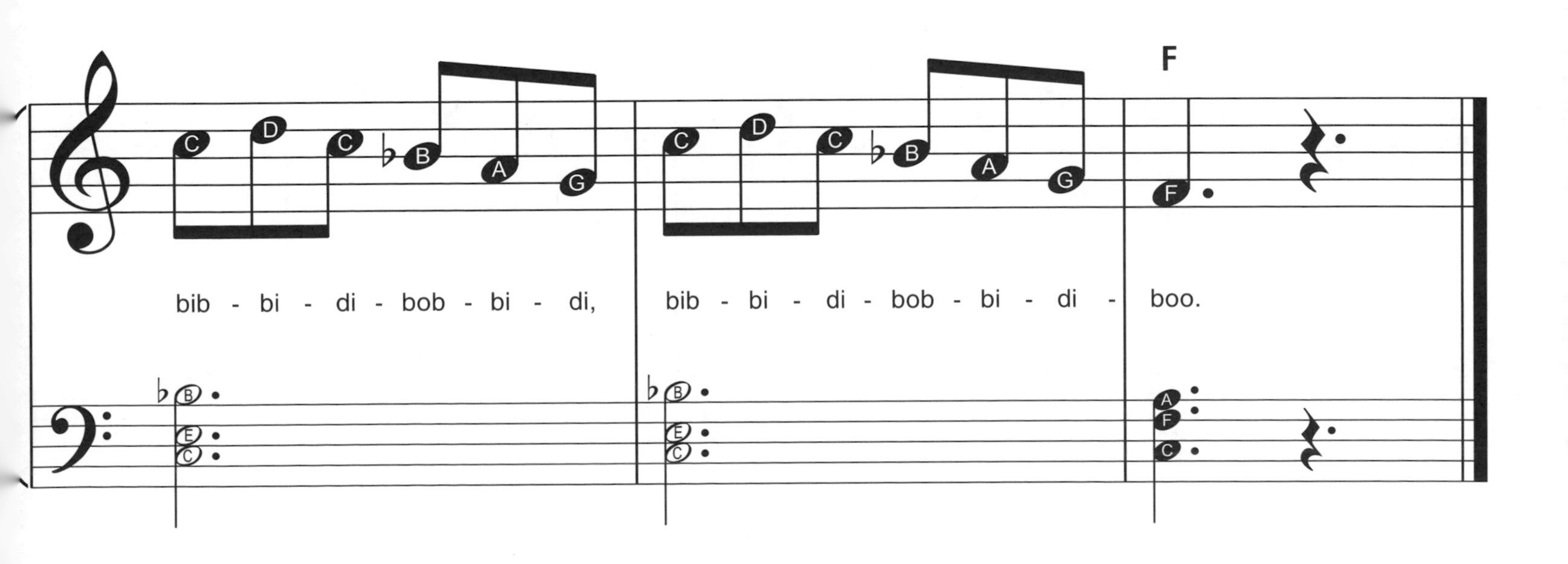
F
C
D
C
B
A
G
F
bib - bi - di - bob - bi - di,
bib - bi - di - bob - bi - di - boo.
B
E
C
A
F
C

Can You Feel the Love Tonight

from THE LION KING

Music by Elton John
Lyrics by Tim Rice

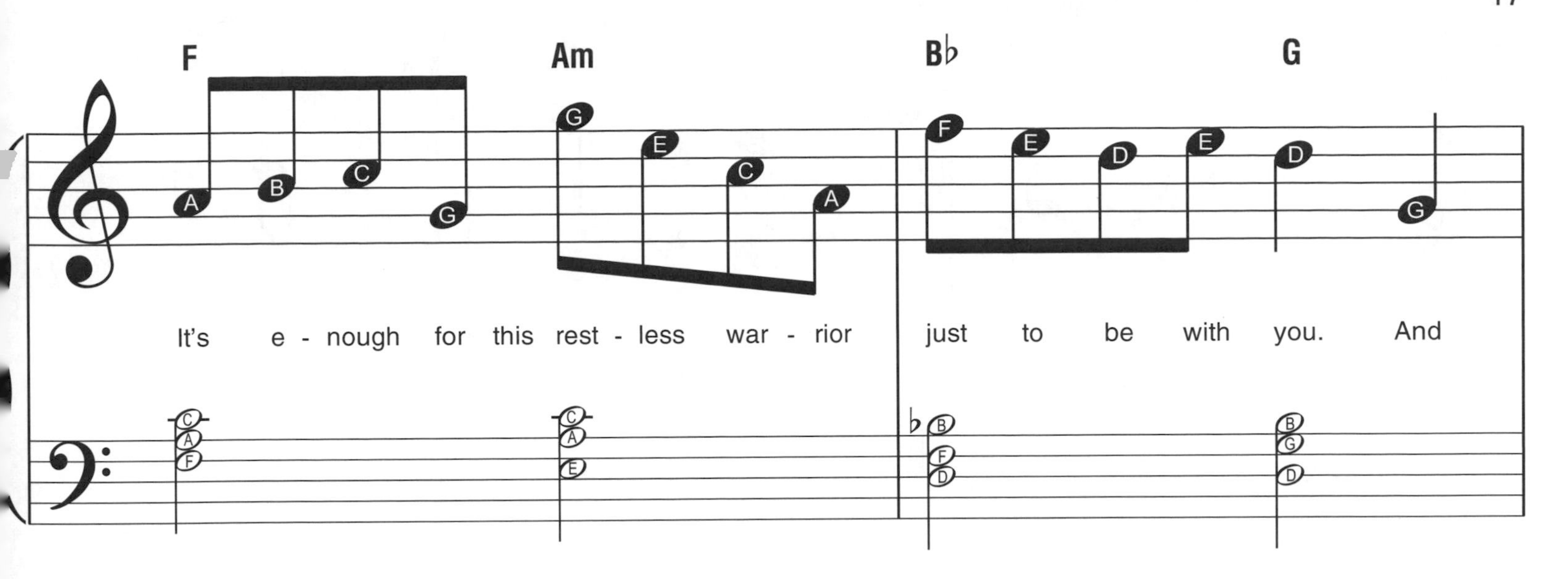
F Am B♭ G
It's e - nough for this rest - less war - rior just to be with you. And

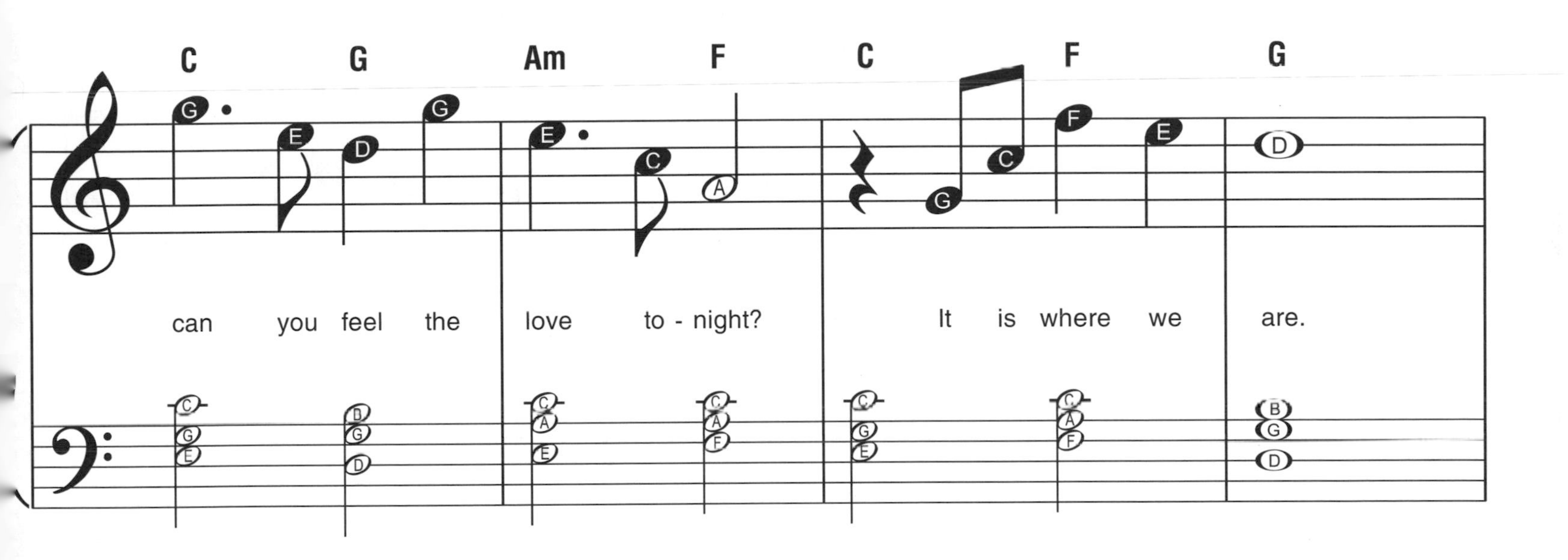
C G Am F C F G
can you feel the love to - night? It is where we are.

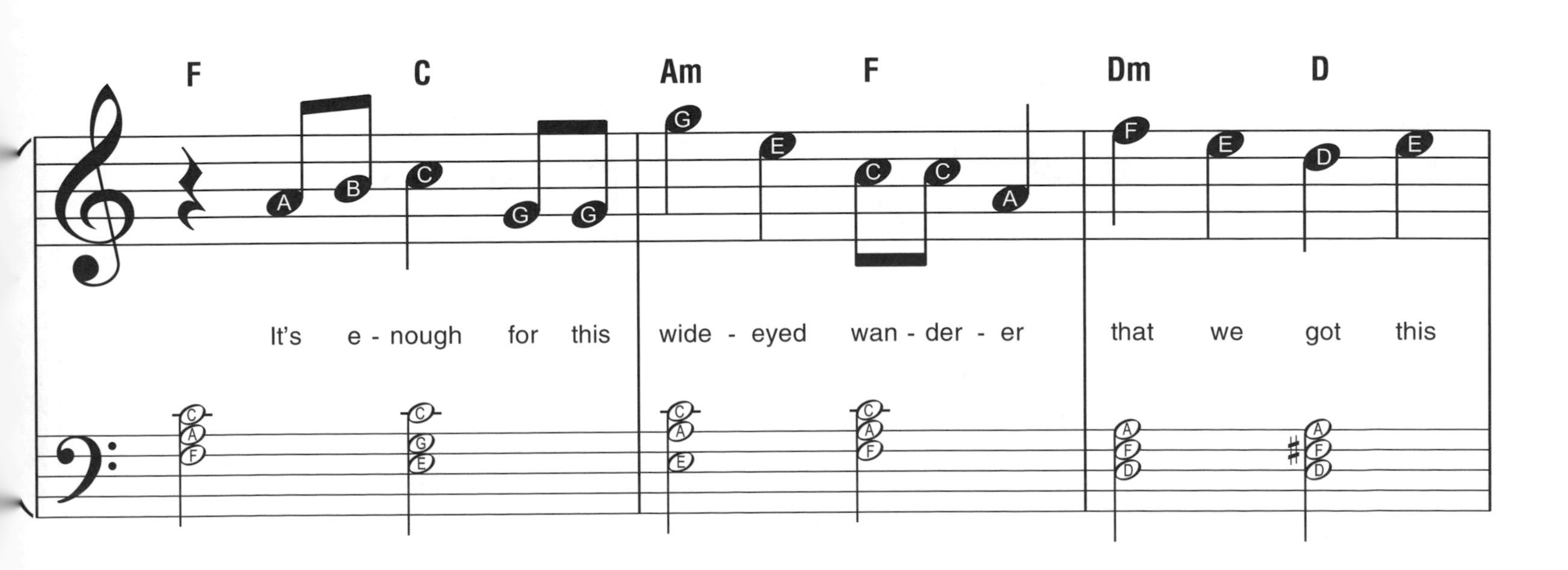
F C Am F Dm D
It's e - nough for this wide - eyed wan - der - er that we got this

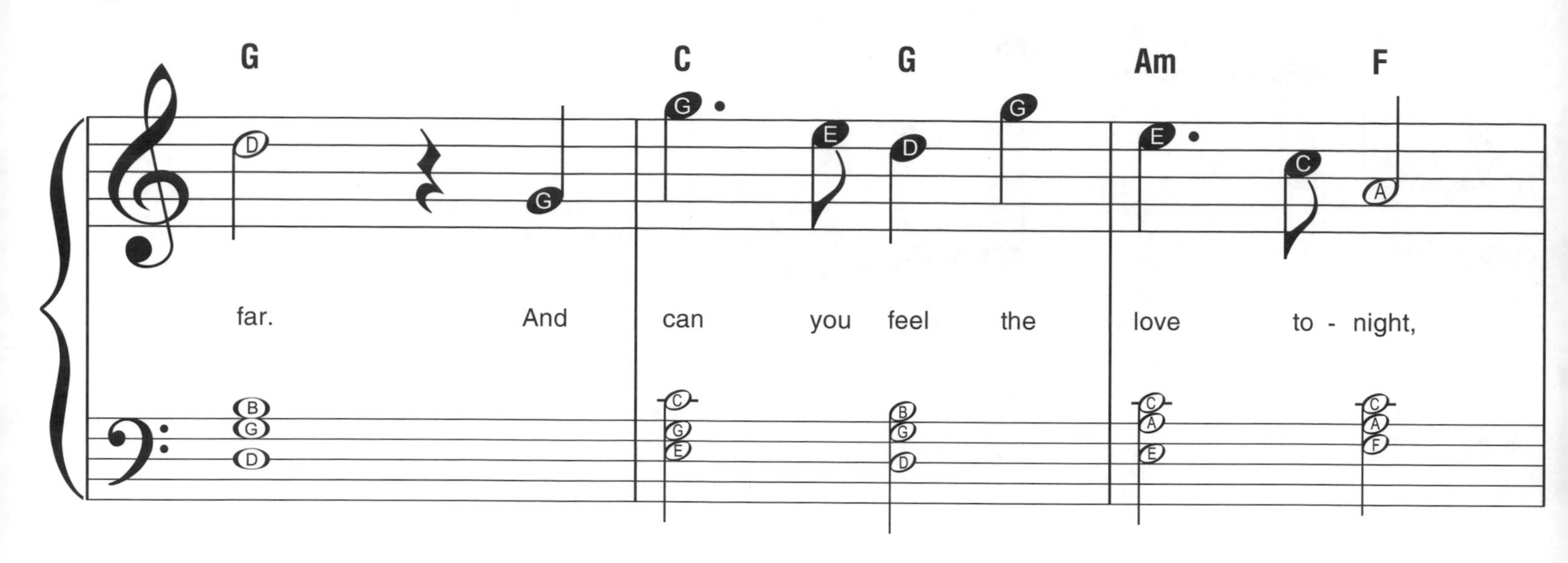
G C G Am F
far. And can you feel the love to - night,

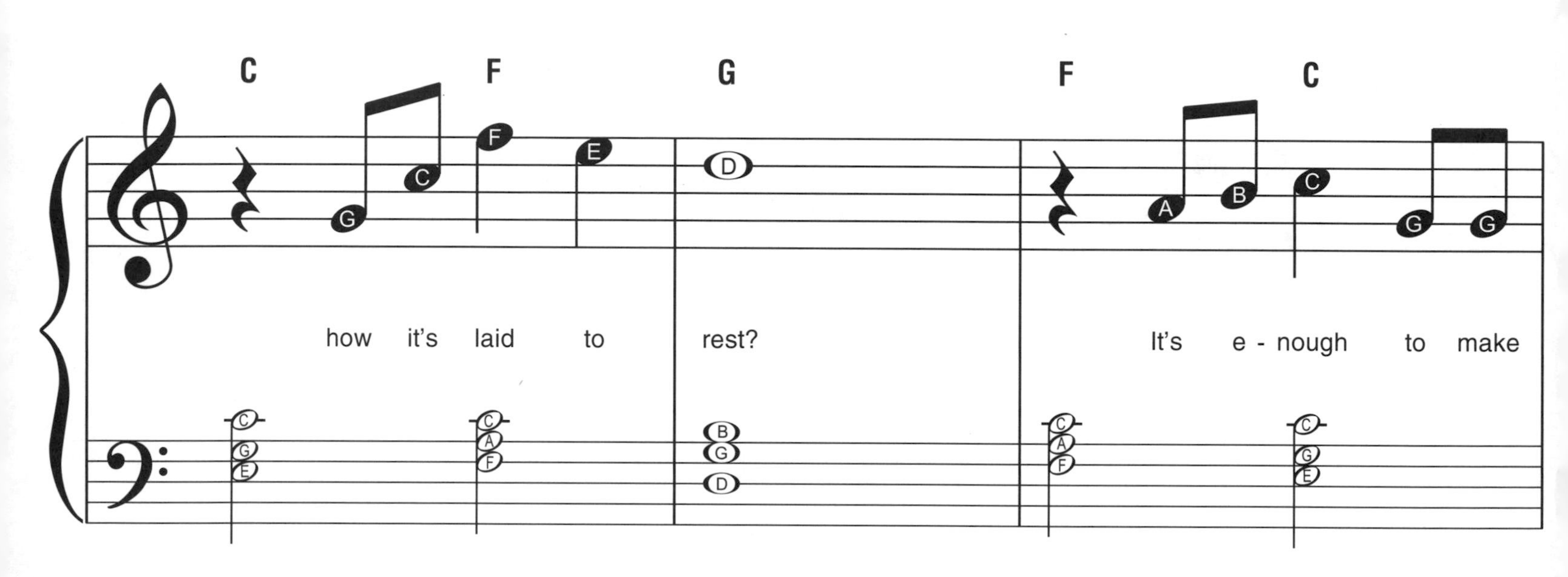
C F G F C
how it's laid to rest? It's e - nough to make

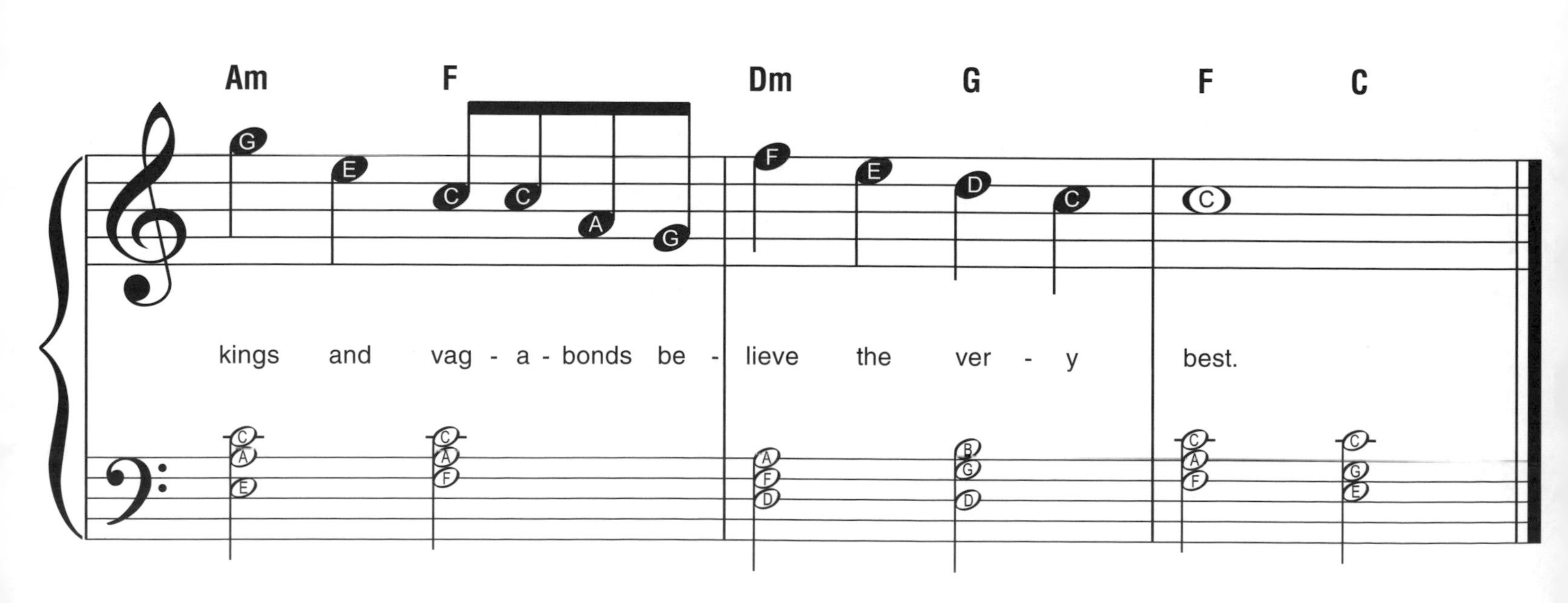
Am F Dm G F C
kings and vag - a - bonds be - lieve the ver - y best.

Circle of Life
from THE LION KING

Music by Elton John
Lyrics by Tim Rice

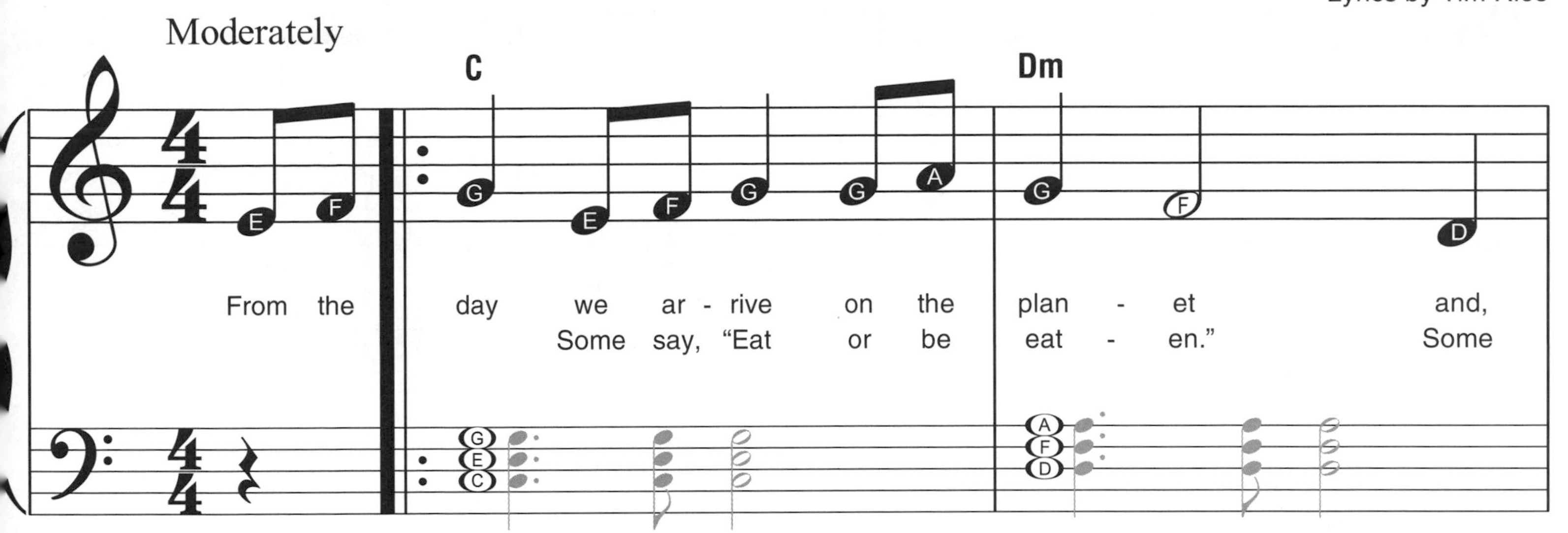

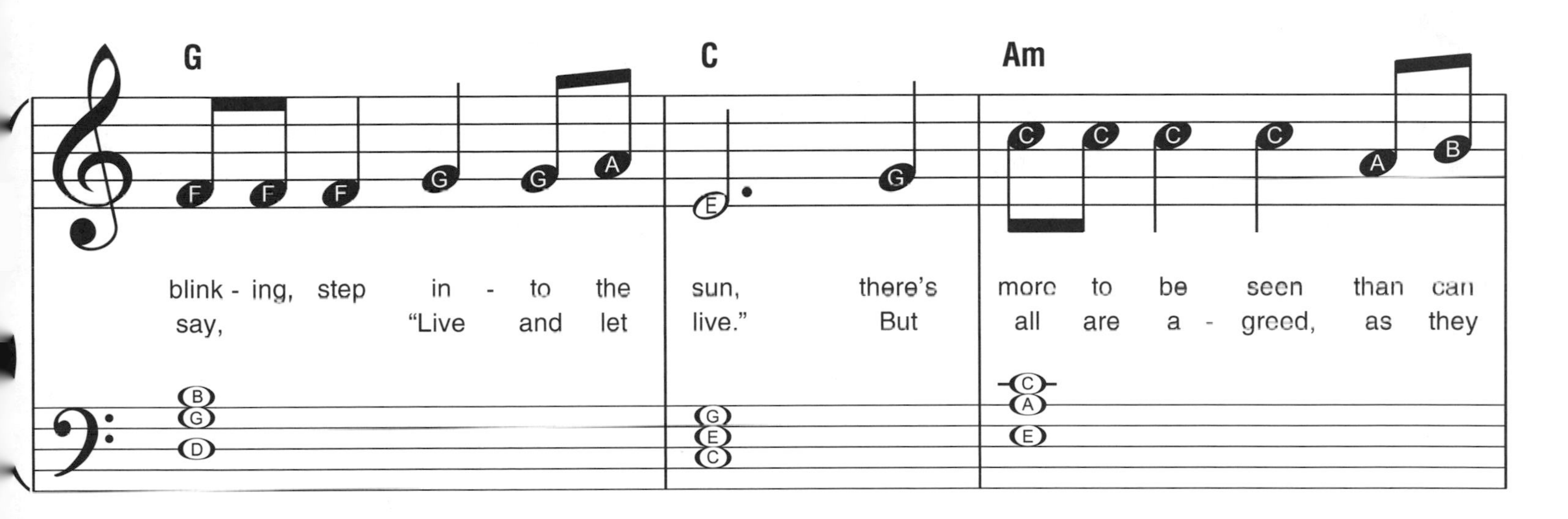

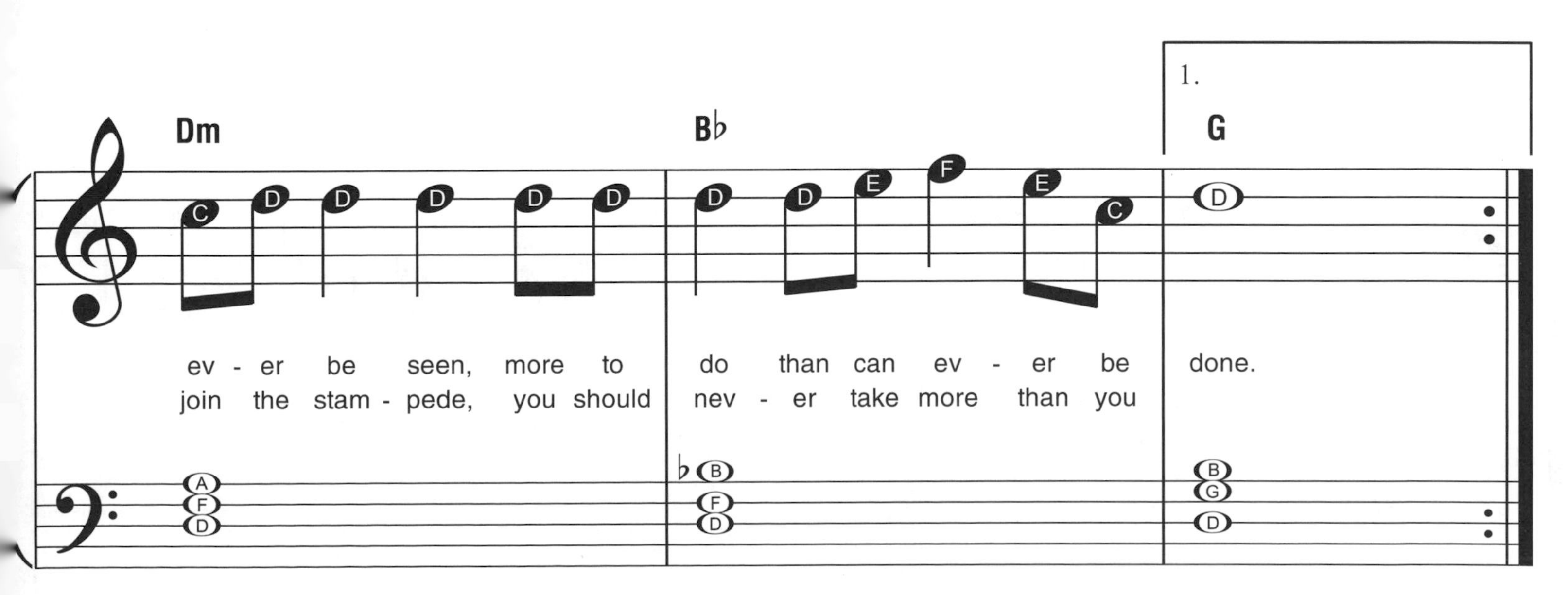

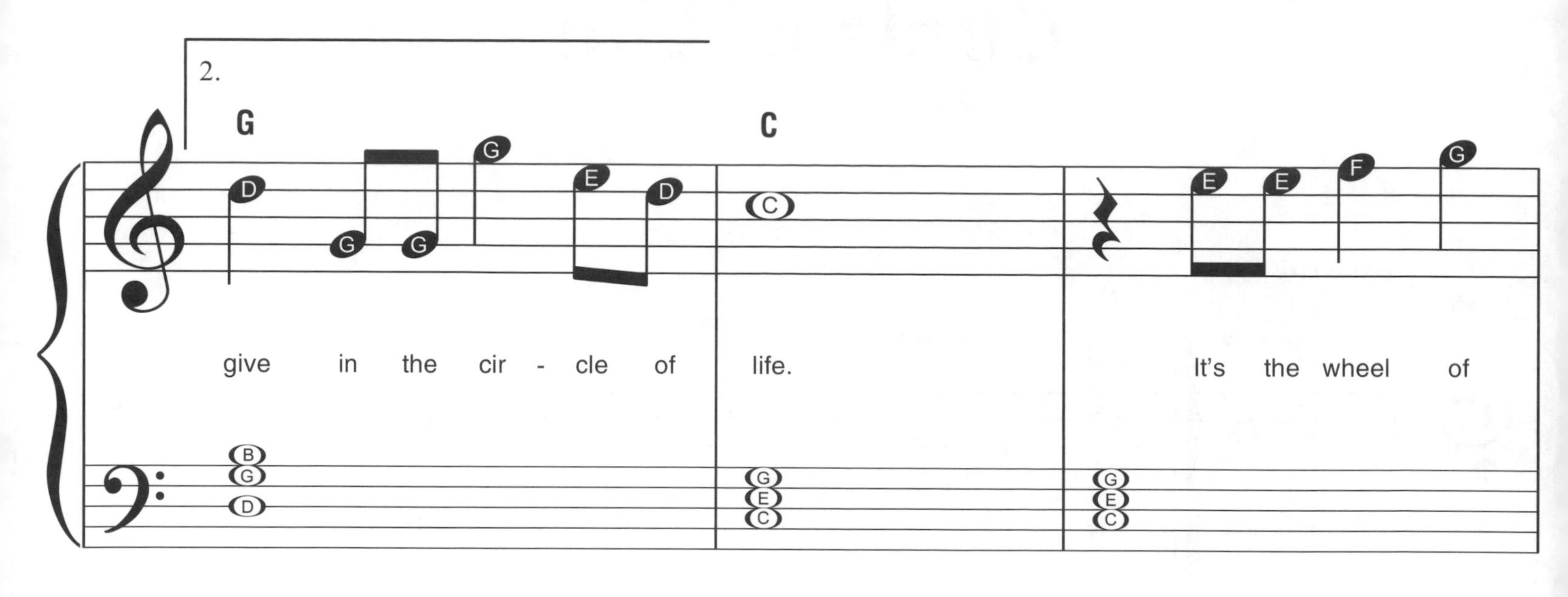
2.
G
C
give in the cir - cle of
life.
It's the wheel of
D G G G E D
C
E E F G
B G D
G E C
G E C

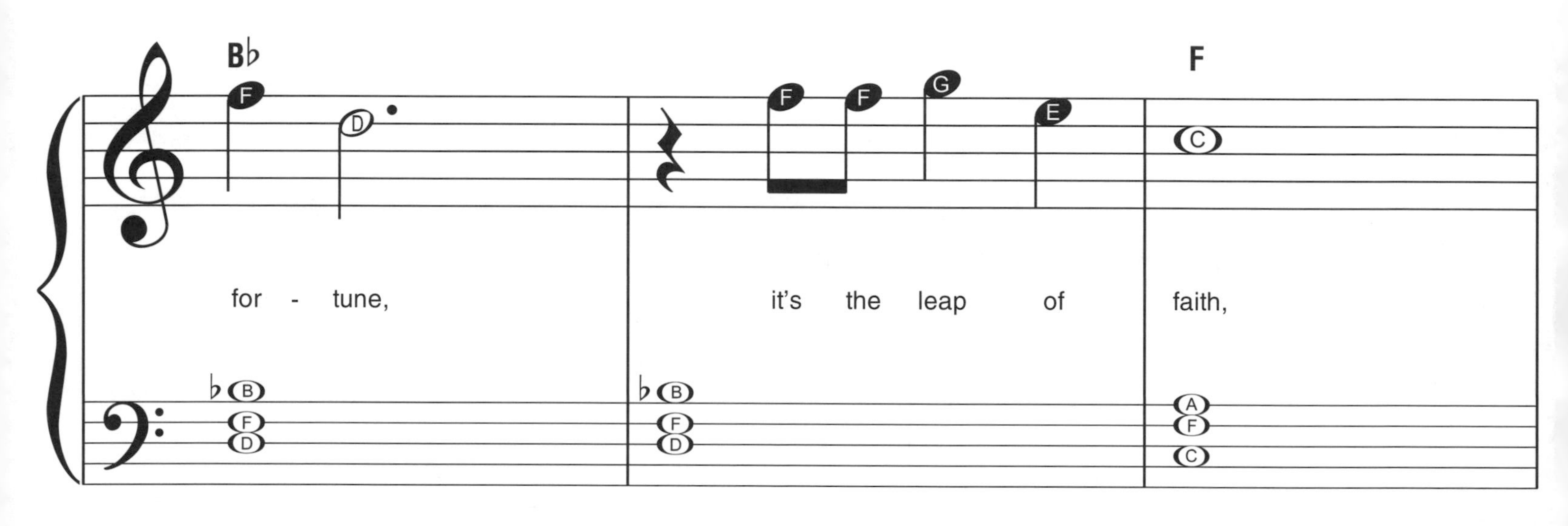
B♭
F
for - tune,
it's the leap of
faith,
F D
F F G E
C
♭B F D
♭B F D
A F C

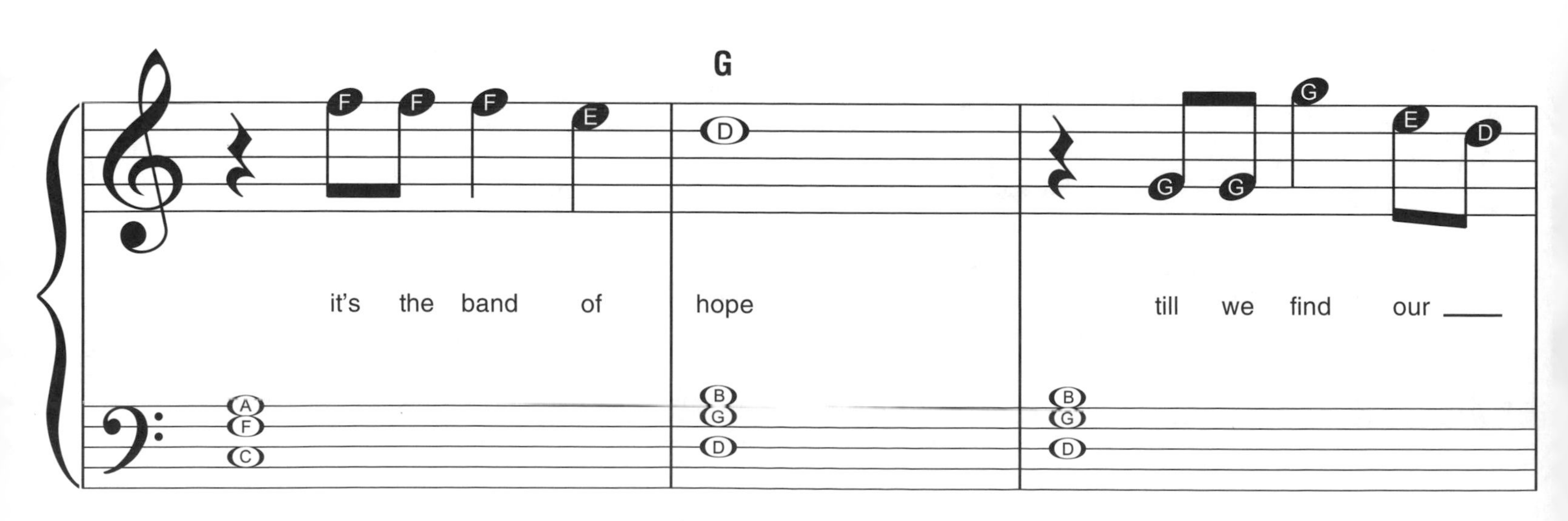
G
it's the band of
hope
till we find our
F F F E
D
G G G E D
A F C
B G D
B G D

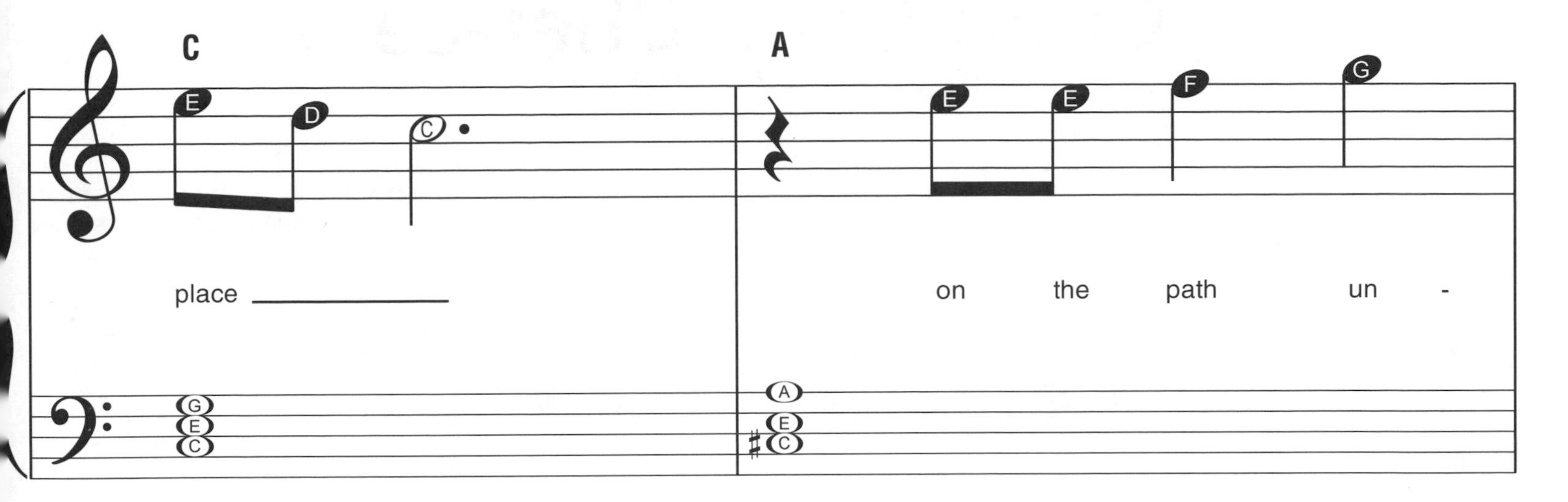
C
A
E D C
E E F G
place
on the path un -
G E C
A E C

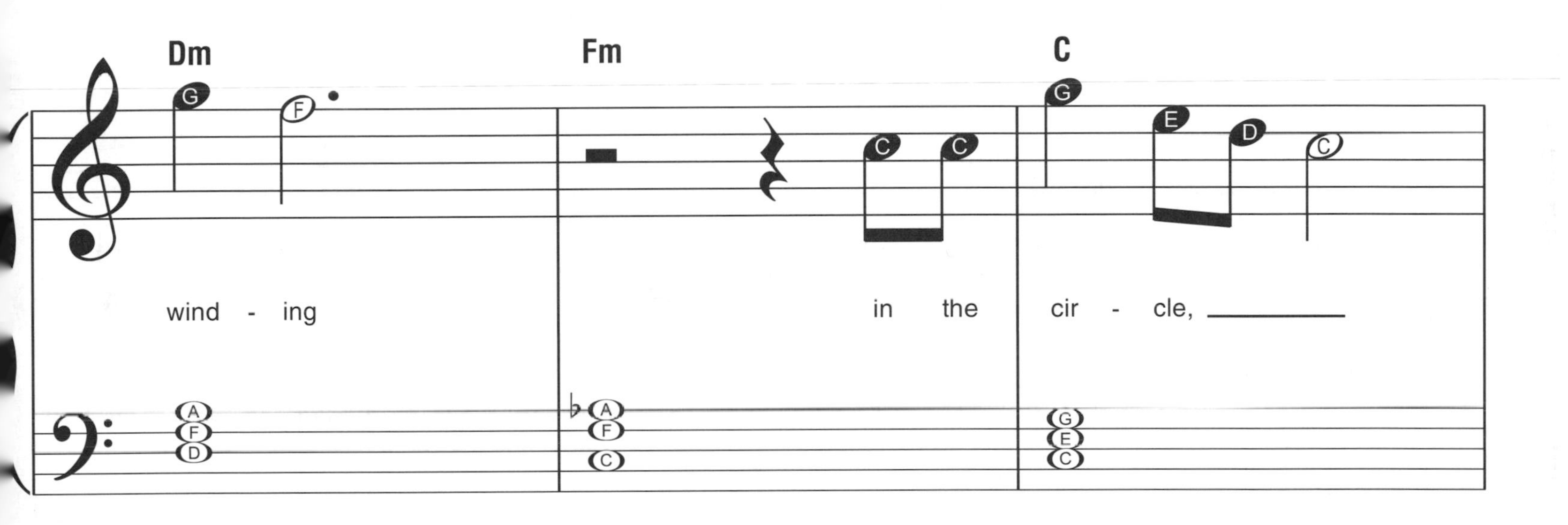
Dm
Fm
C
G F
C C
G E D C
wind - ing
in the
cir - cle,
A F D
A F C
G E C

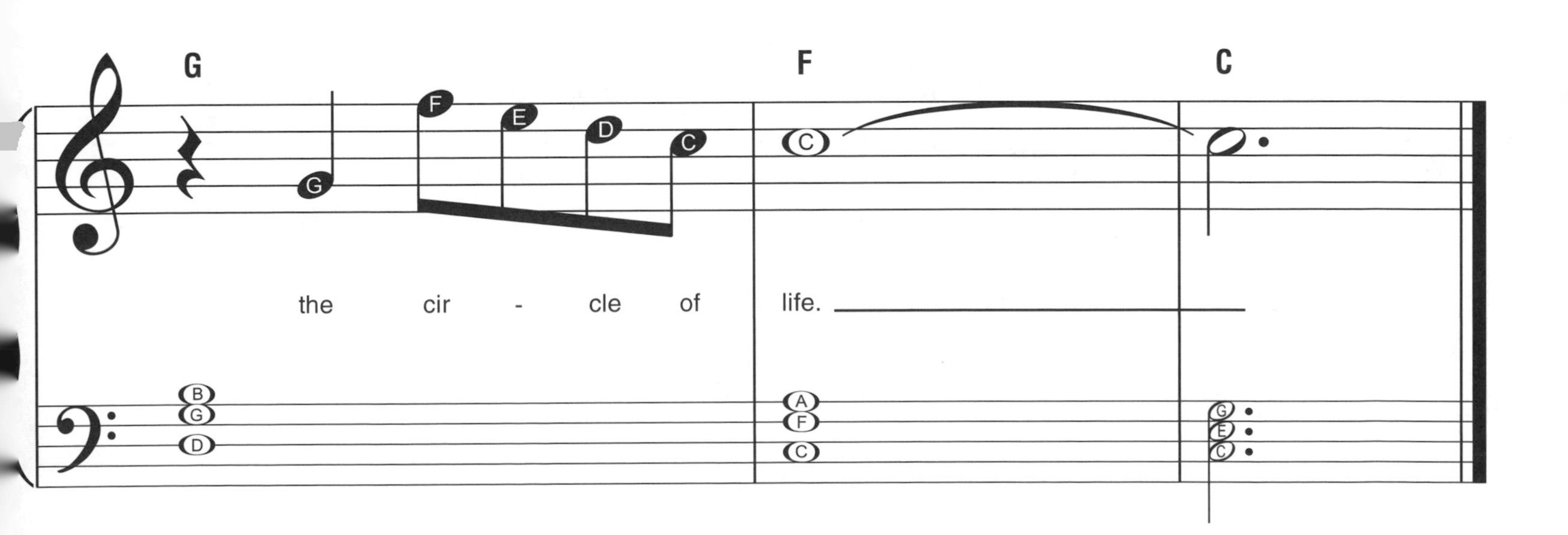
G
F
C
G F E D C
C
the cir - cle of
life.
B G D
A F C
G E C

Chim Chim Cher-ee

from MARY POPPINS

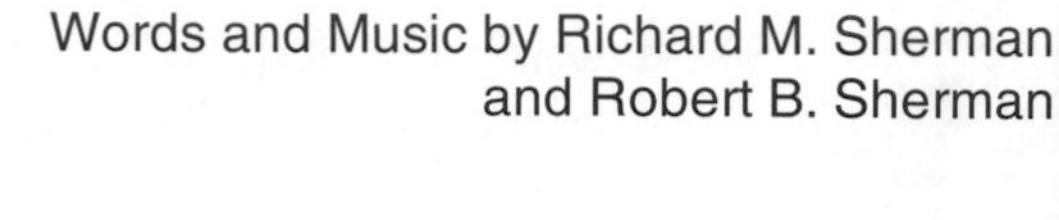

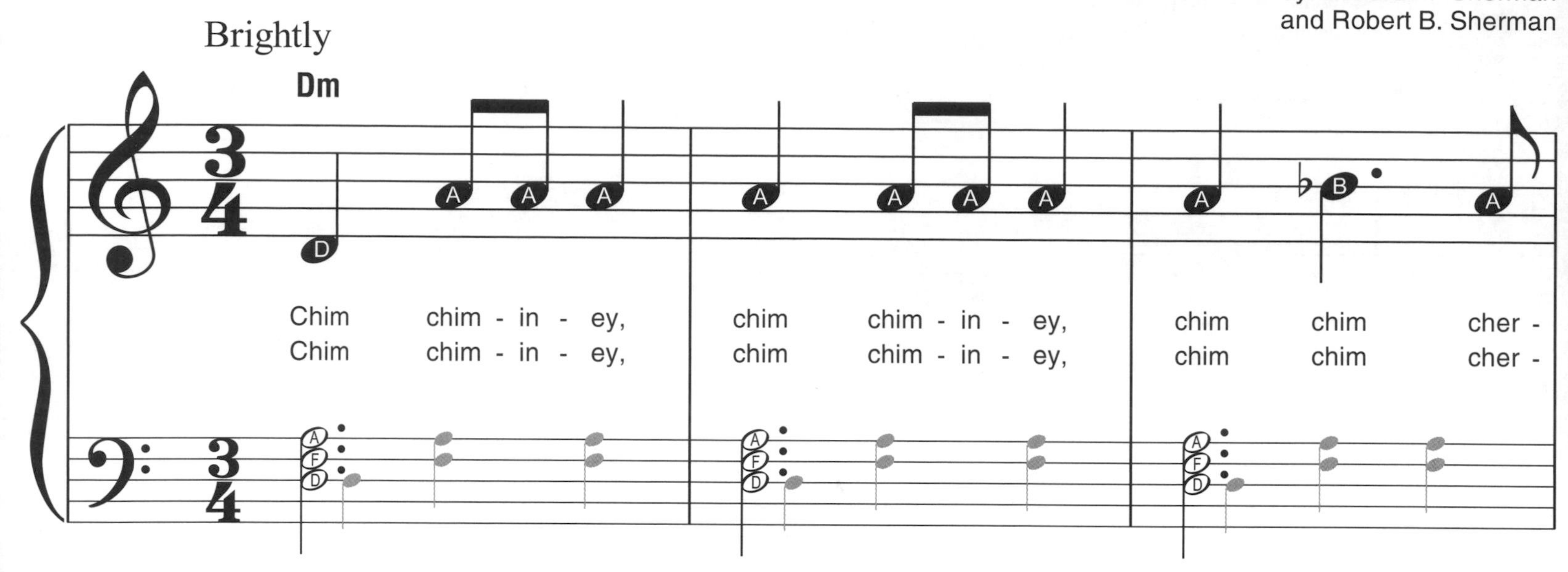

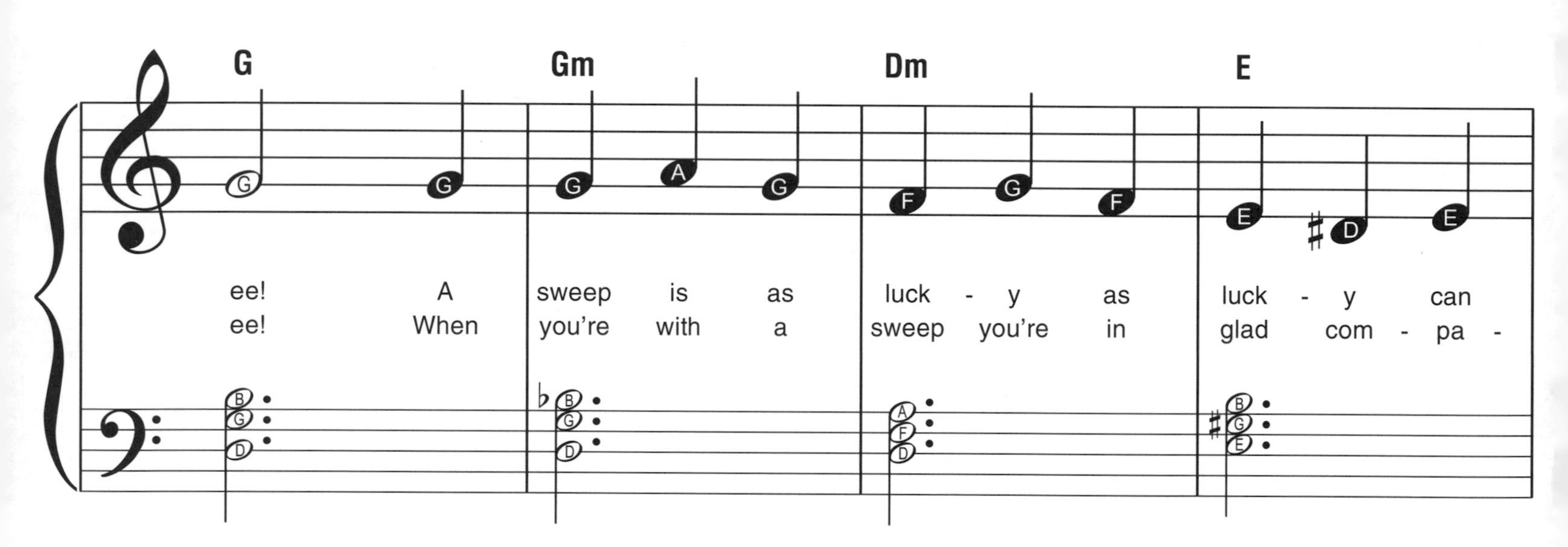

G Gm Dm
oo! Good luck will rub off when I
crew than them wot sings, "Chim chim cher -
A
1.
Dm Gm
shakes 'ands with you. Or blow me a
ee, chim cher -
Dm A Dm
kiss, and that's luck - y, too.
2.
Dm
oo!"
Gm Dm A Dm
Chim chim - in - ey, chim chim, cher - ee, chim cher - oo!

Colors of the Wind
from POCAHONTAS

Music by Alan Menken
Lyrics by Stephen Schwartz

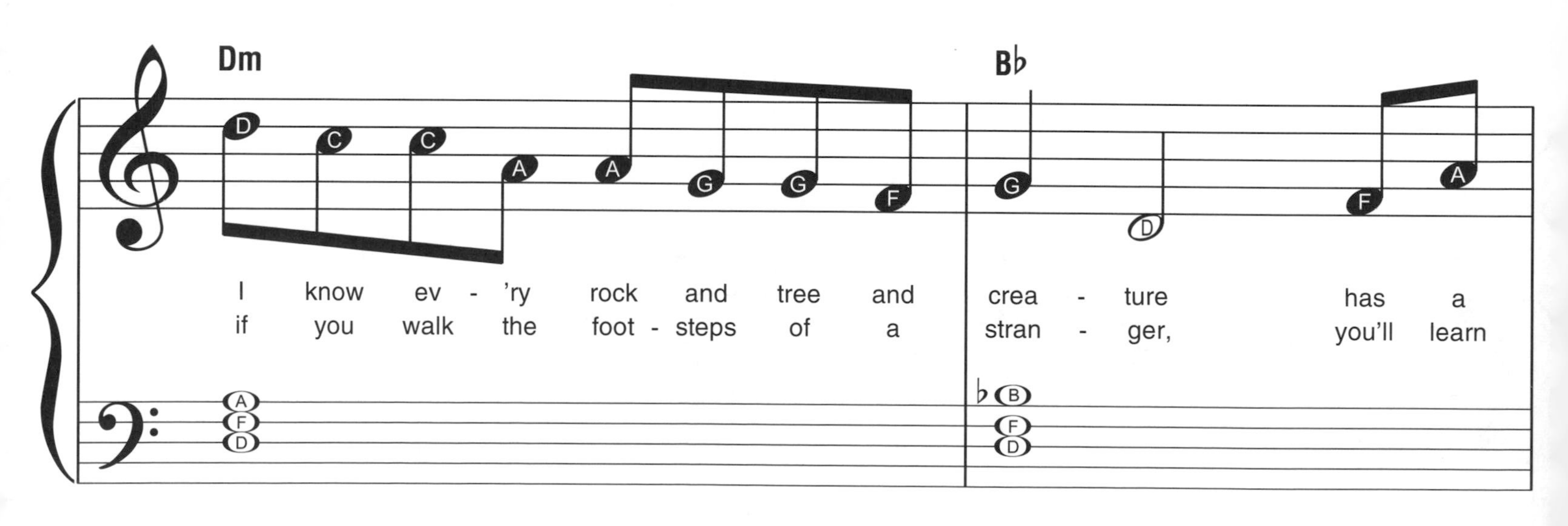

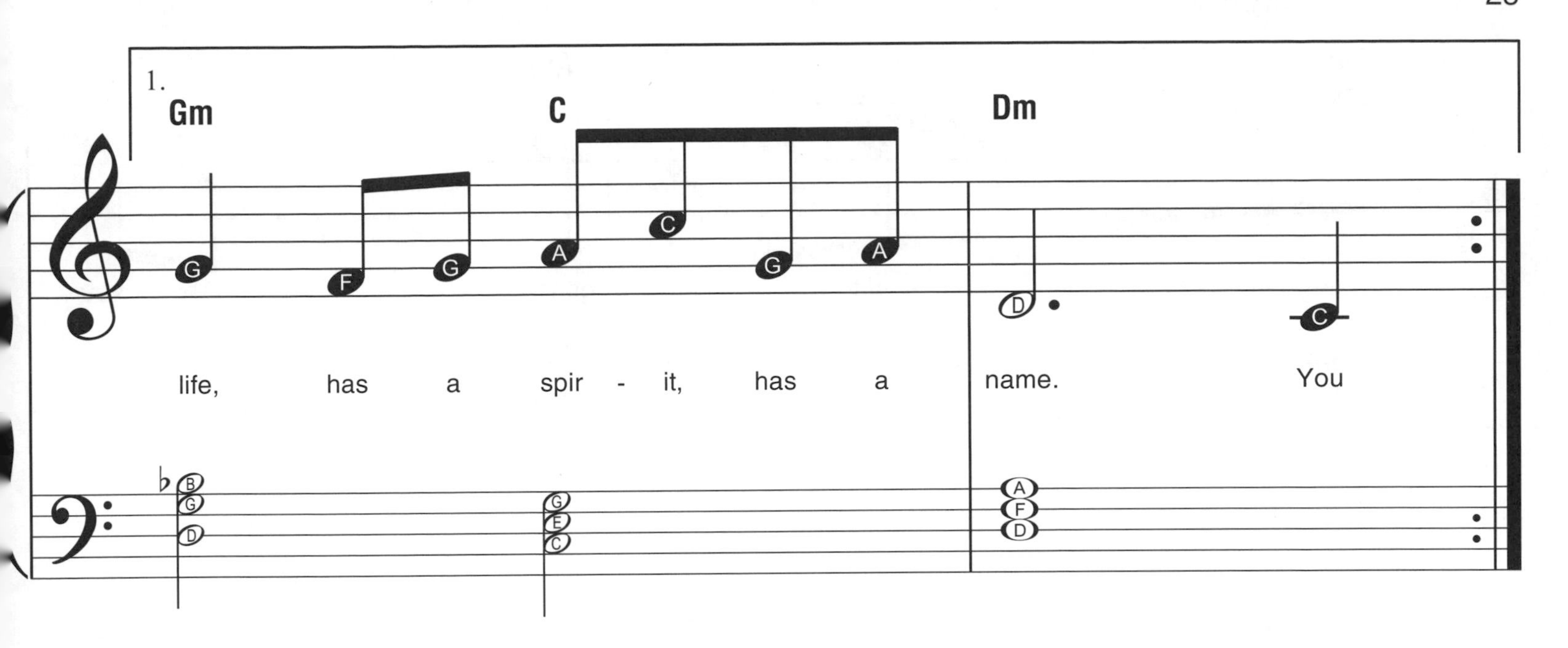
1.
Gm
C
Dm
life, has a spir - it, has a name. You

2.
Gm
C
F
things you nev - er knew you nev - er knew. Have you

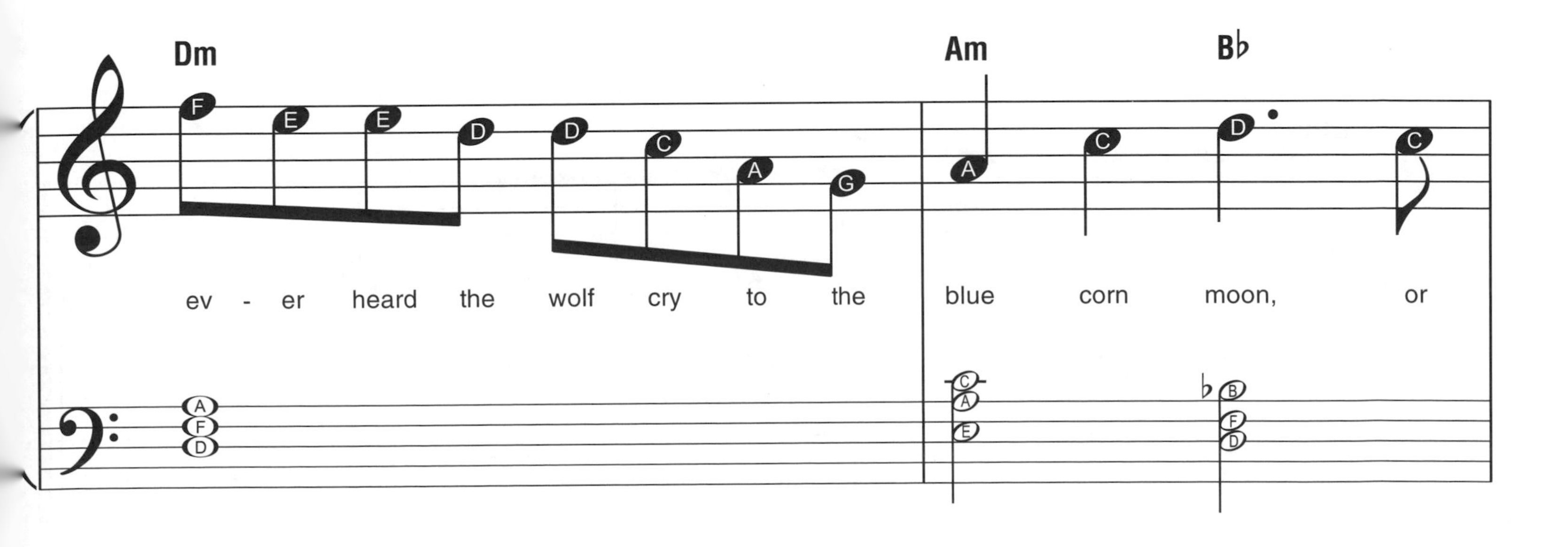
Dm
Am
B♭
ev - er heard the wolf cry to the blue corn moon, or

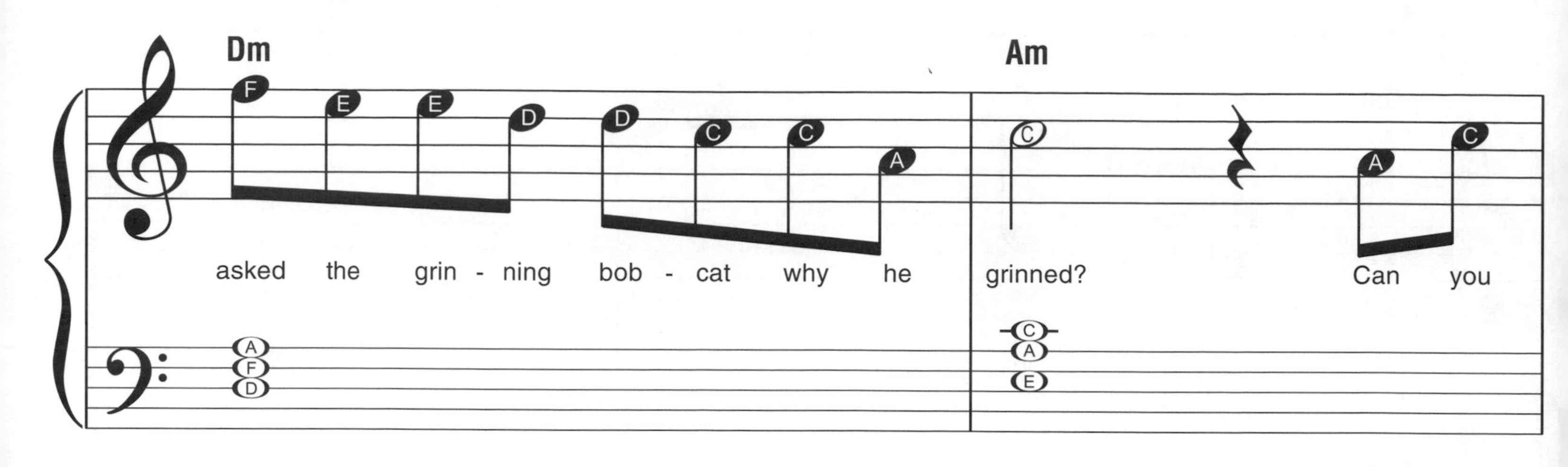
Dm
Am
F E E D D C C A
C A C
asked the grin - ning bob - cat why he grinned? Can you
A F D
C A E

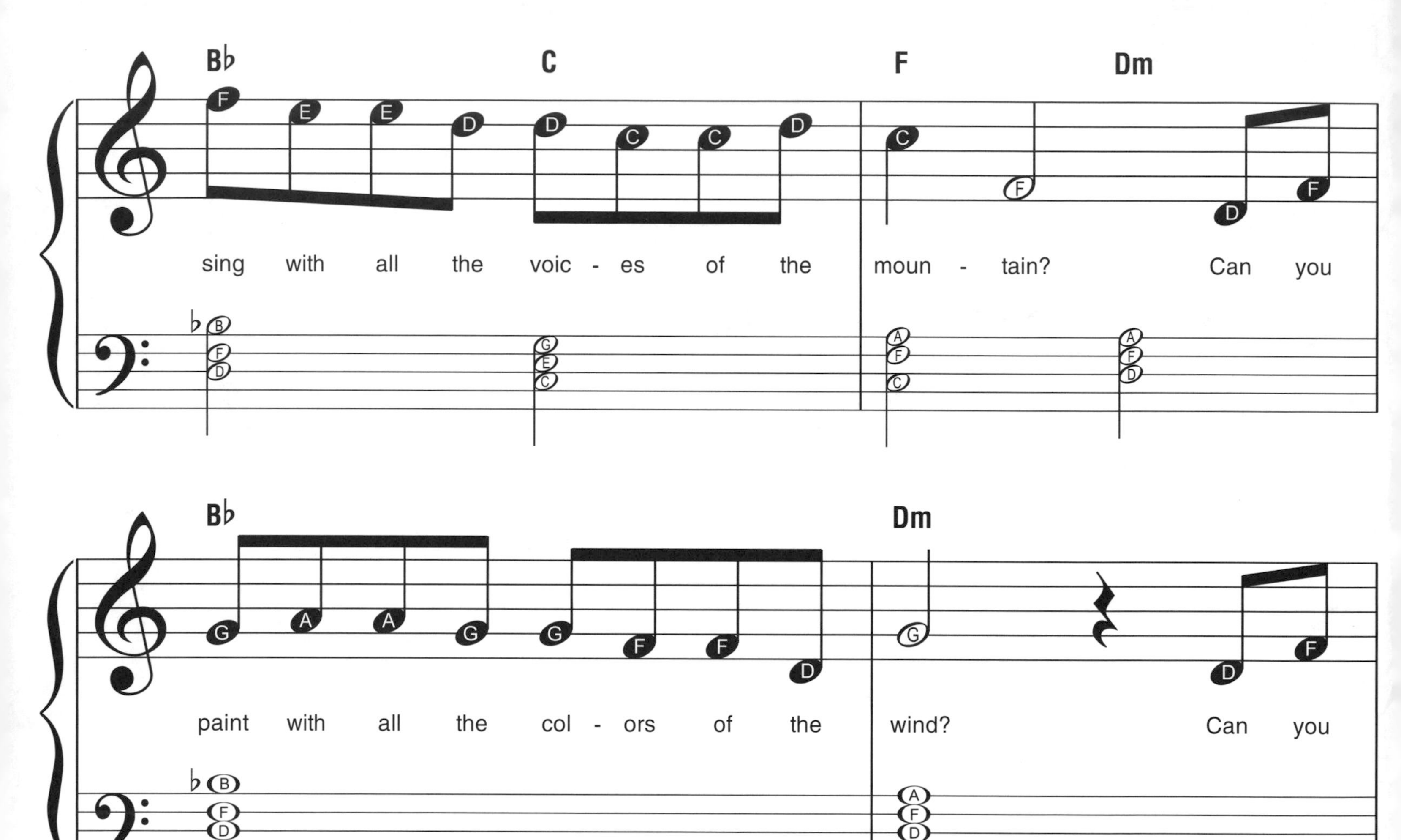
B♭
C
F
Dm
F E E D D C C D
C F D F
sing with all the voic - es of the moun - tain? Can you
B F D
G E C
A F C
A F D
B♭
Dm
G A A G G F F D
G D F
paint with all the col - ors of the wind? Can you
B F D
A F D

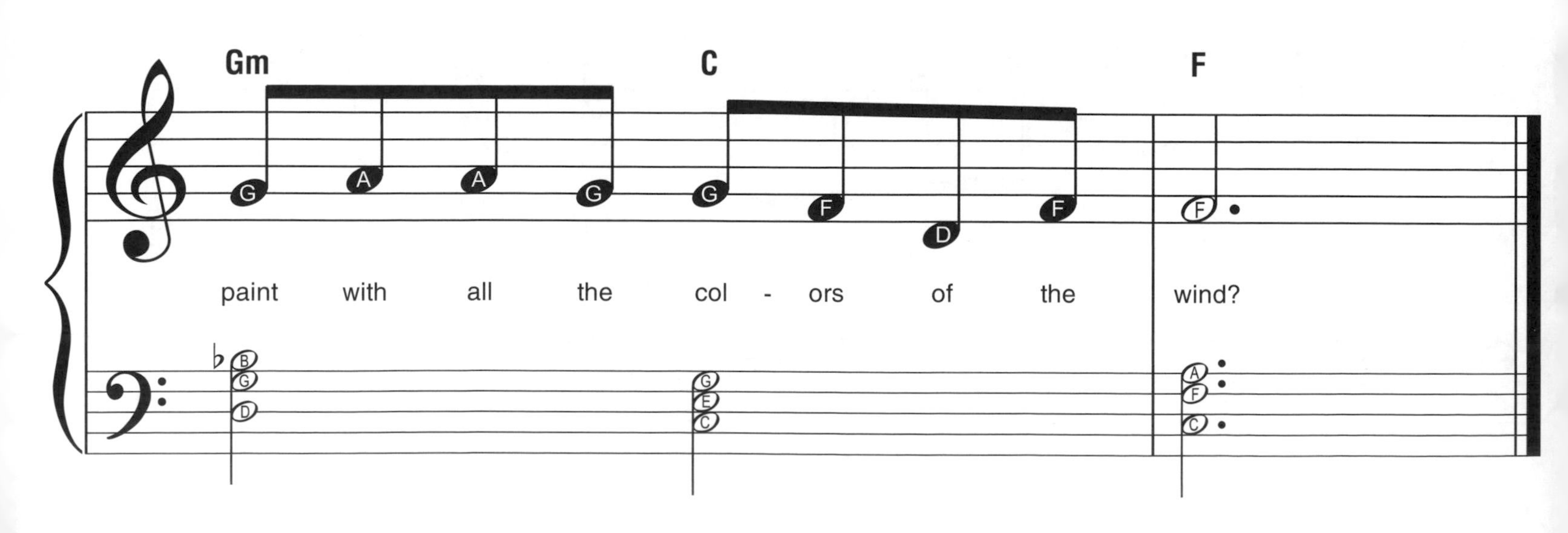
Gm
C
F
G A A G G F D F
F
paint with all the col - ors of the wind?
B G D
G E C
A F C

A Dream Is a Wish Your Heart Makes

from CINDERELLA

Music by Mack David and Al Hoffman
Lyrics by Jerry Livingston

Moderately fast

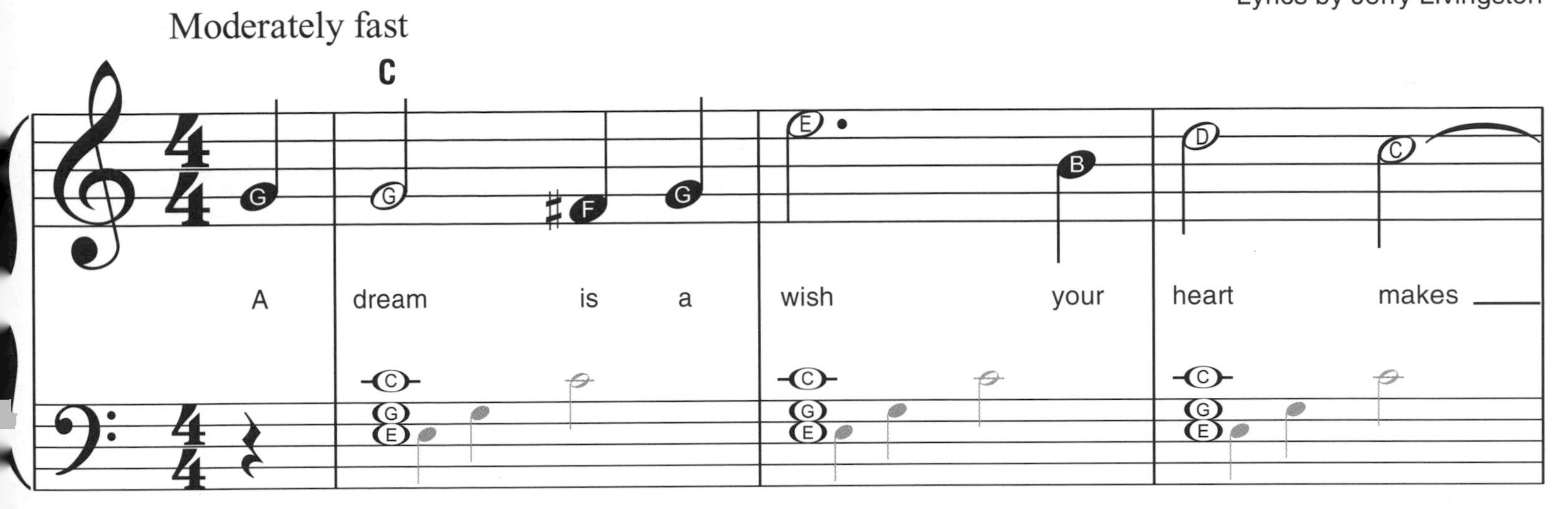

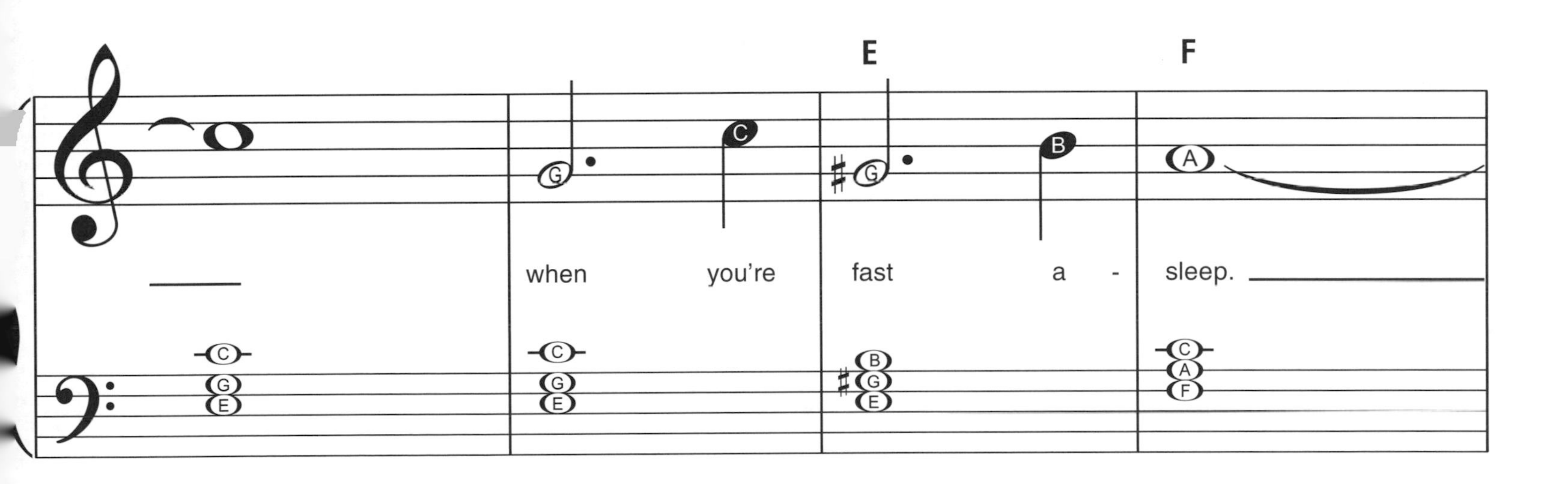

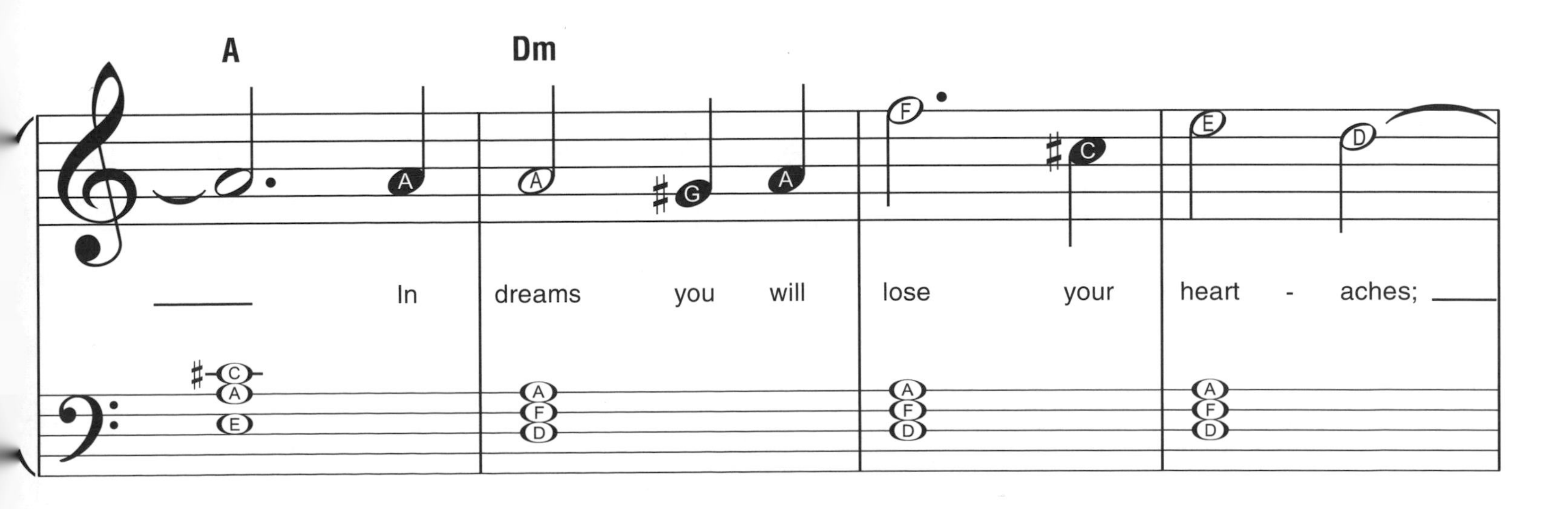

G
C
what - ev - er you wish for you keep.
E C D A C B G E
A F D A F D B G D C G E

Have faith in your dreams and some - day
G G F G E B D C
C G E C G E C G E C G E

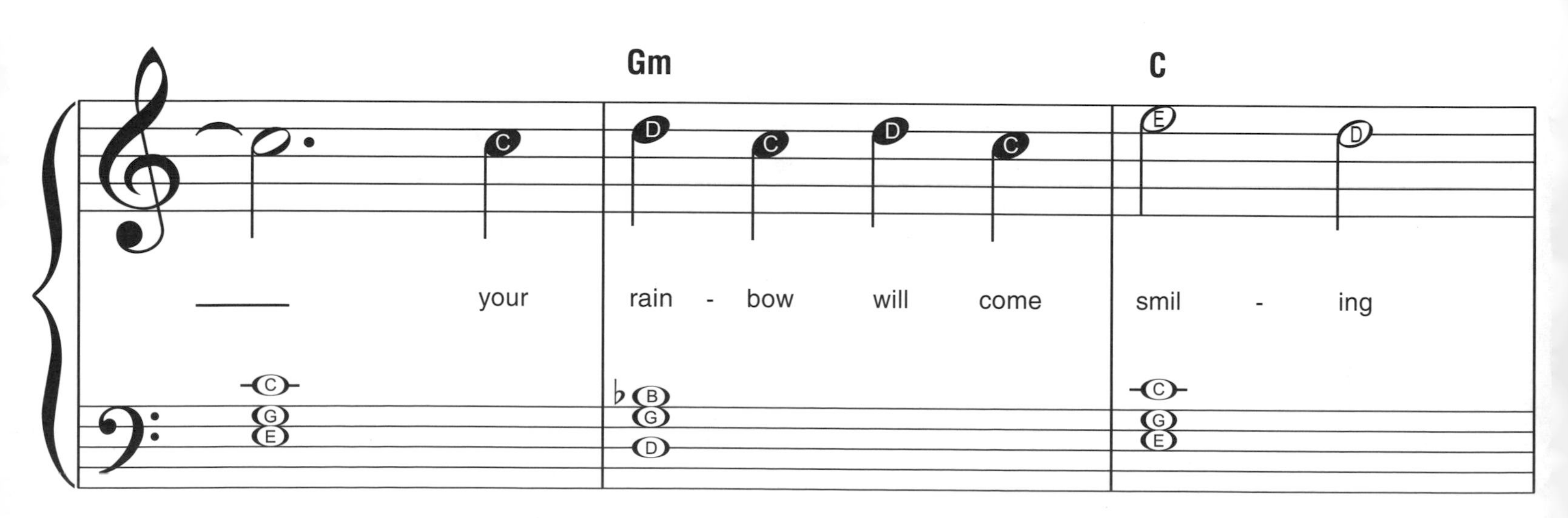
Gm
C
your rain - bow will come smil - ing
C D C D C E D
C G E B G D C G E

F
Dm
through.
No mat - ter
how your heart is

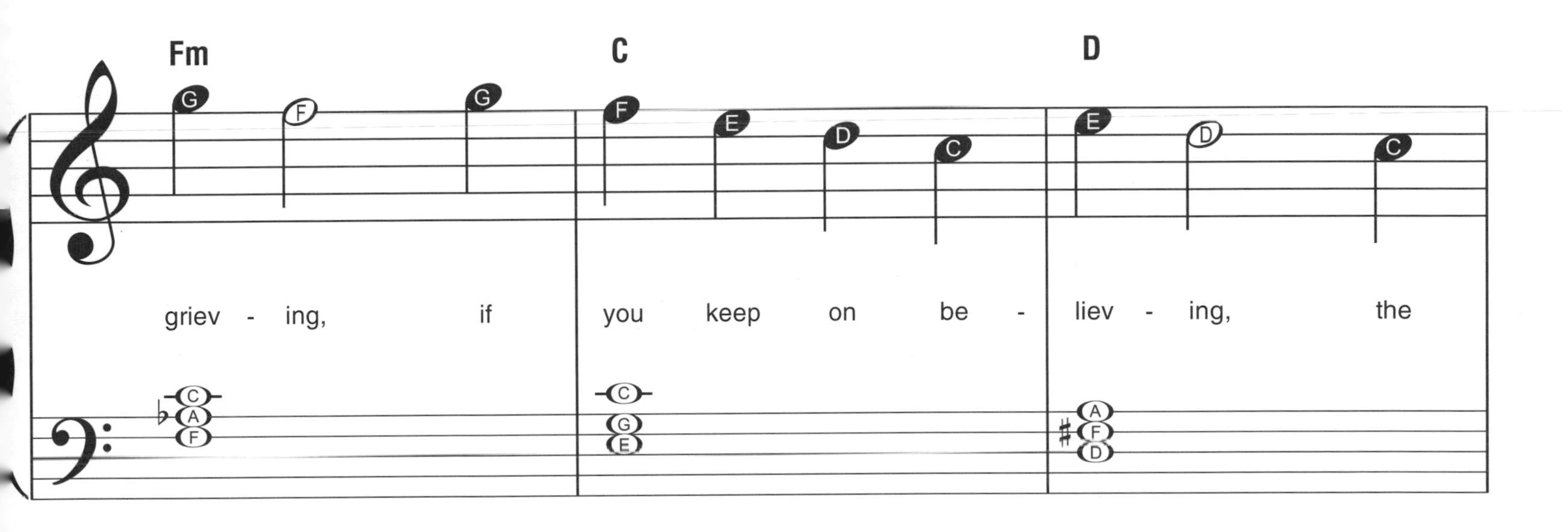
Fm
C
D
griev - ing, if
you keep on be -
liev - ing, the

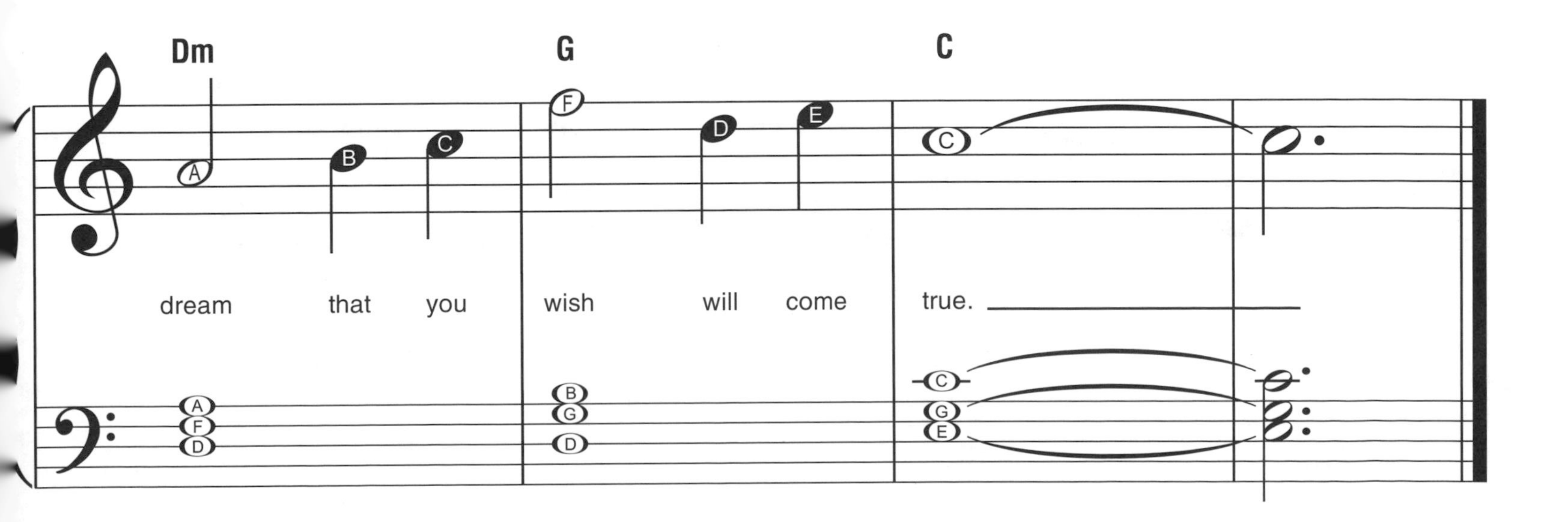
Dm
G
C
dream that you
wish will come
true.

Evermore
from BEAUTY AND THE BEAST

Music by Alan Menken
Lyrics by Tim Rice

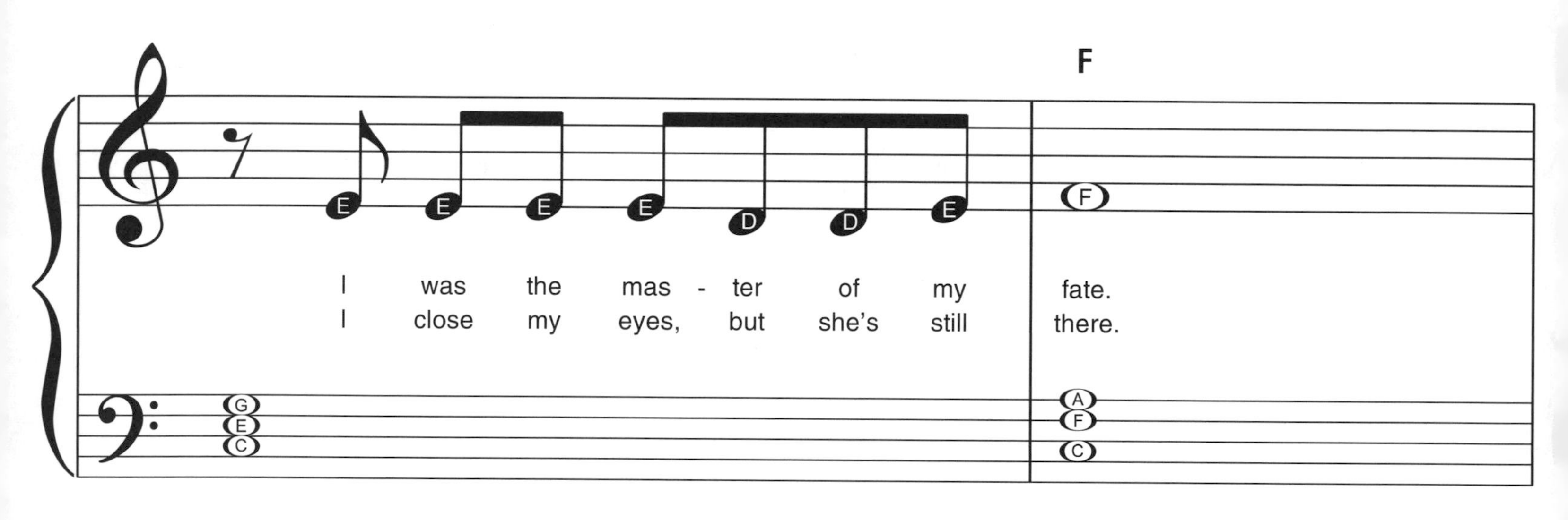

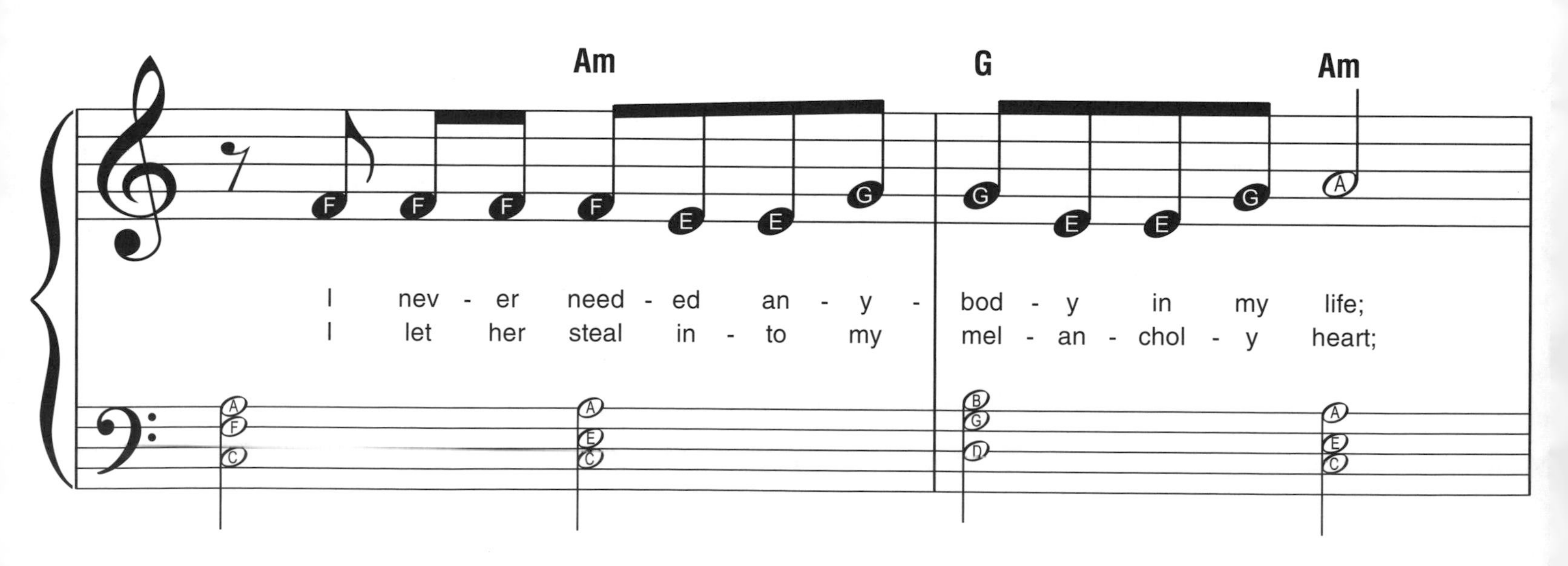

1.
2.
F
C
G
G
I learned the truth too late.
it's more than I can take.
F
G
F
C
Now I know she'll nev - er leave me, e - ven
F
C
F
E
as she runs a - way. She will still tor - ment me,
Am
Dm
D
G
calm me, hurt me, move me, come what may.

F
C
D D D C F E G C
A F C
G E C
Wast - ing in my lone - ly tow - er,

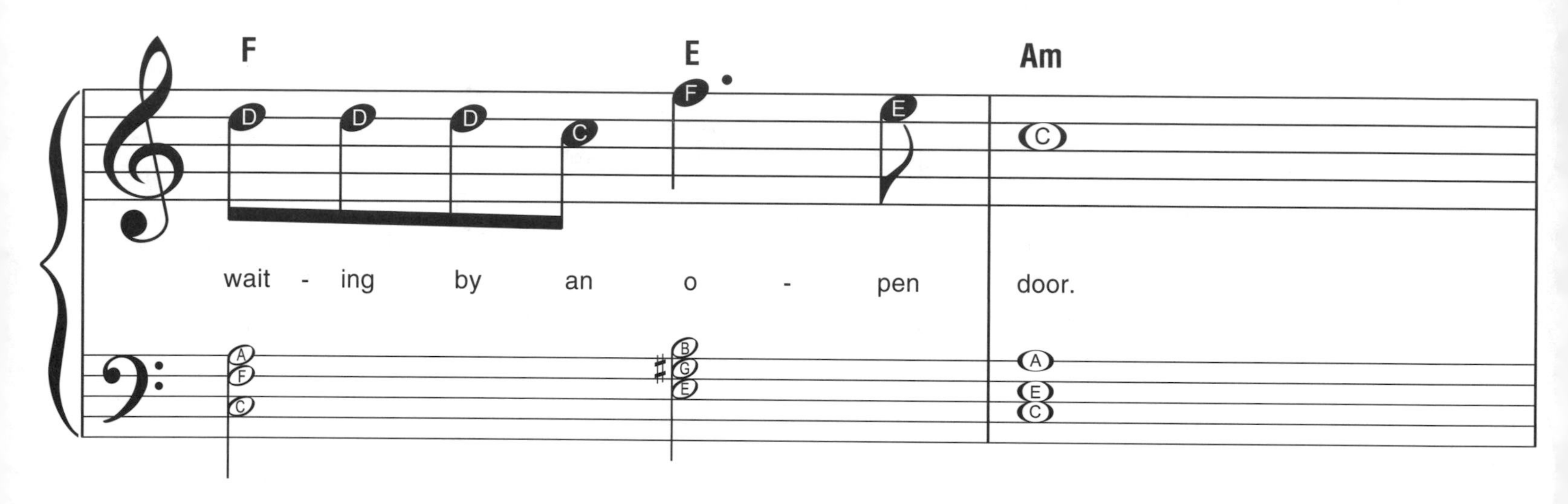
F
E
Am
D D D C F E C
A F C
B G E
A E C
wait - ing by an o - pen door.

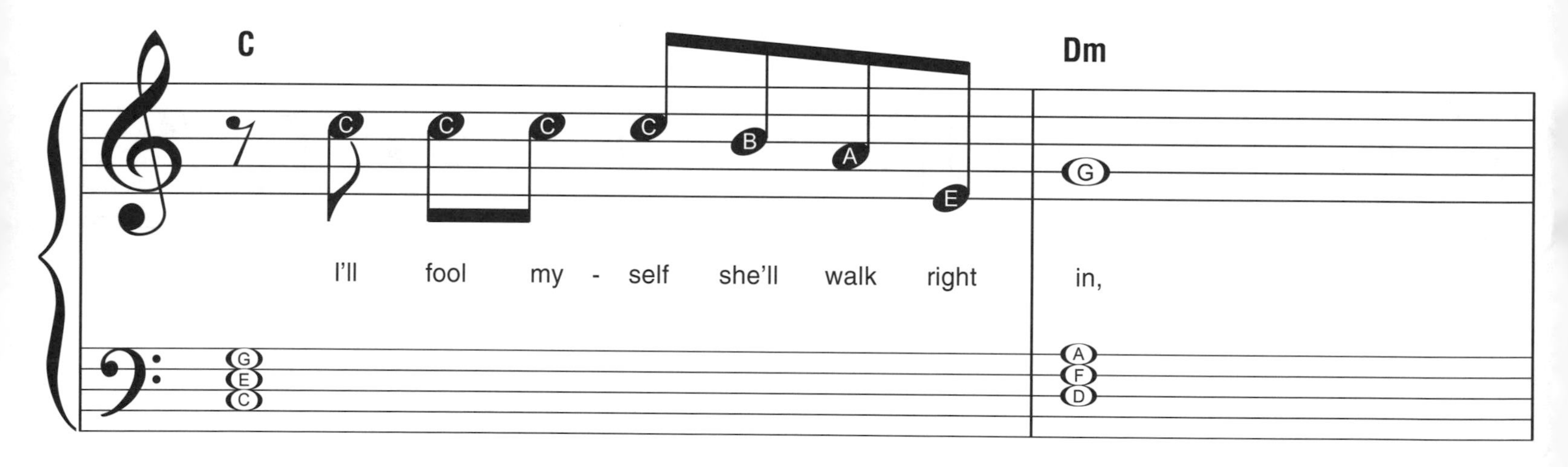
C
Dm
C C C C B A E G
G E C
A F D
I'll fool my - self she'll walk right in,

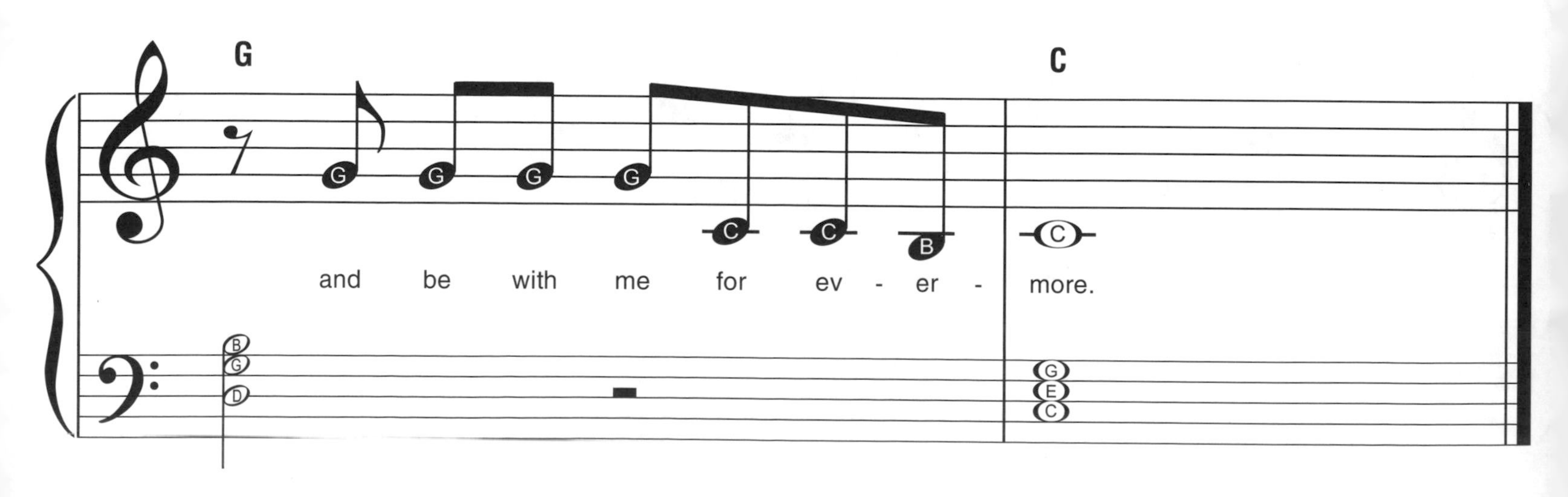
G
C
G G G G C C B C
B G D
G E C
and be with me for ev - er - more.

How Does a Moment Last Forever

from BEAUTY AND THE BEAST

Music by Alan Menken
Lyrics by Tim Rice

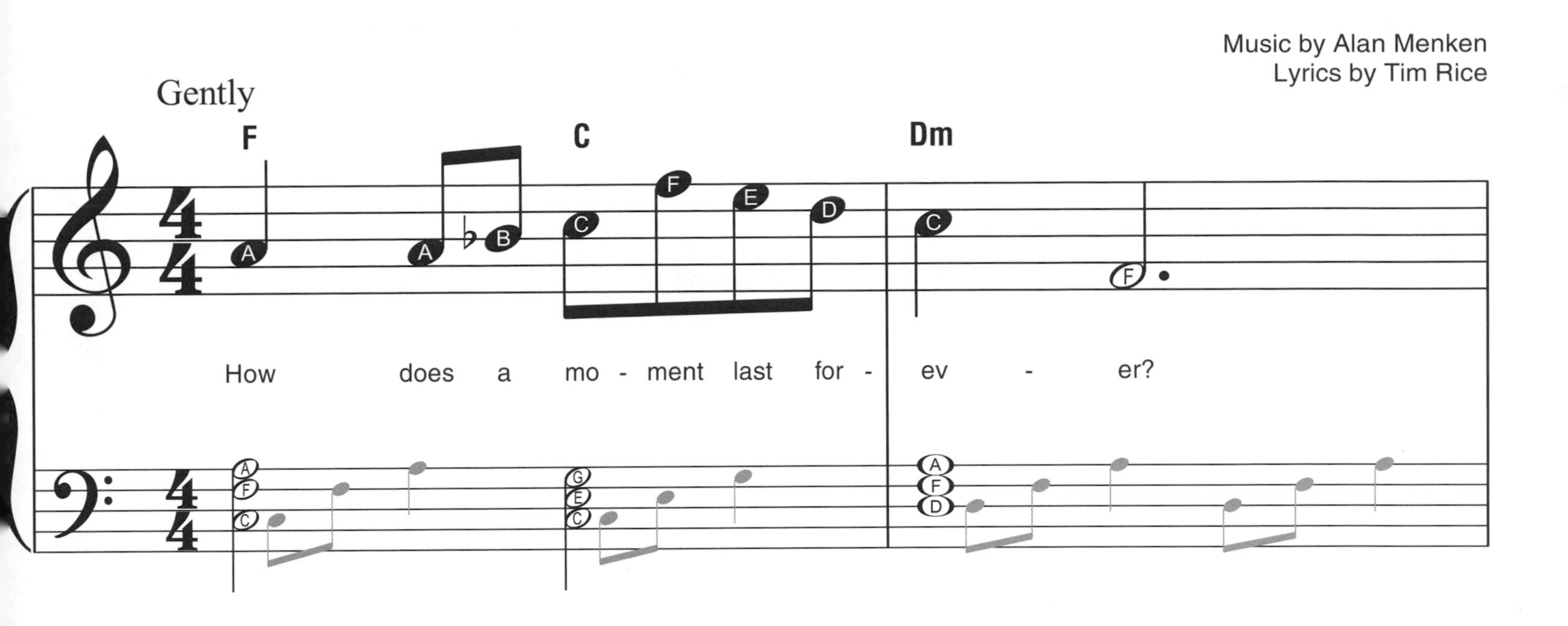

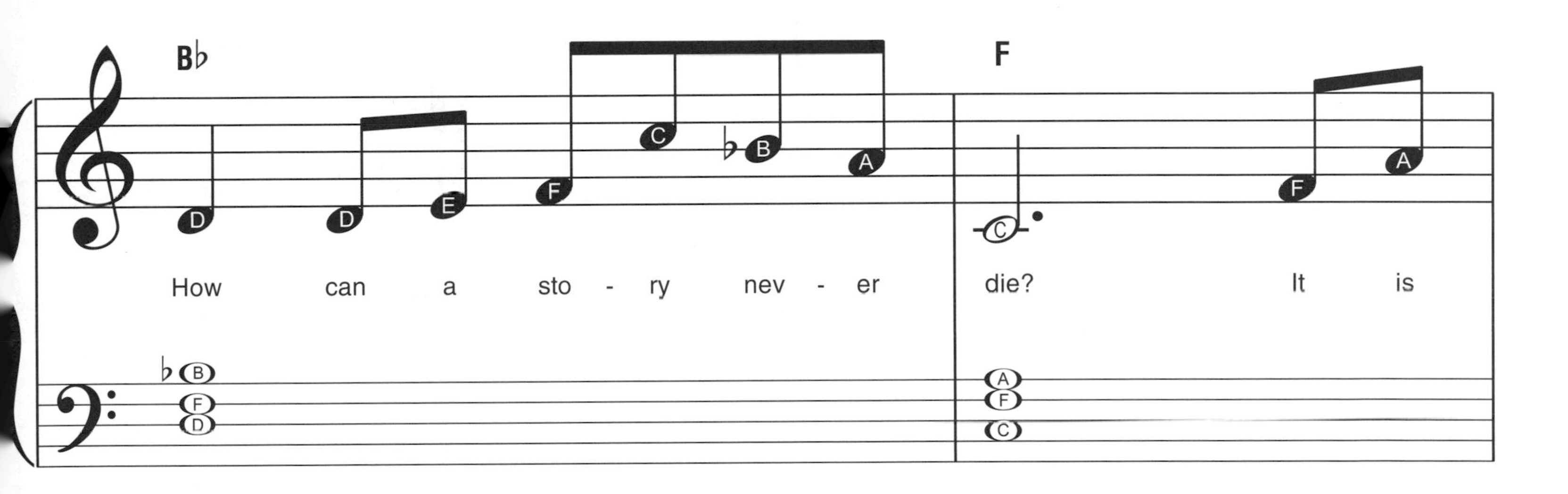

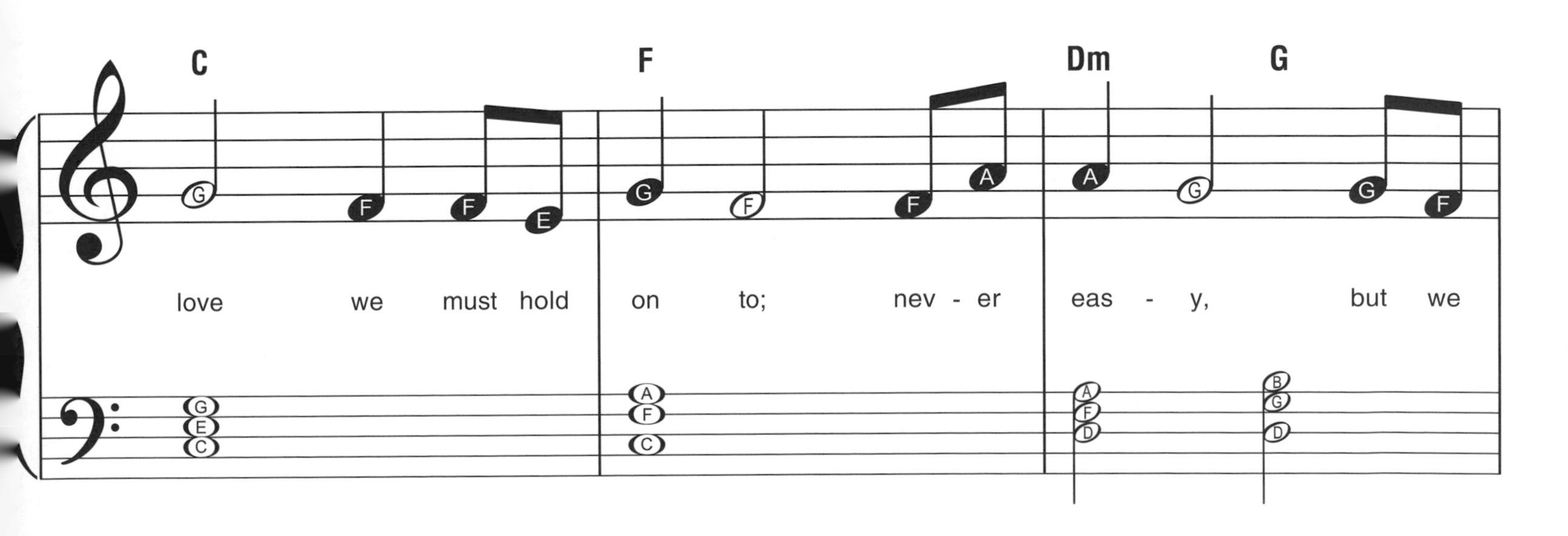

C
F
C
Dm
try.
Some - times our hap - pi - ness seems cap - tured;

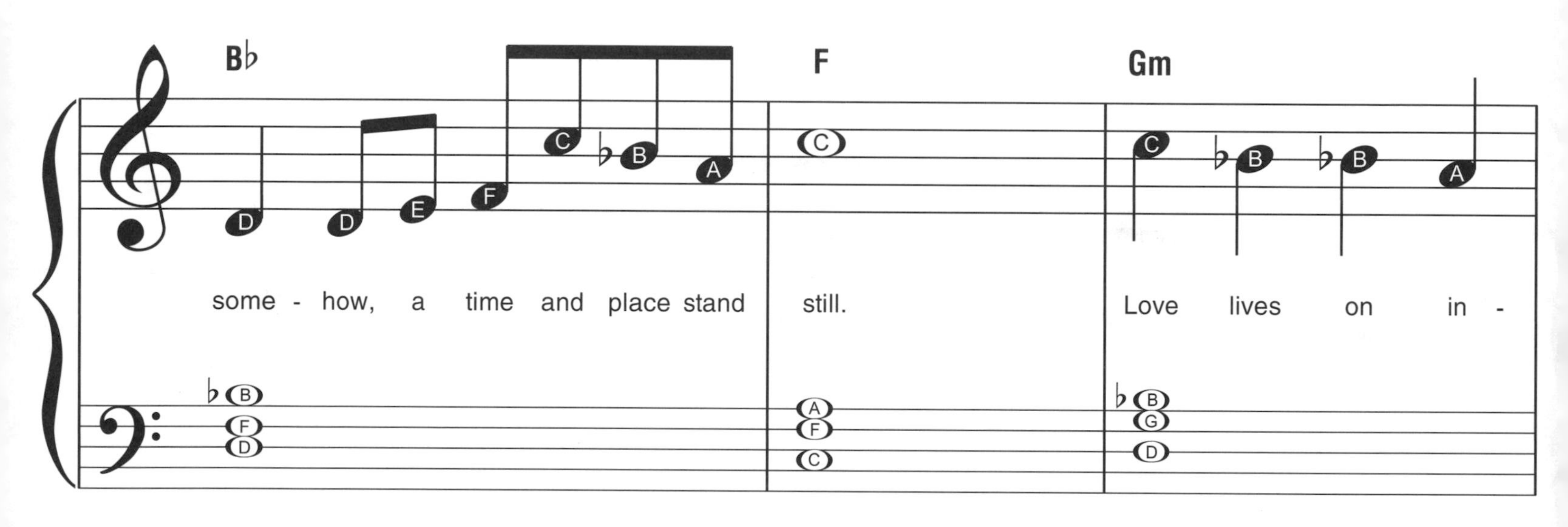
B♭
F
Gm
some - how, a time and place stand still.
Love lives on in -

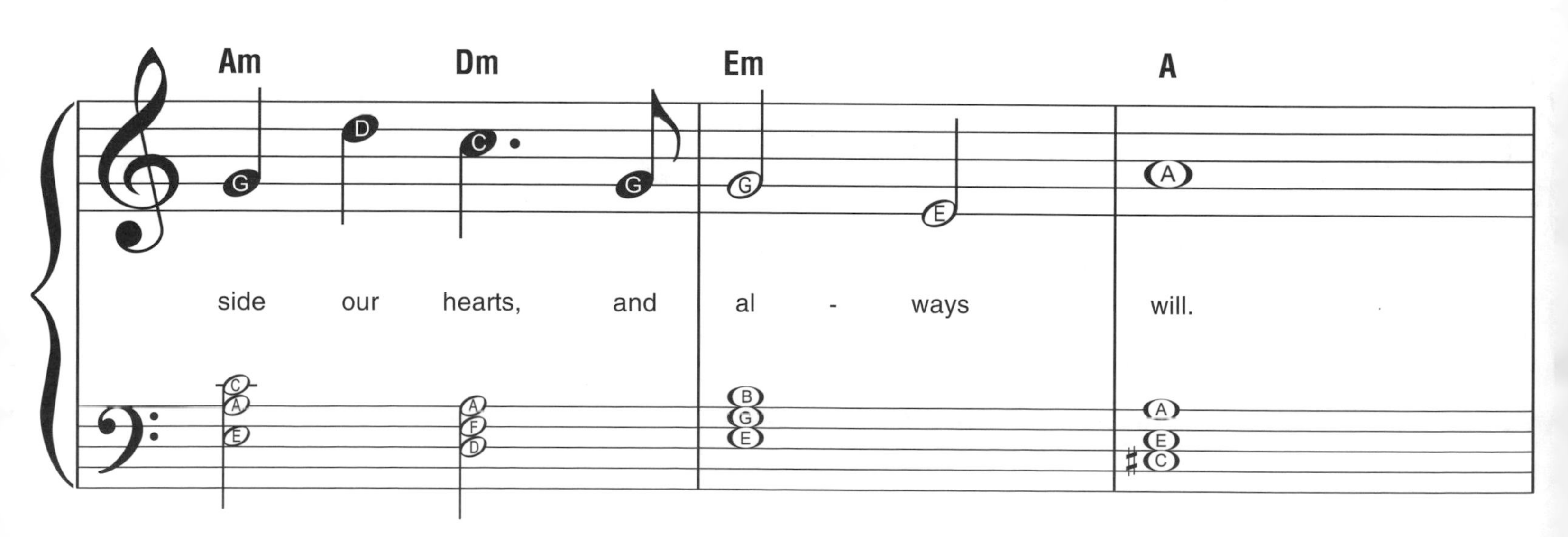
Am
Dm
Em
A
side our hearts, and al - ways will.

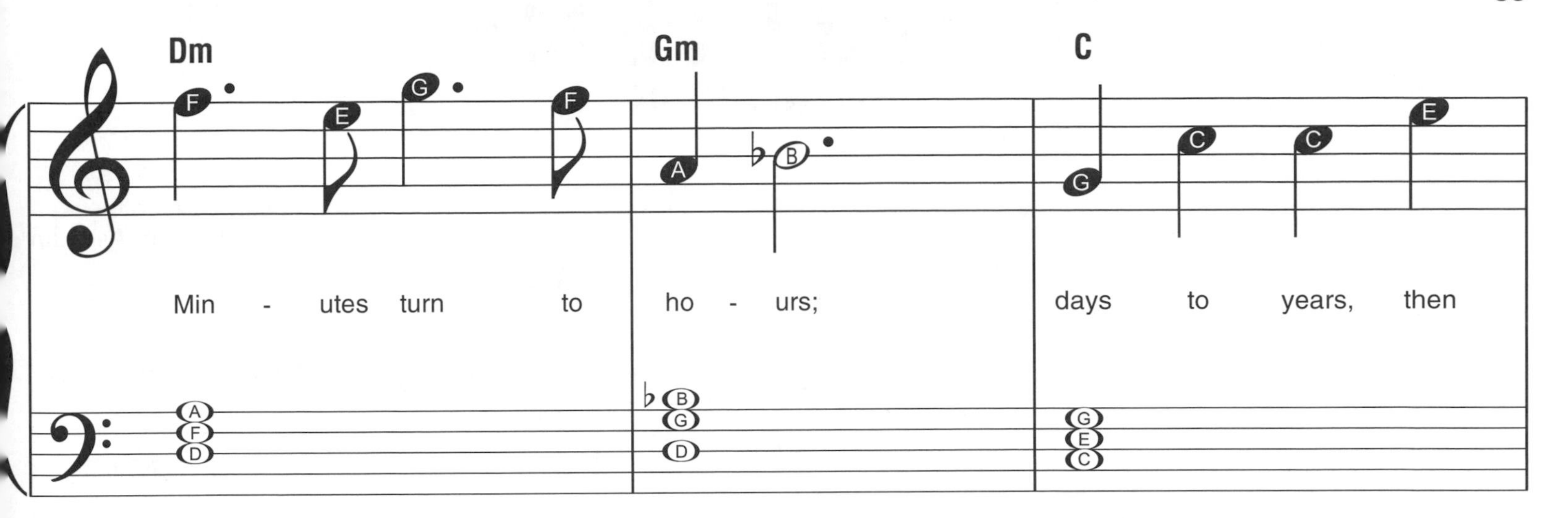
Dm
Gm
C
F
E
G
F
A
B
G
C
C
E
Min - utes turn to
ho - urs;
days to years, then
A
F
D
B
G
D
G
E
C

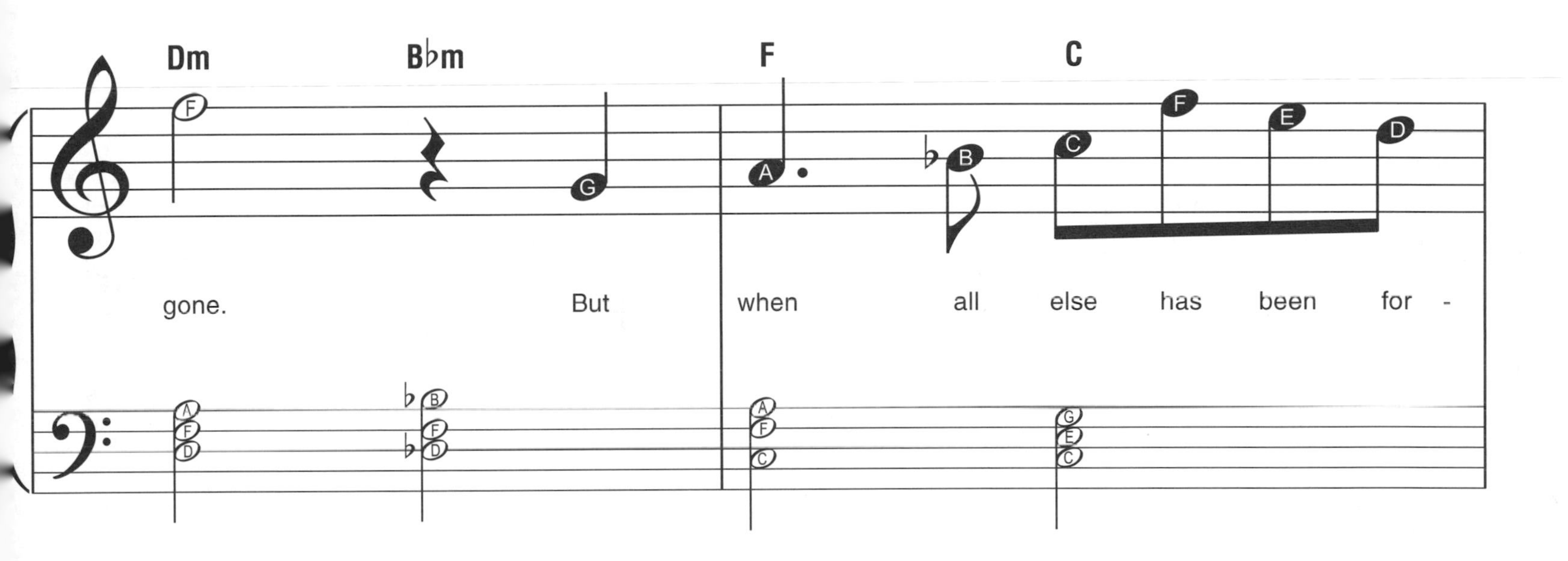
Dm
B♭m
F
C
F
G
A
B
C
F
E
D
gone.
But
when all else has been for -
A
F
D
B
F
D
A
F
C
G
E
C

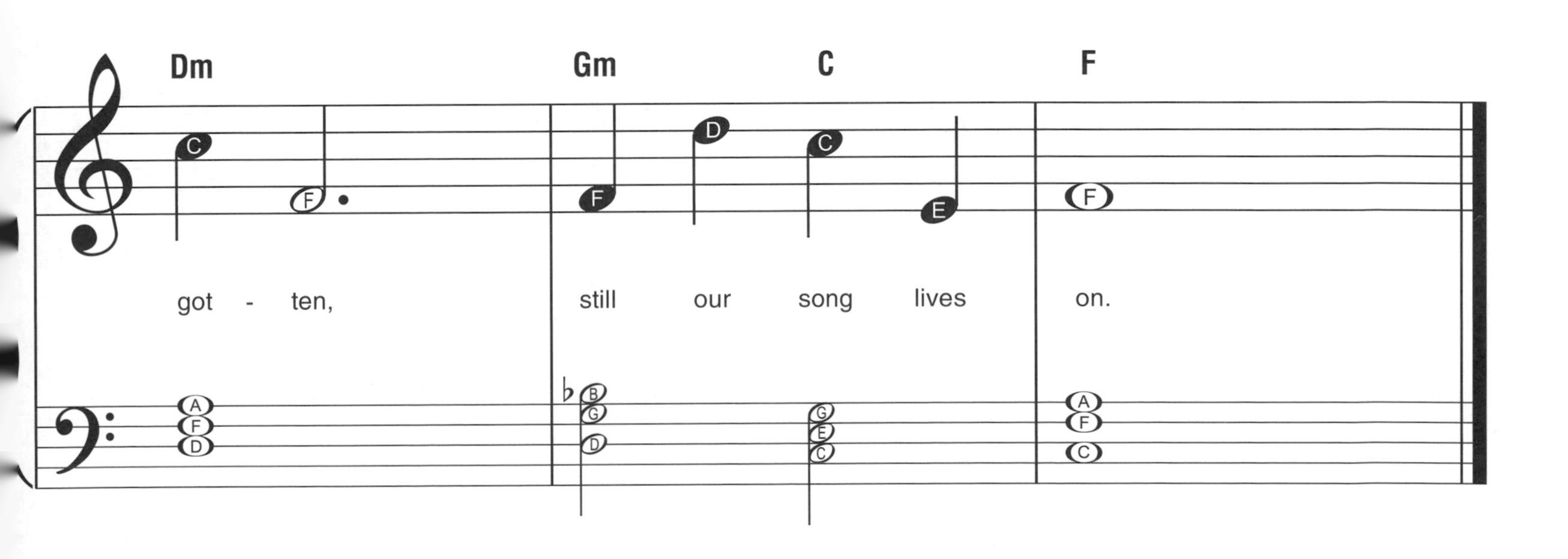
Dm
Gm
C
F
C
F
F
D
C
E
F
got - ten,
still our song lives
on.
A
F
D
B
G
D
G
E
C
A
F
C

Friend Like Me

from ALADDIN

Music by Alan Menken
Lyrics by Howard Ashman

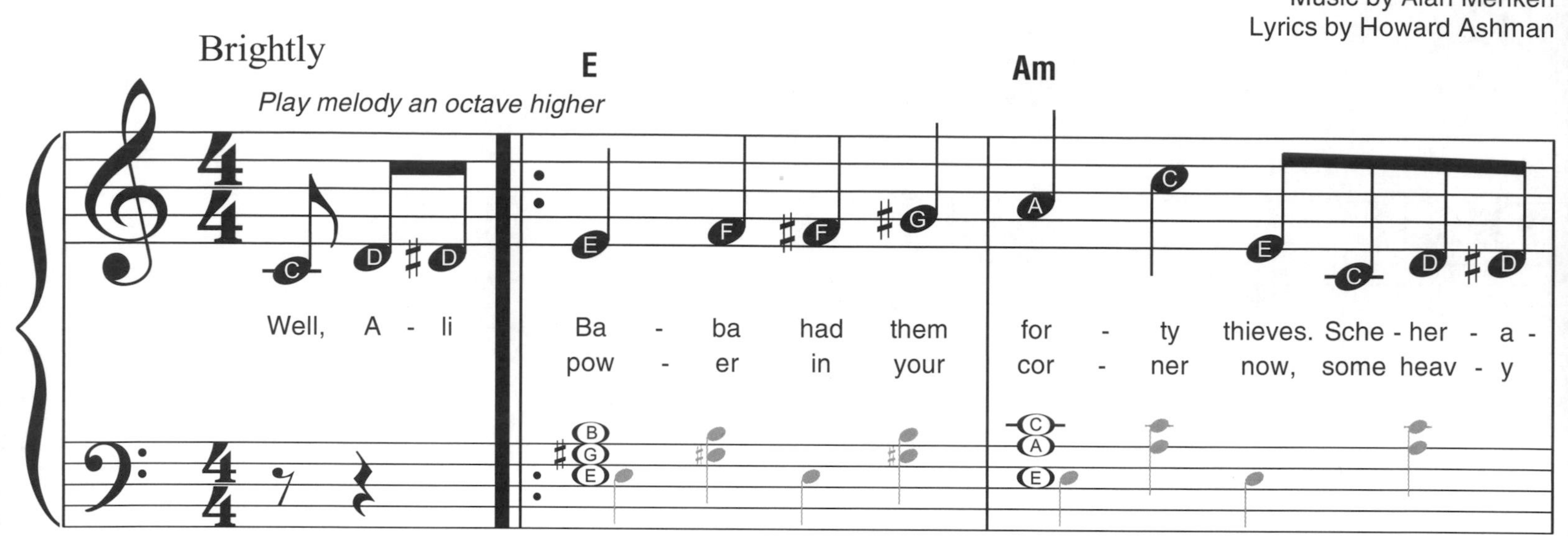

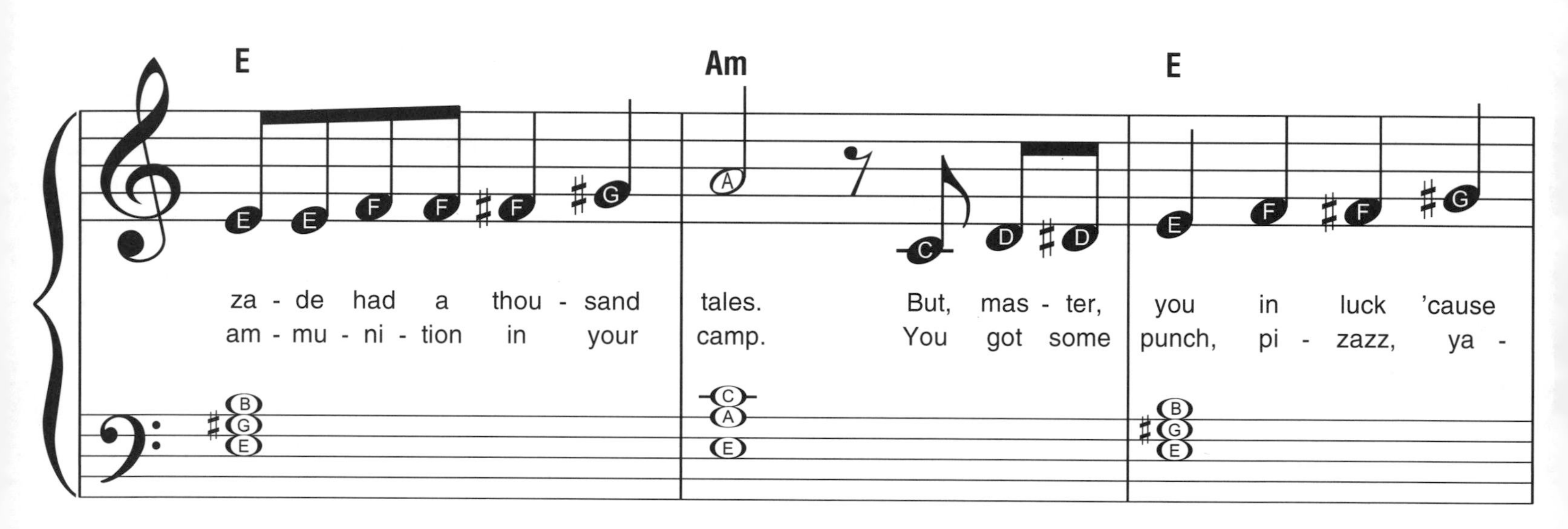

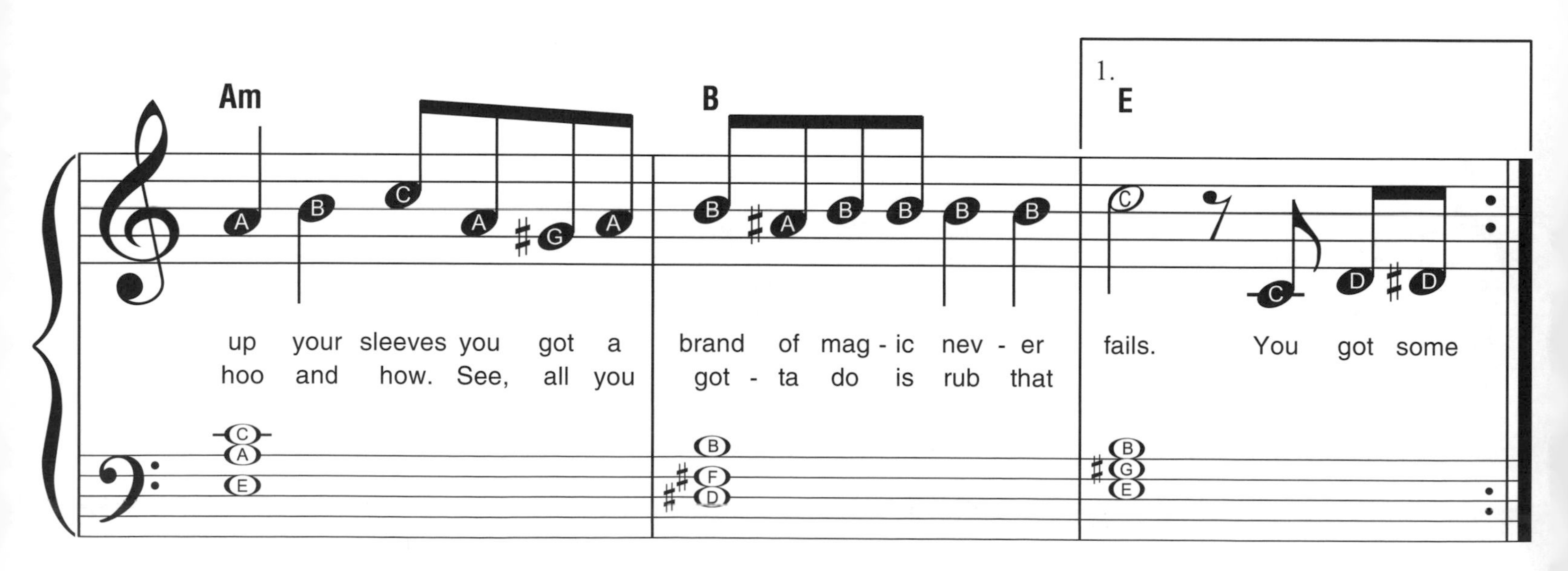

2.
E
Am
F
E
Am
lamp. And I'll say:
Mis - ter A - lad - din, sir, what will your pleas - ure
Life is your res - tau - rant and I'm your mai - tre

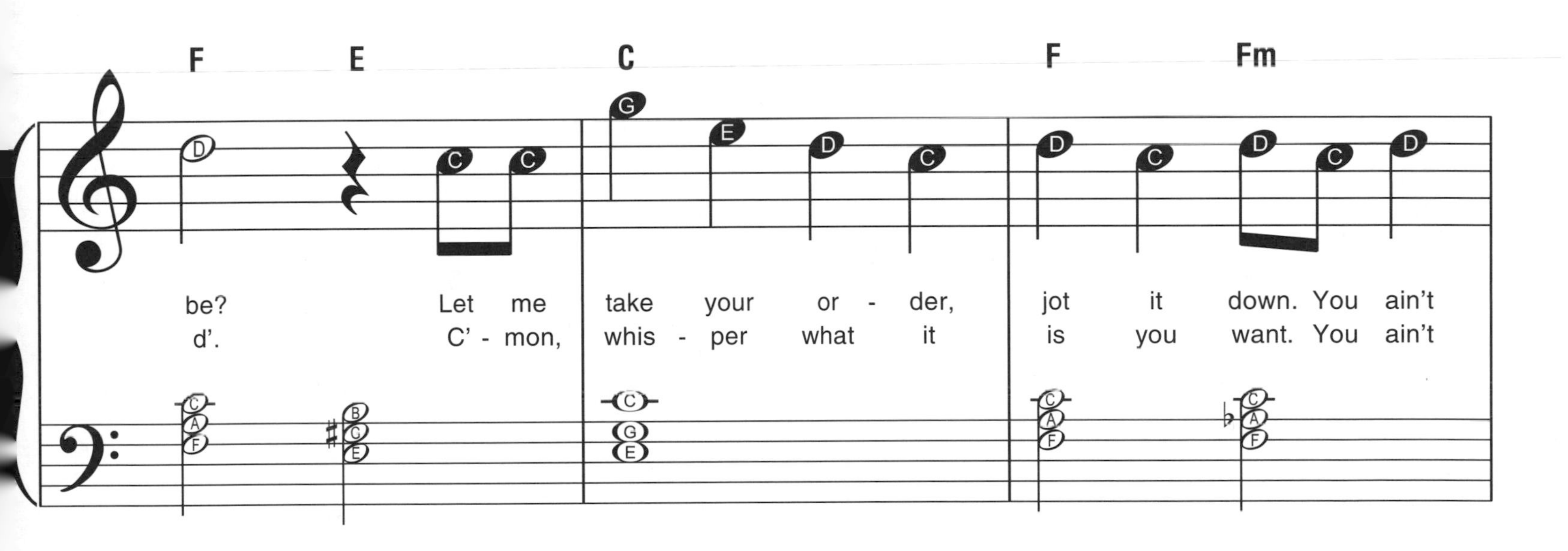
F
E
C
F
Fm
be? Let me take your or - der, jot it down. You ain't
d'. C' - mon, whis - per what it is you want. You ain't

1.
2.
C
E
Am
E
Am
nev - er had a friend like me. No, no, no.
nev - er had a friend like me.

God Help the Outcasts

from THE HUNCHBACK OF NOTRE DAME

Music by Alan Menken
Lyrics by Stephen Schwartz

Prayerfully

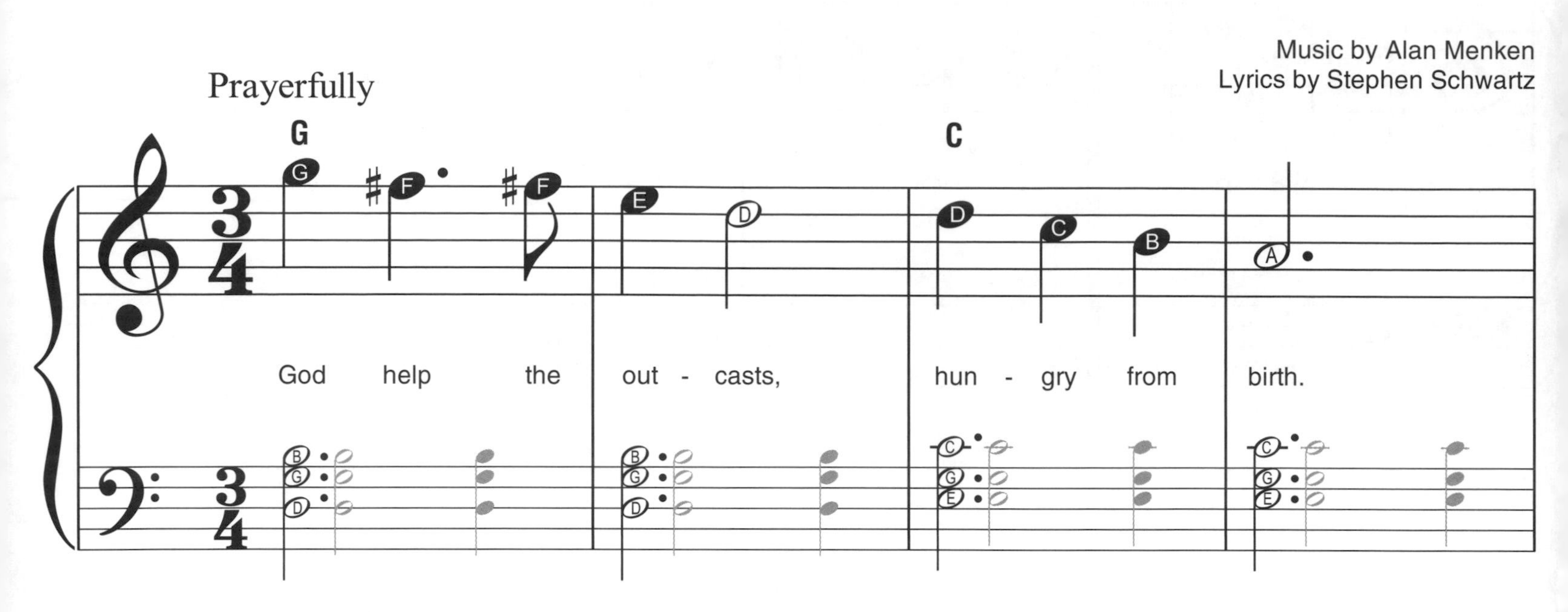

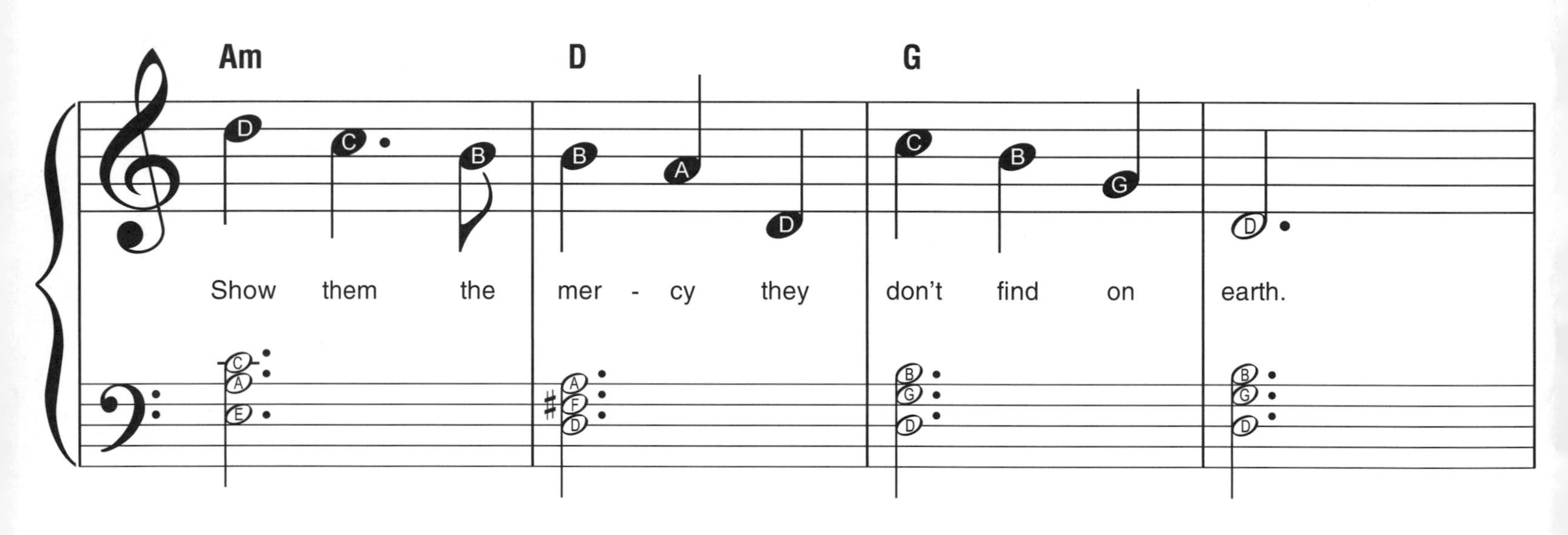

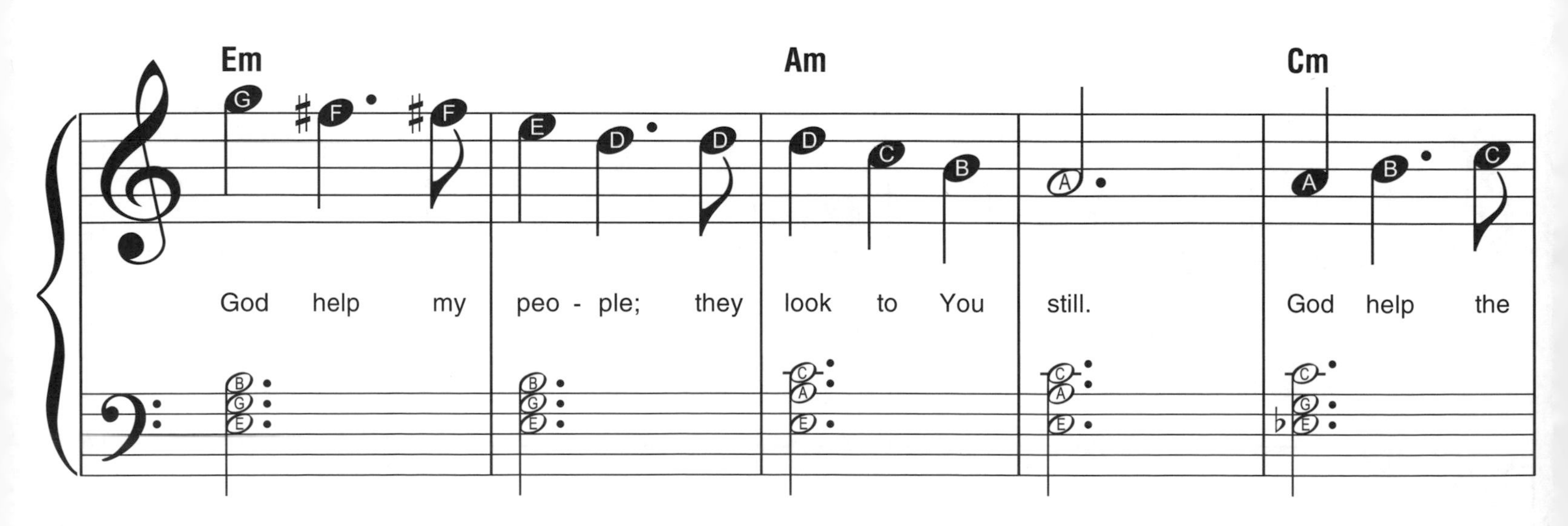

G
D
G
out - casts or
no - bod - y
will.
I ask for
noth - ing;
C
Am
D
G
I can get
by. But
I know so
man - y less
luck - y than
Em
Am
I.
Please help my
peo - ple, the
poor and down -
Cm
G
D
G
trod.
I thought we
all were the
chil - dren of
God.

How Far I'll Go

from MOANA

Music and Lyrics by
Lin-Manuel Miranda

Moderately

F Gm

I've been star - ing at the edge of the wa - ter long

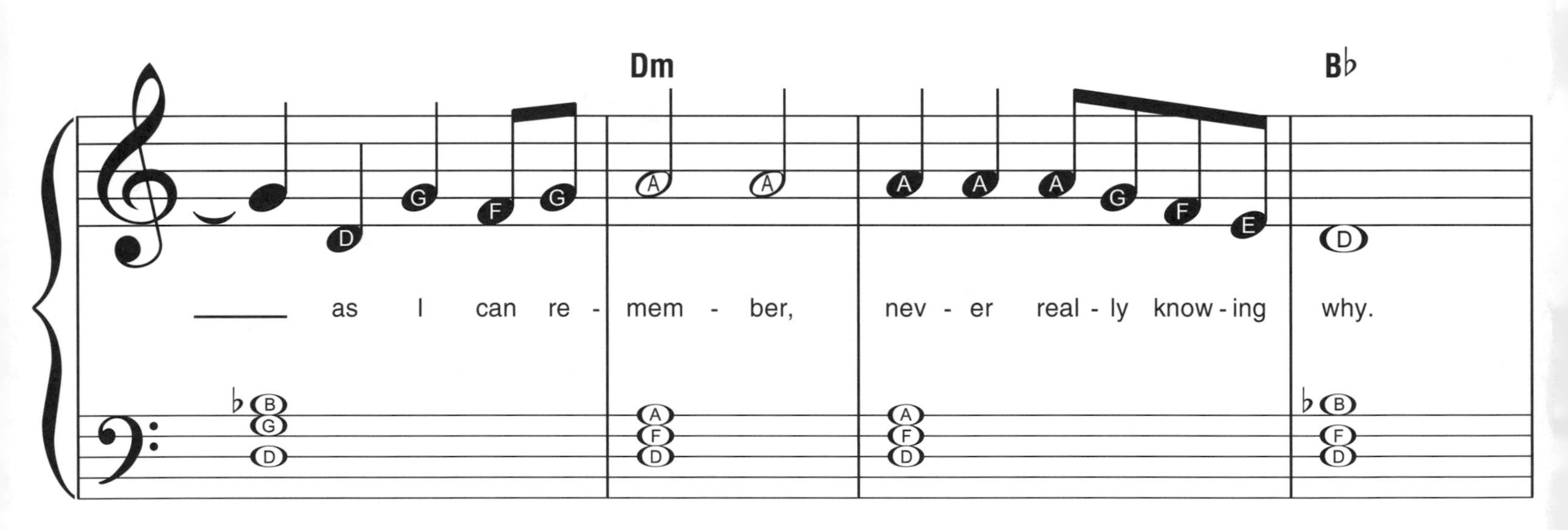

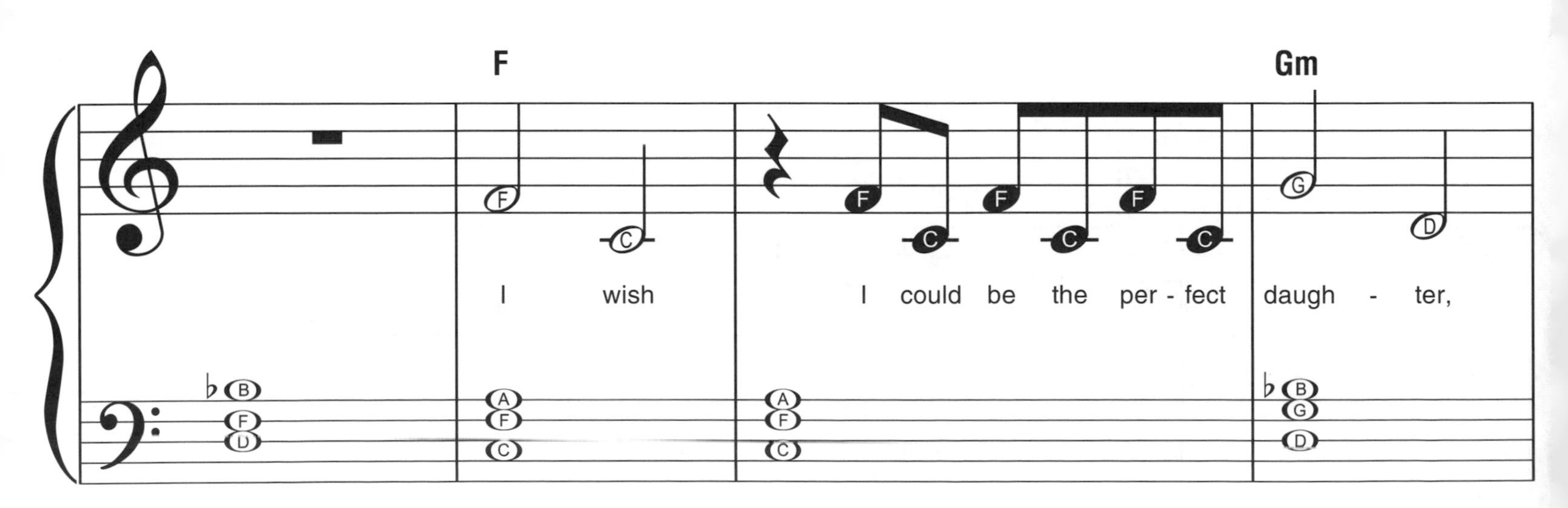

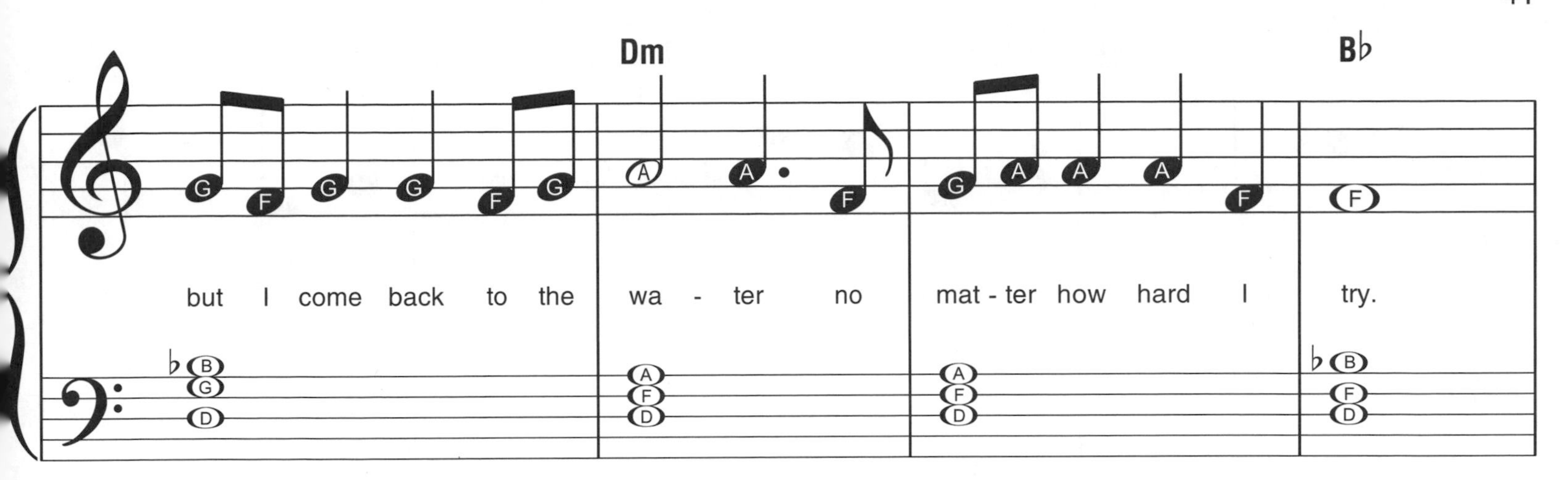
Dm
B♭
but I come back to the wa - ter no mat - ter how hard I try.

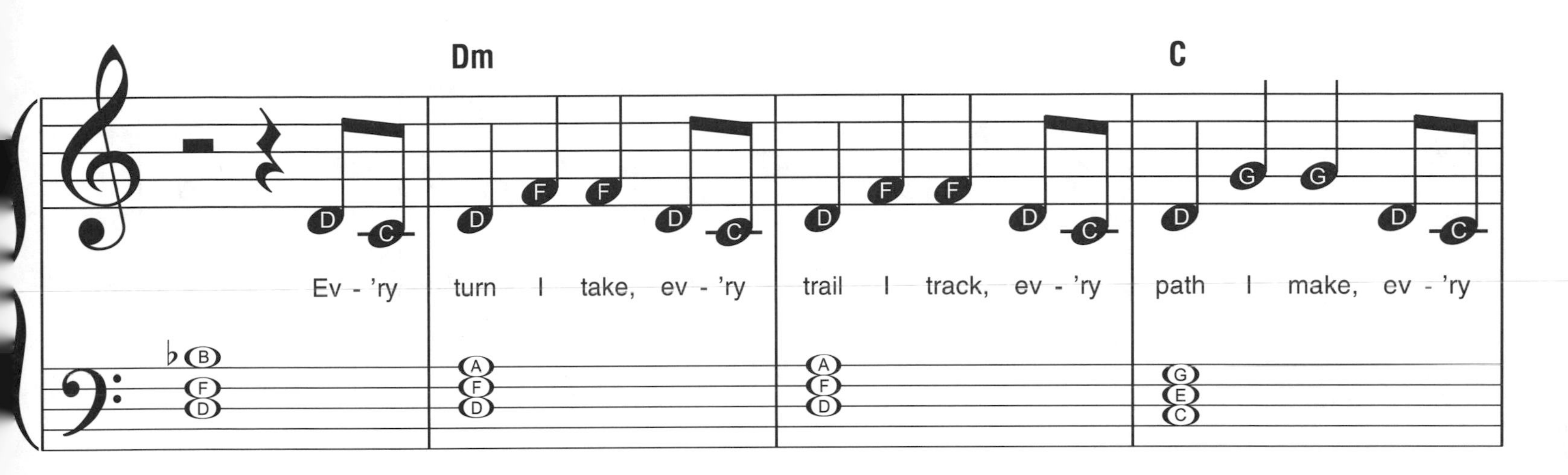
Dm
C
Ev - 'ry turn I take, ev - 'ry trail I track, ev - 'ry path I make, ev - 'ry

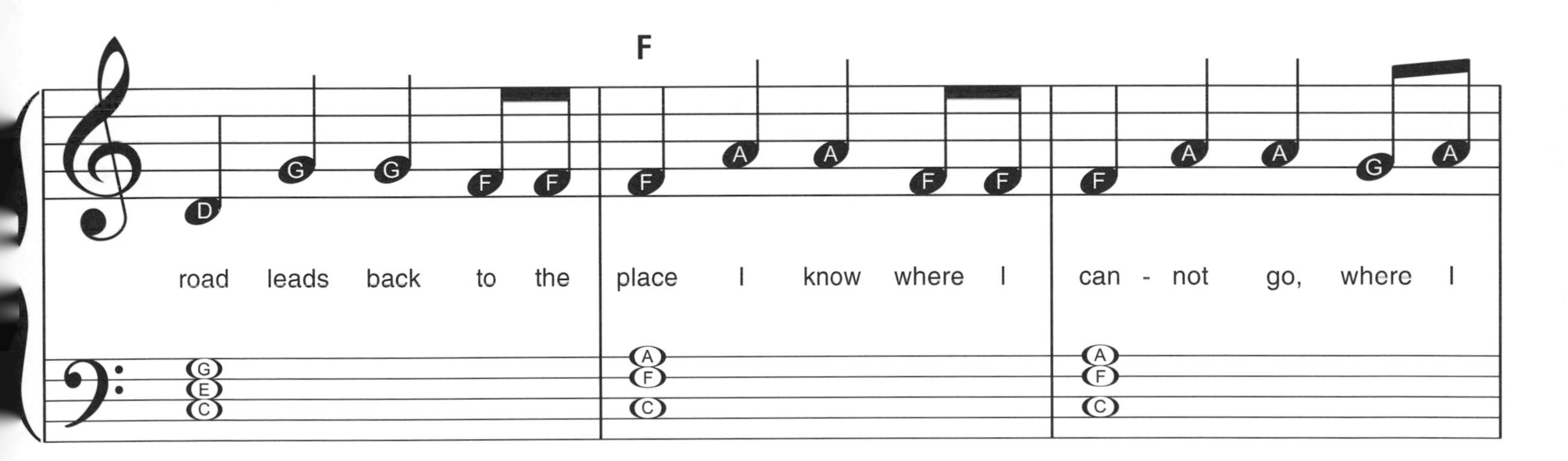
F
road leads back to the place I know where I can - not go, where I

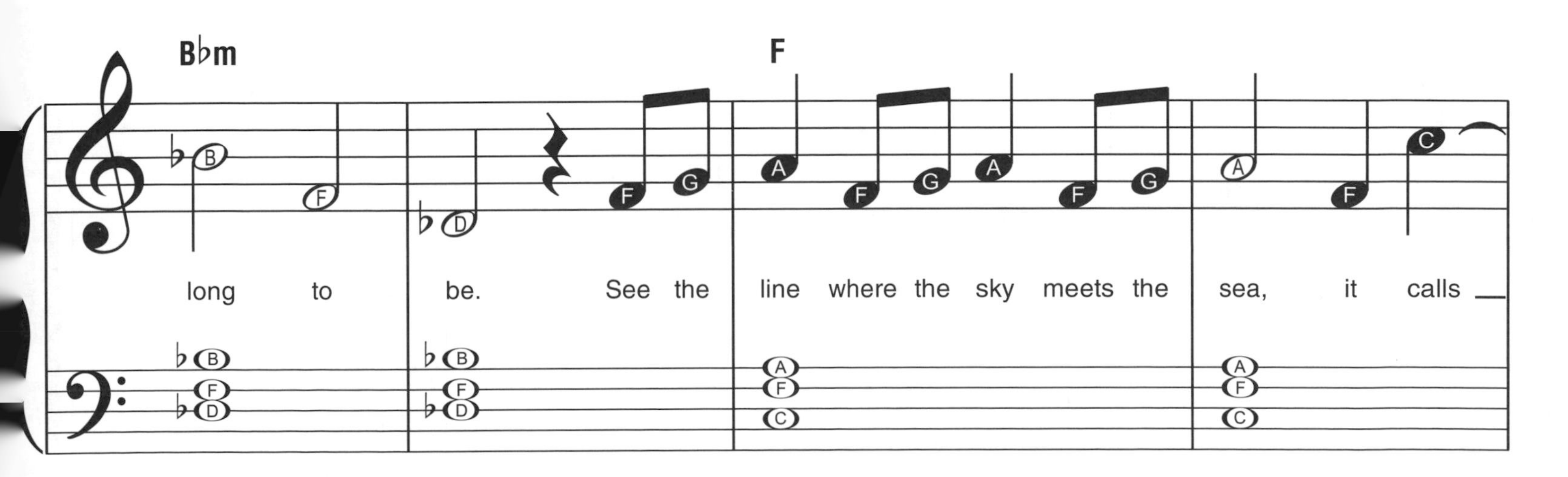
B♭m
F
long to be. See the line where the sky meets the sea, it calls

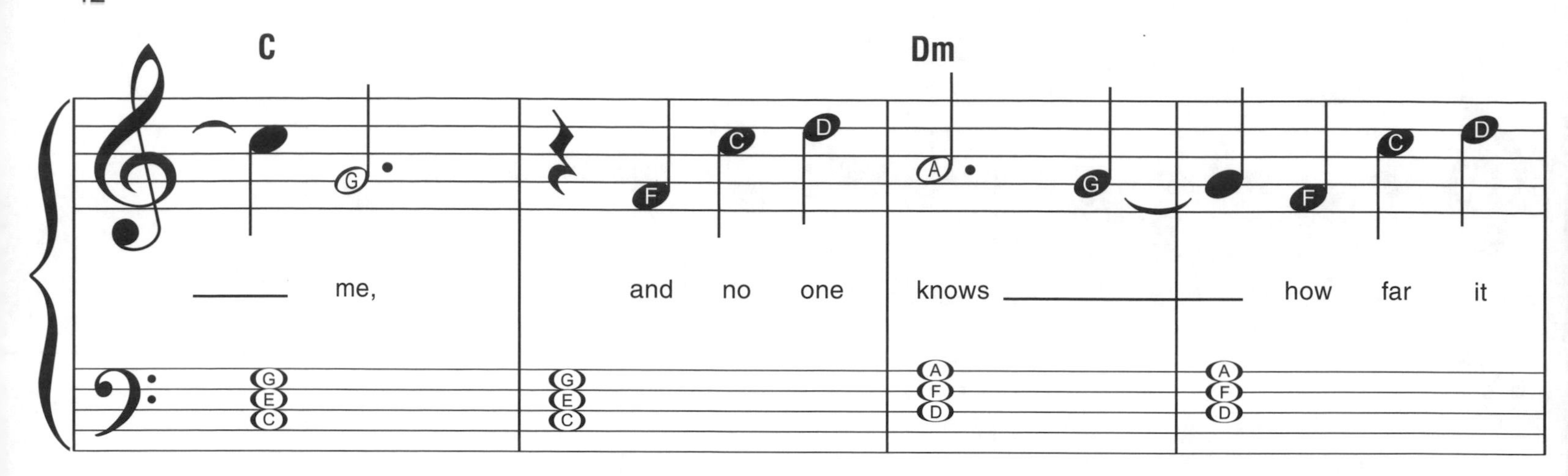
C
Dm
me,
and no one
knows
how far it

B♭
F
goes.
If the
wind in my sail on the
sea stays be - hind

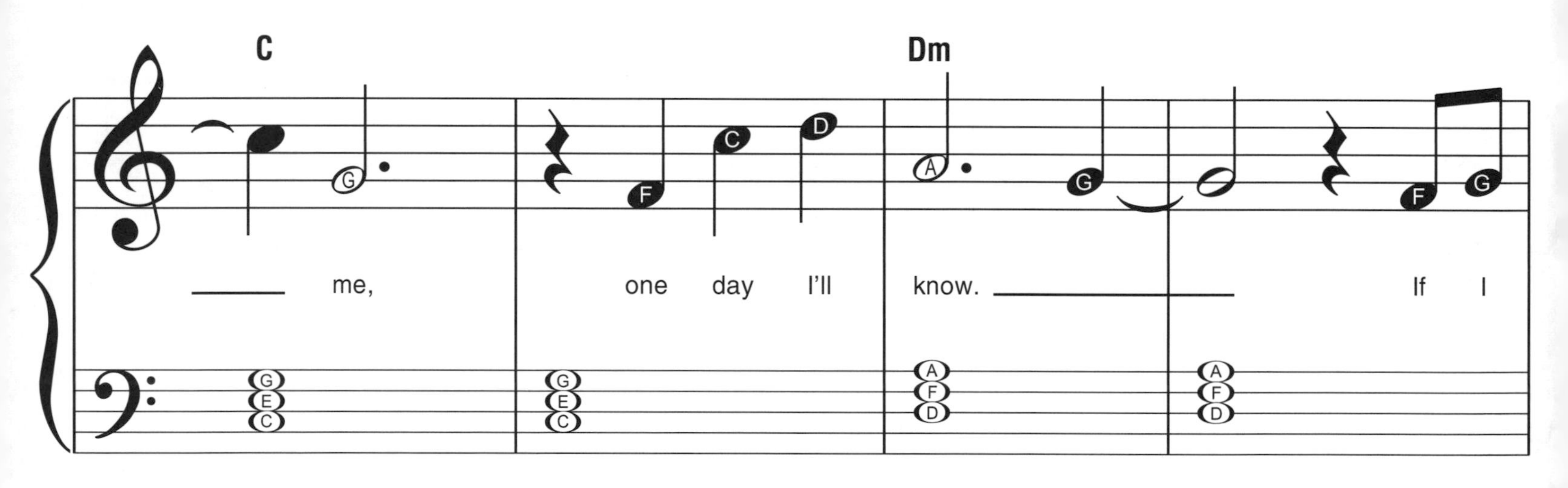
C
Dm
me,
one day I'll
know.
If I

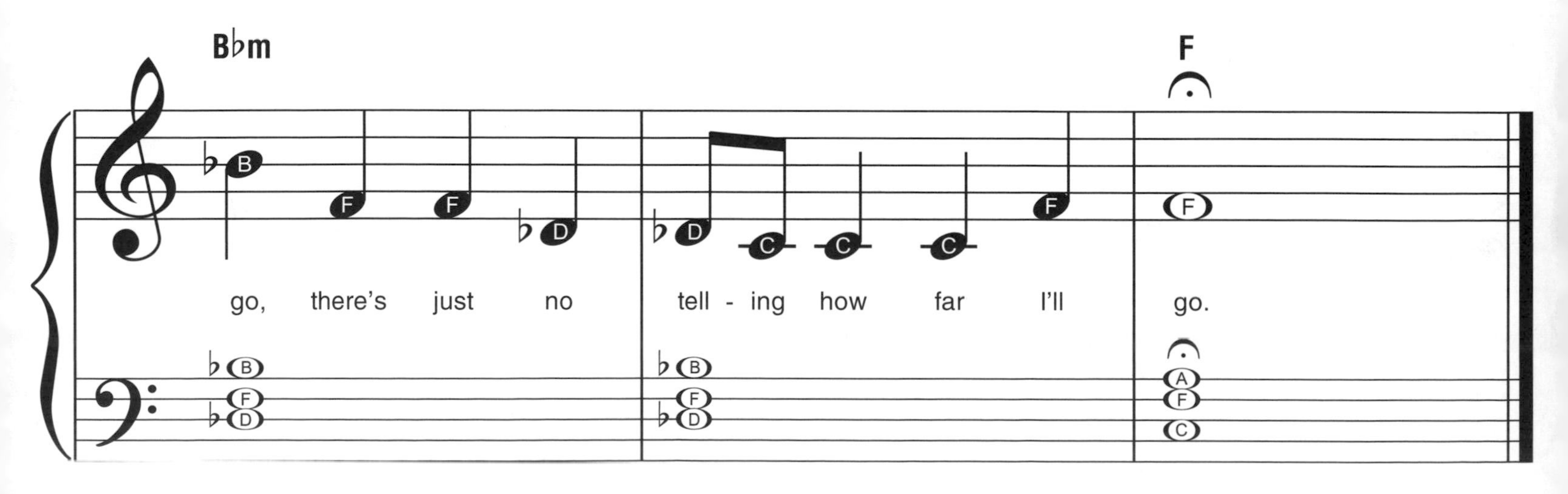
B♭m
F
go, there's just no
tell - ing how far I'll
go.

I See the Light

from TANGLED

Music by Alan Menken
Lyrics by Glenn Slater

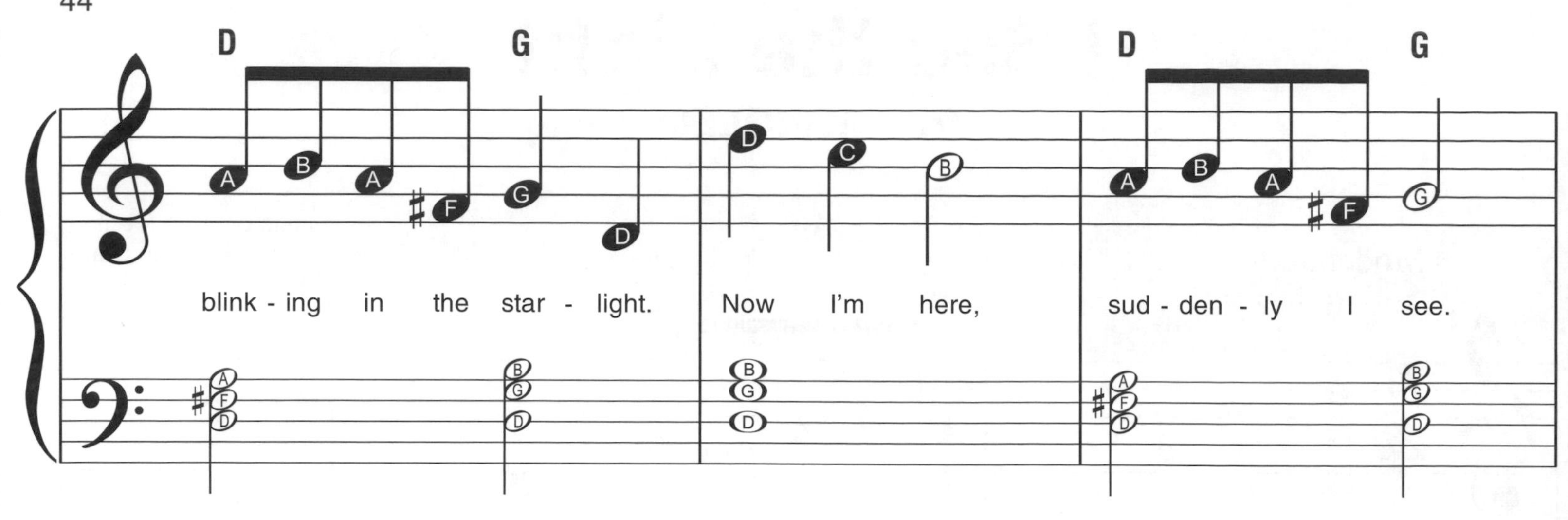
D G D G
blink - ing in the star - light. Now I'm here, sud - den - ly I see.

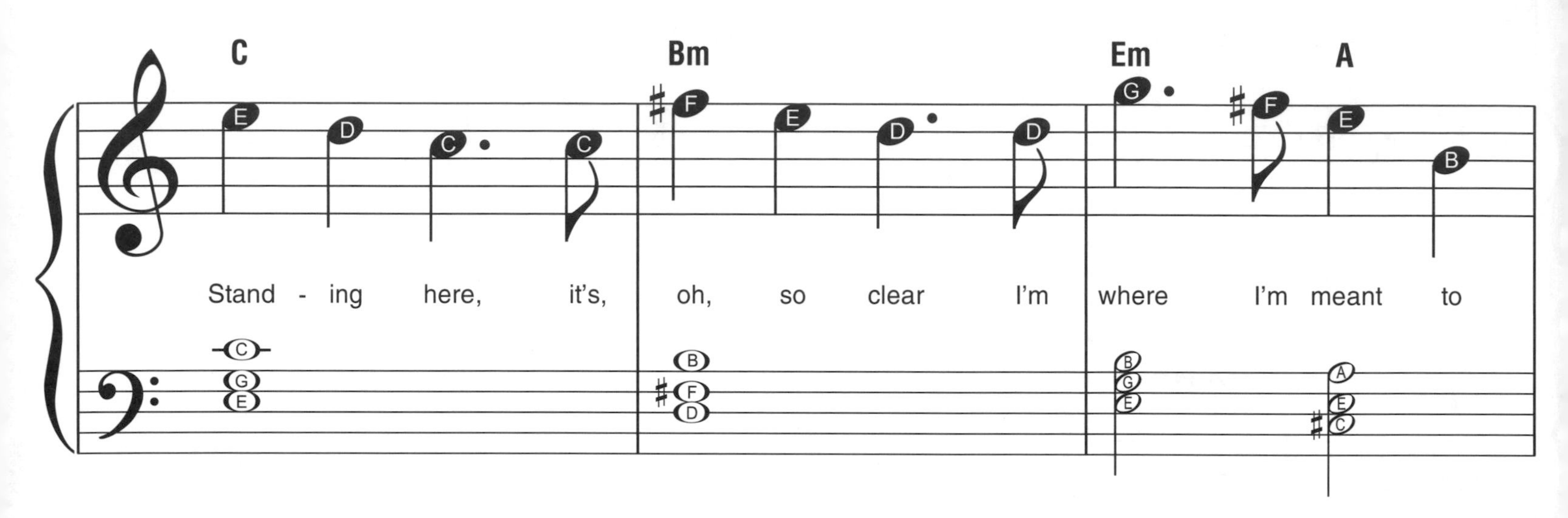
C Bm Em A
Stand - ing here, it's, oh, so clear I'm where I'm meant to

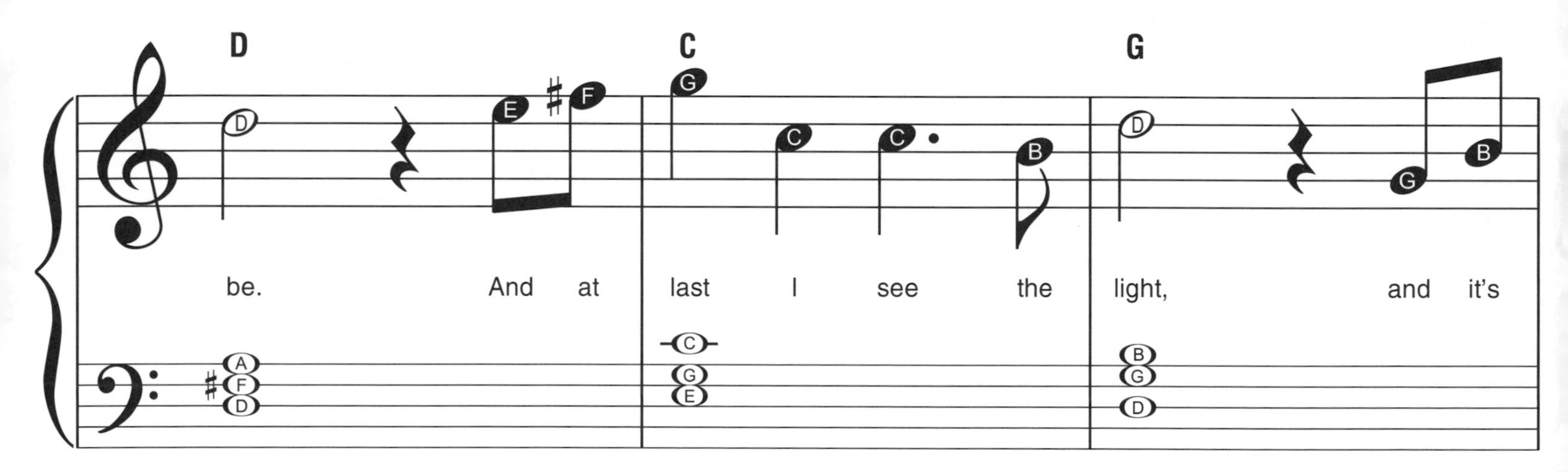
D C G
be. And at last I see the light, and it's

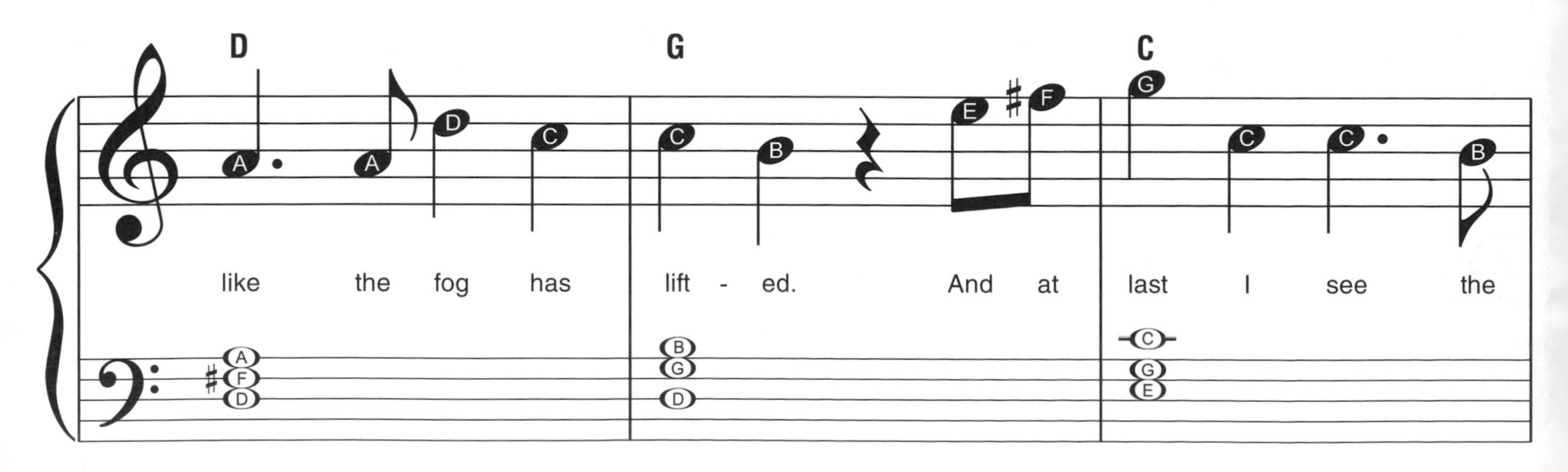
D G C
like the fog has lift - ed. And at last I see the

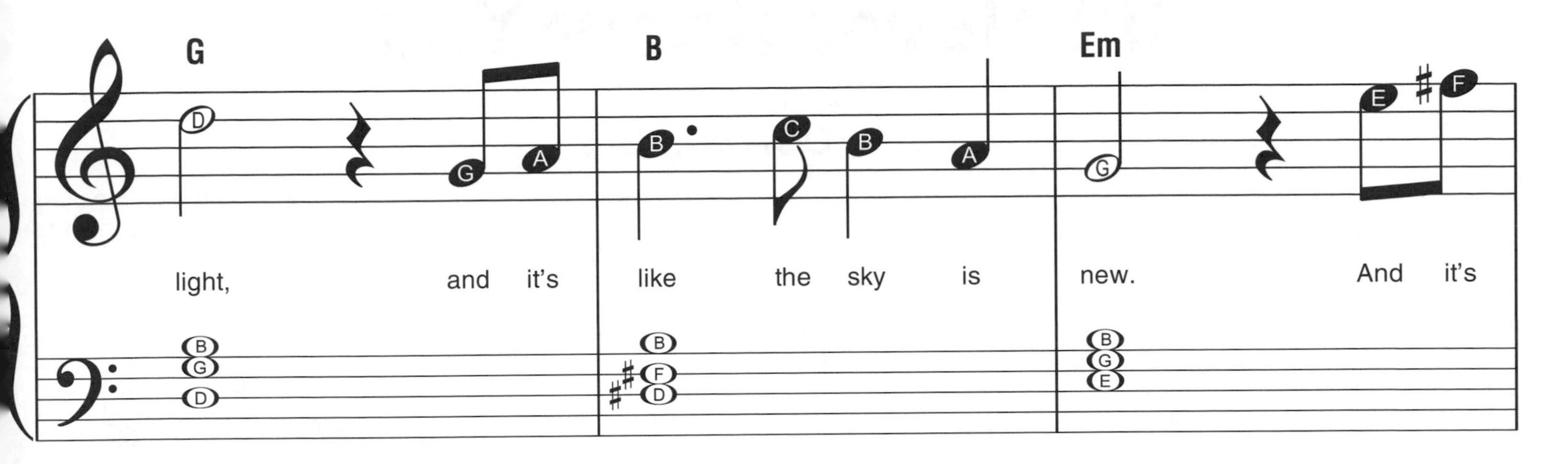
G
B
Em
light, and it's like the sky is new. And it's

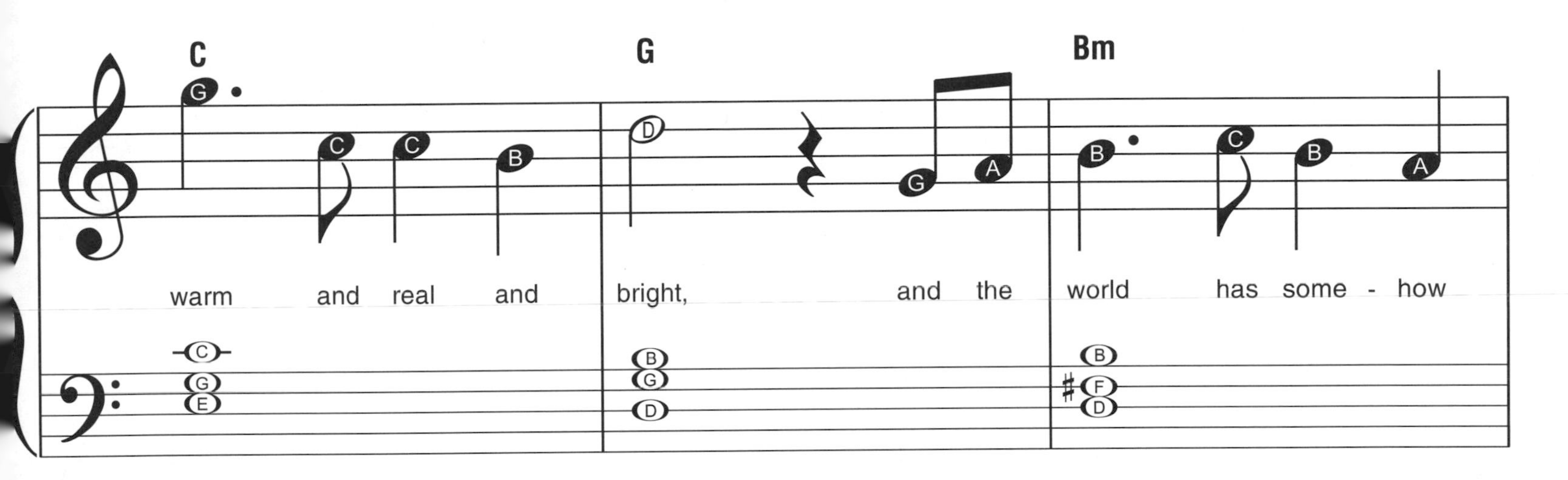
C
G
Bm
warm and real and bright, and the world has some - how

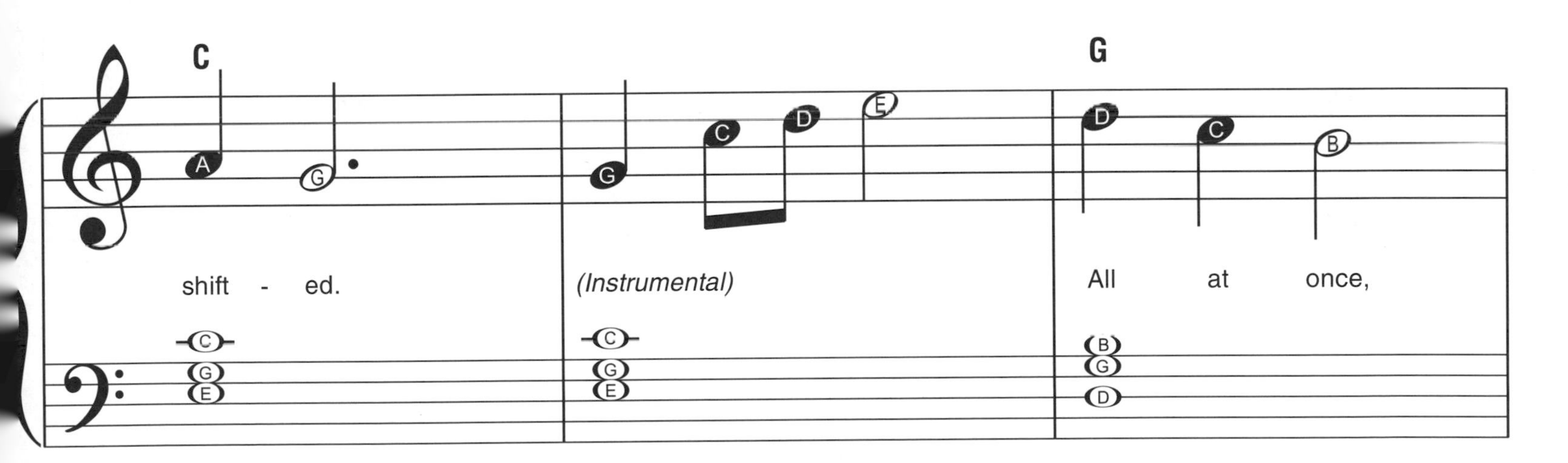
C
G
shift - ed.
(Instrumental)
All at once,

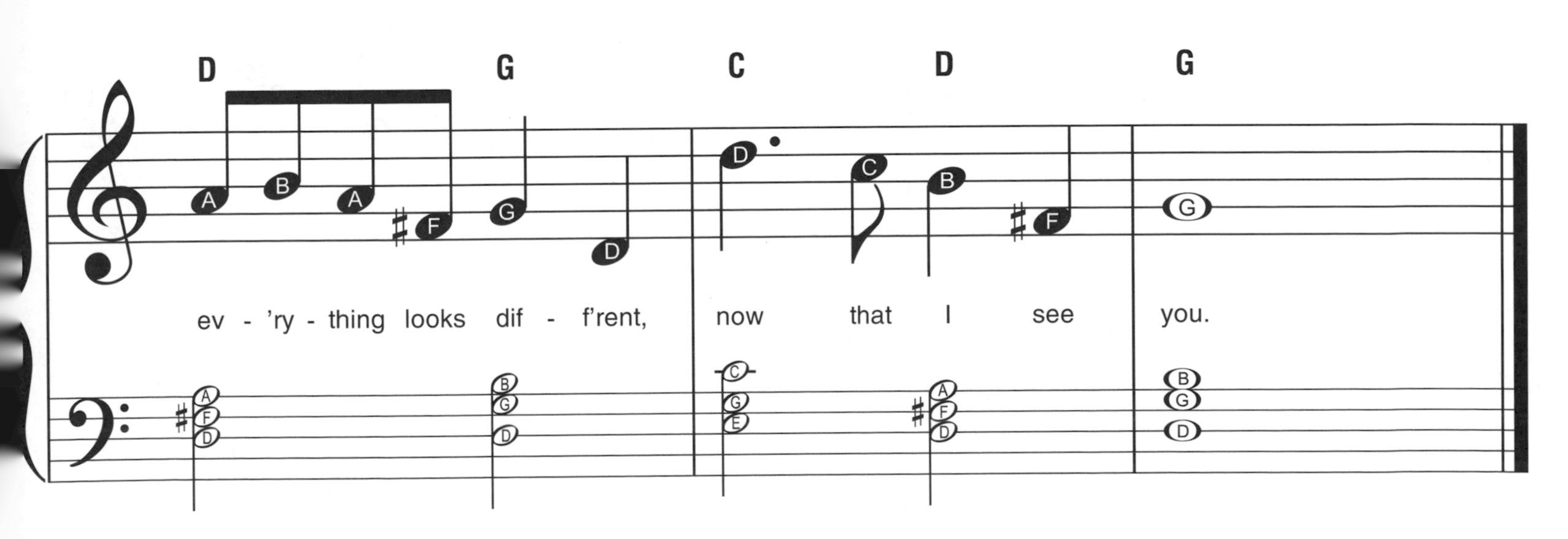
D
G
C
D
G
ev - 'ry - thing looks dif - f'rent, now that I see you.

If I Never Knew You

(End Title)
from POCAHONTAS

Music by Alan Menken
Lyrics by Stephen Schwartz

Moderately slow

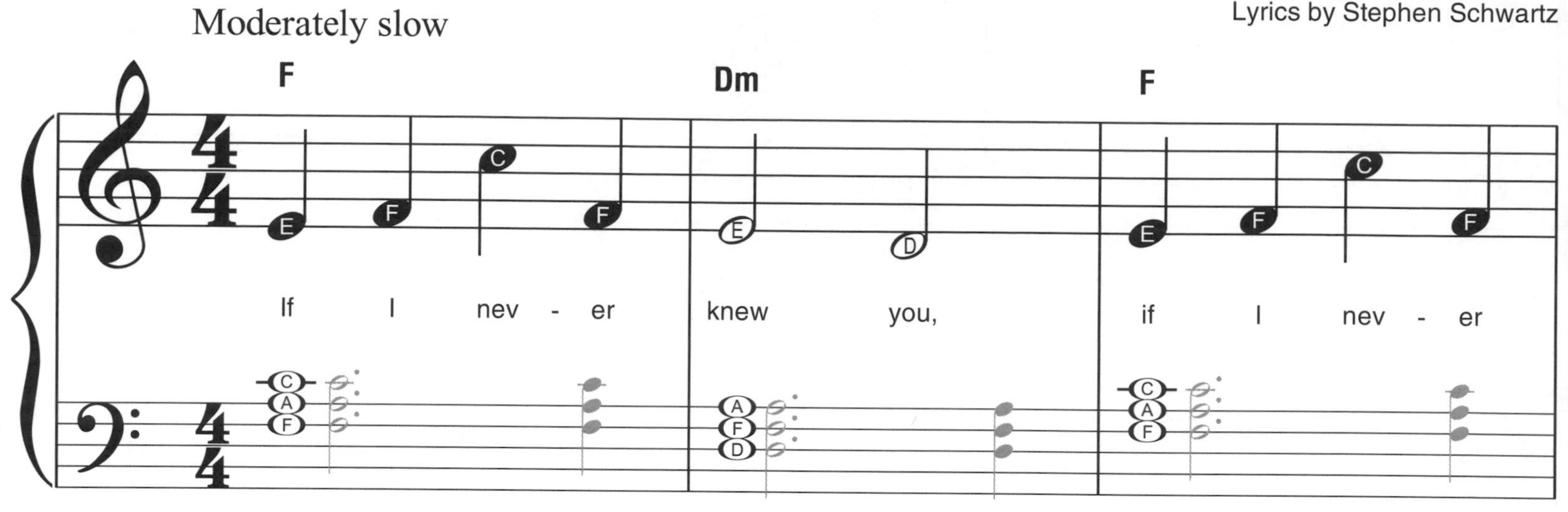

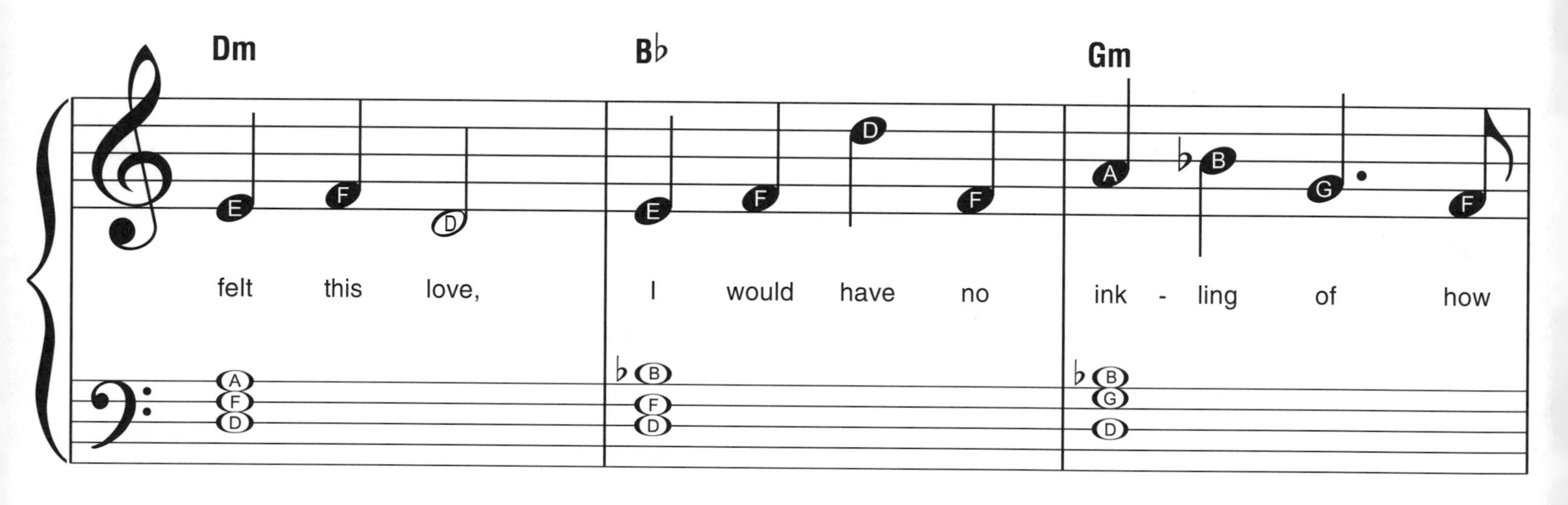

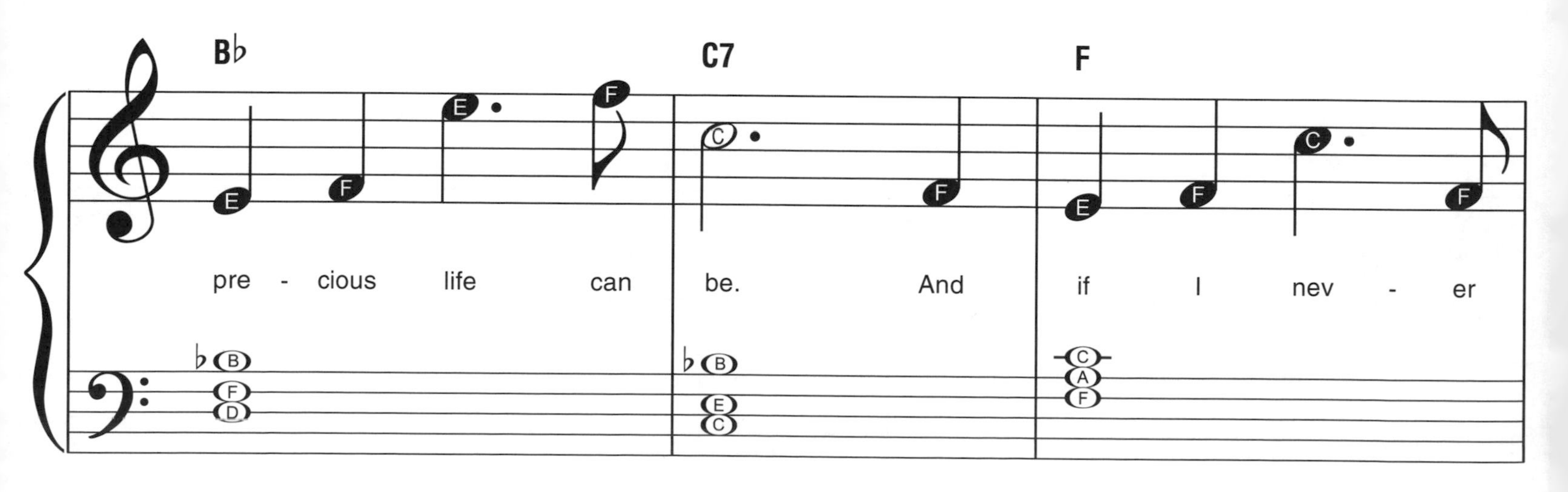

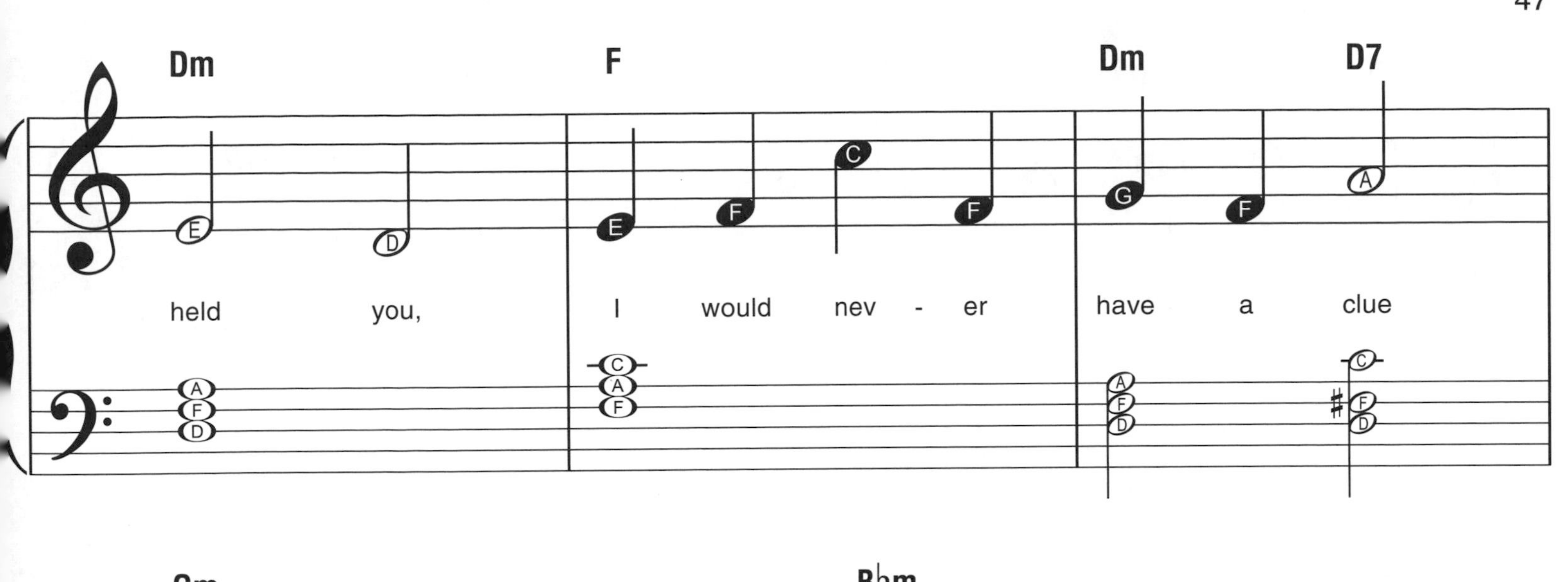
Dm F Dm D7
held you, I would nev - er have a clue

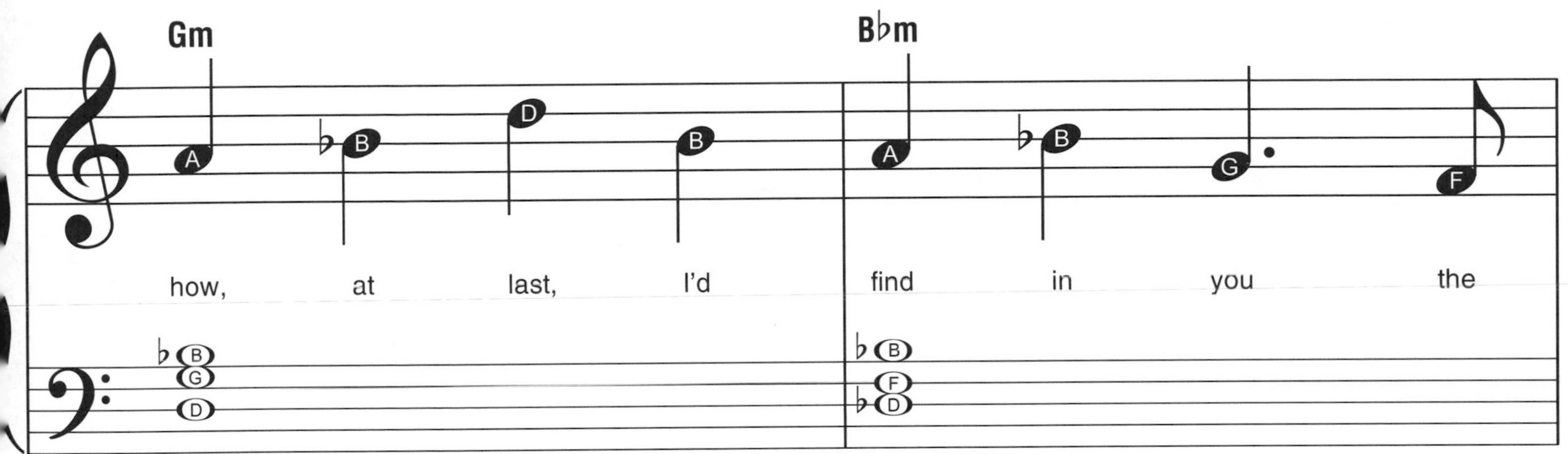
Gm B♭m
how, at last, I'd find in you the

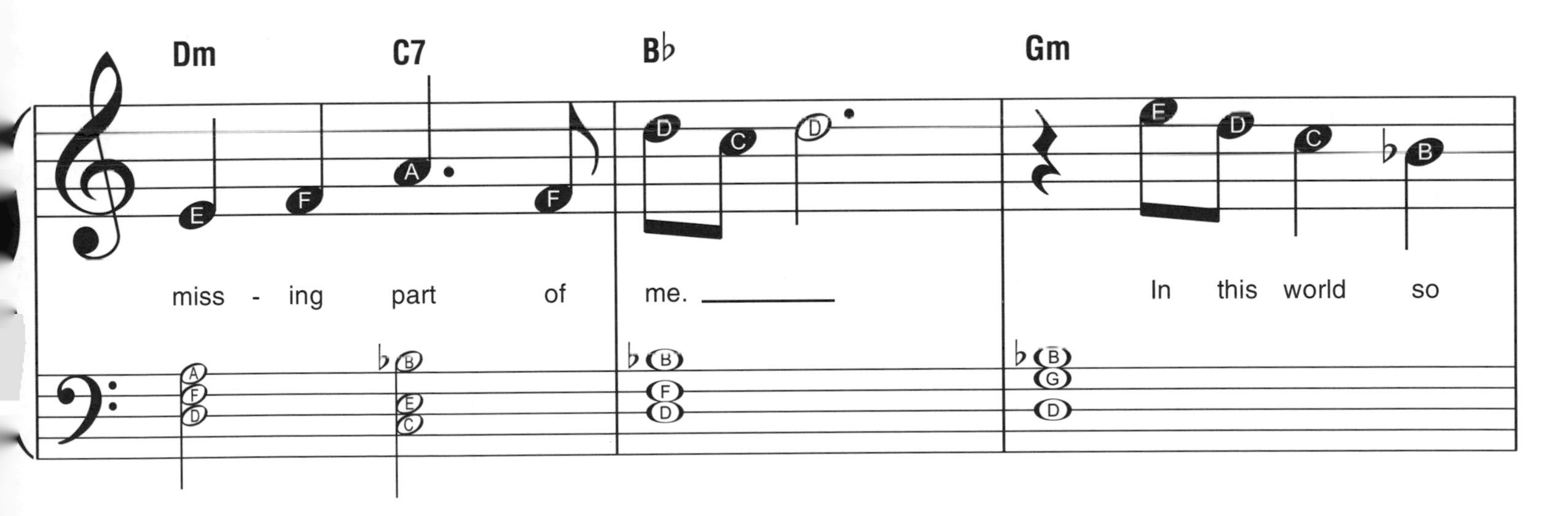
Dm C7 B♭ Gm
miss - ing part of me. In this world so

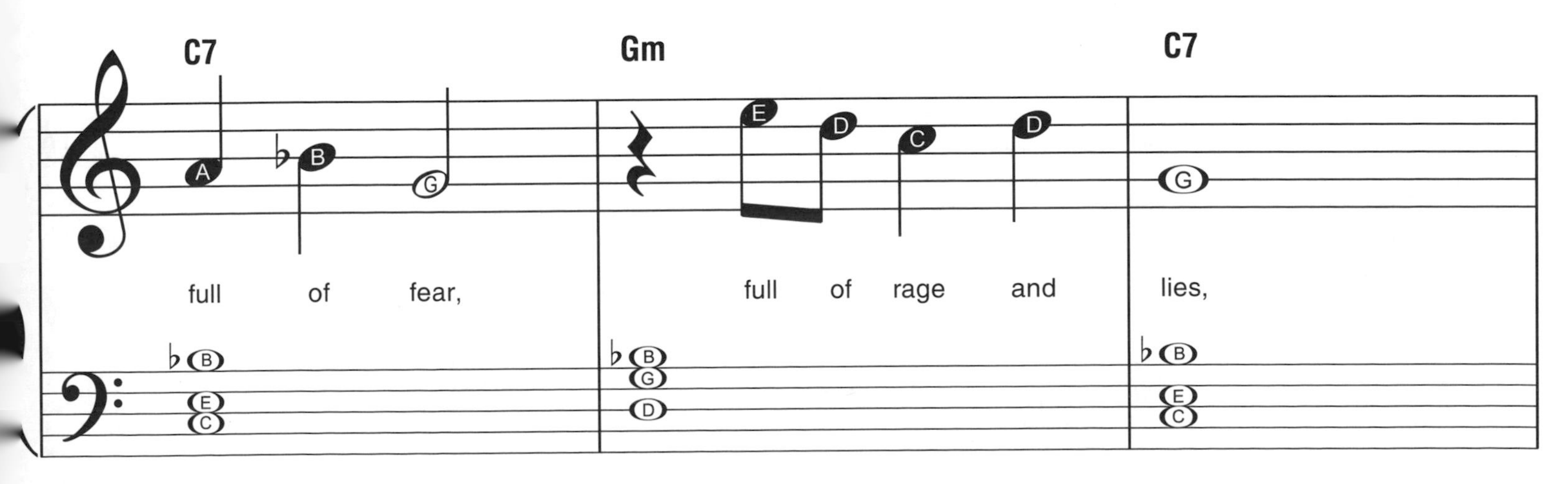
C7 Gm C7
full of fear, full of rage and lies,

Am A Dm B♭
I can see the truth so clear in your eyes, so

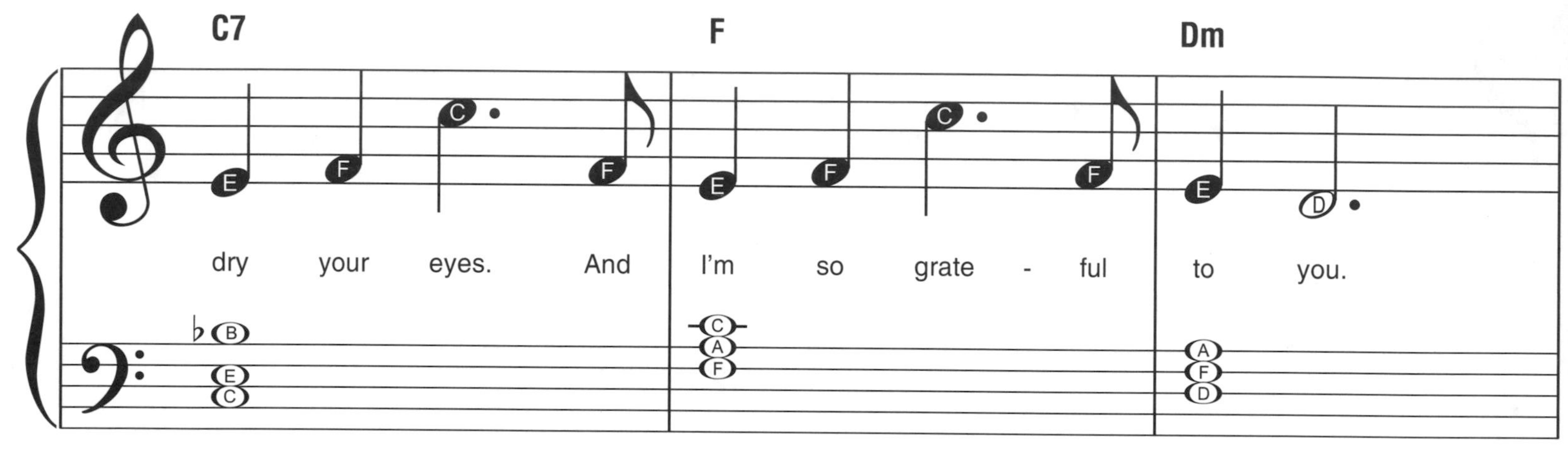
C7 F Dm
dry your eyes. And I'm so grate - ful to you.

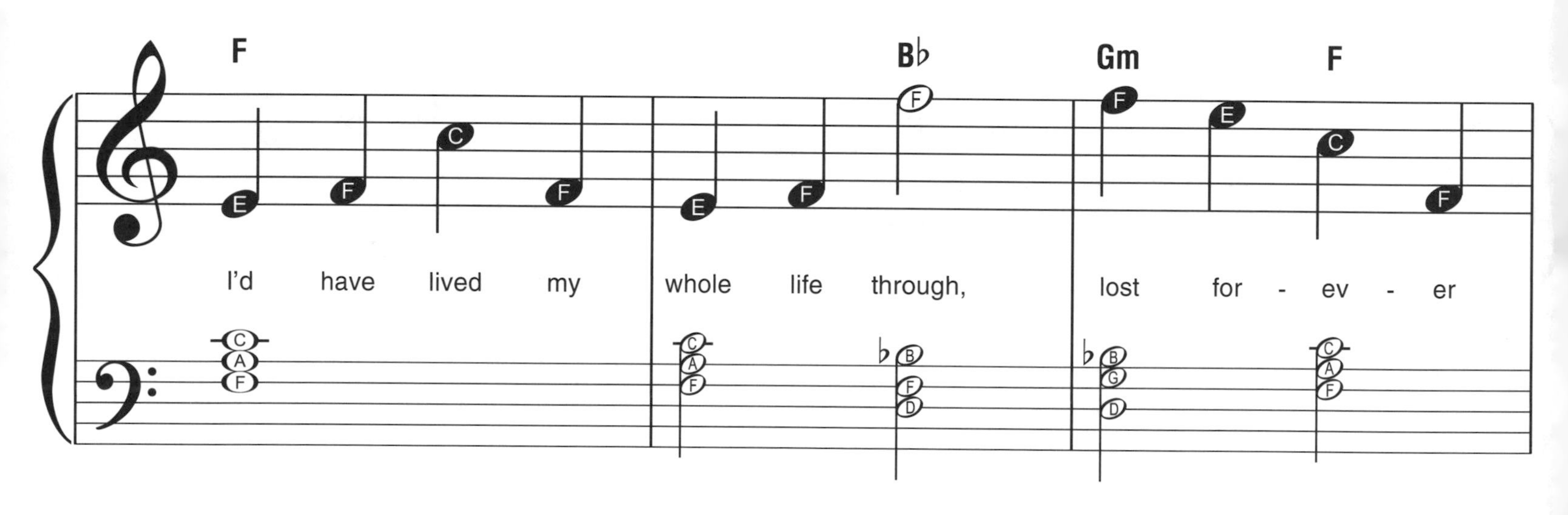
F B♭ Gm F
I'd have lived my whole life through, lost for - ev - er

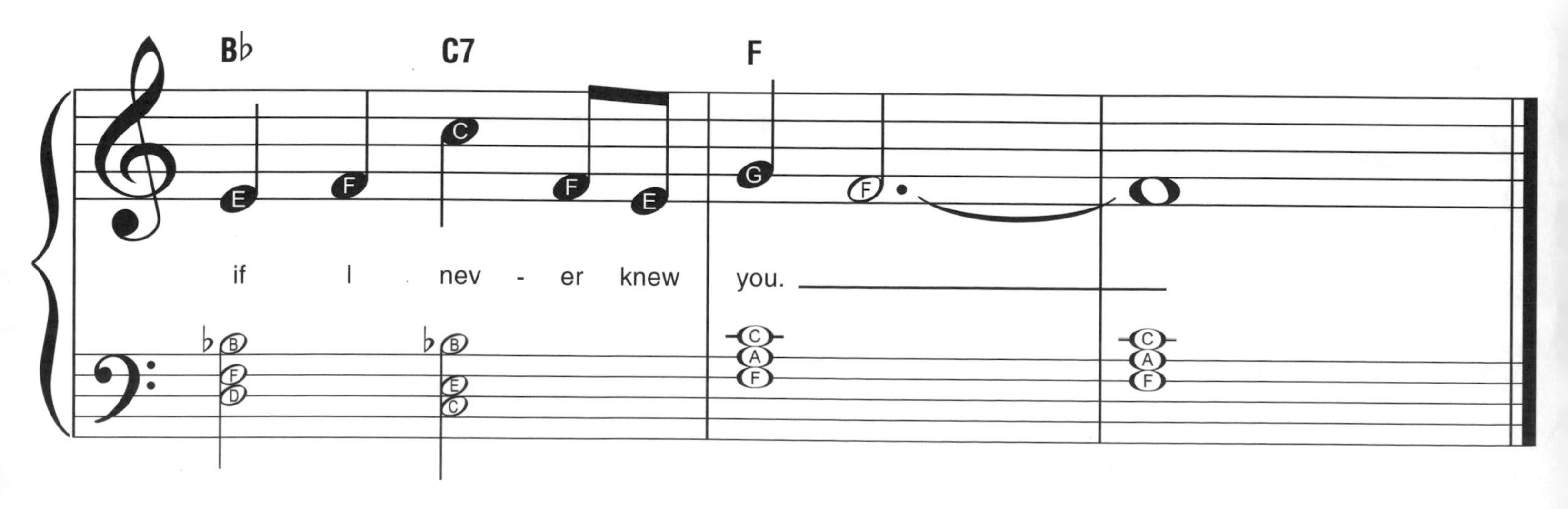
B♭ C7 F
if I nev - er knew you.

Lava

from LAVA

Music and Lyrics by
James Ford Murphy

Moderately bright

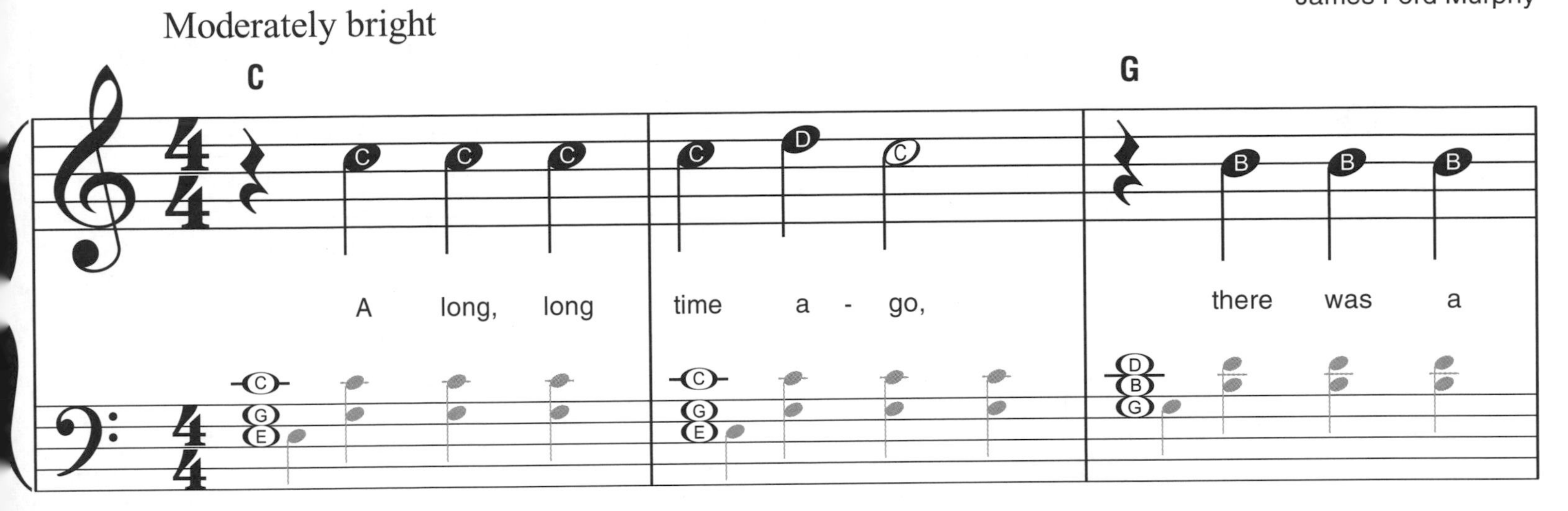

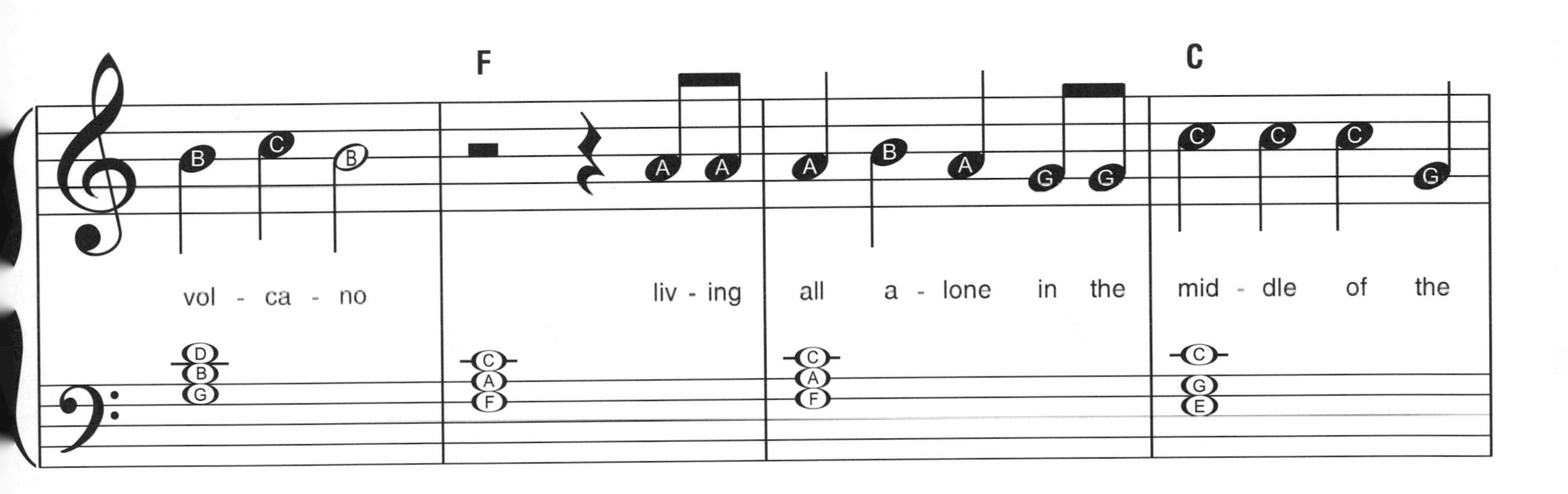

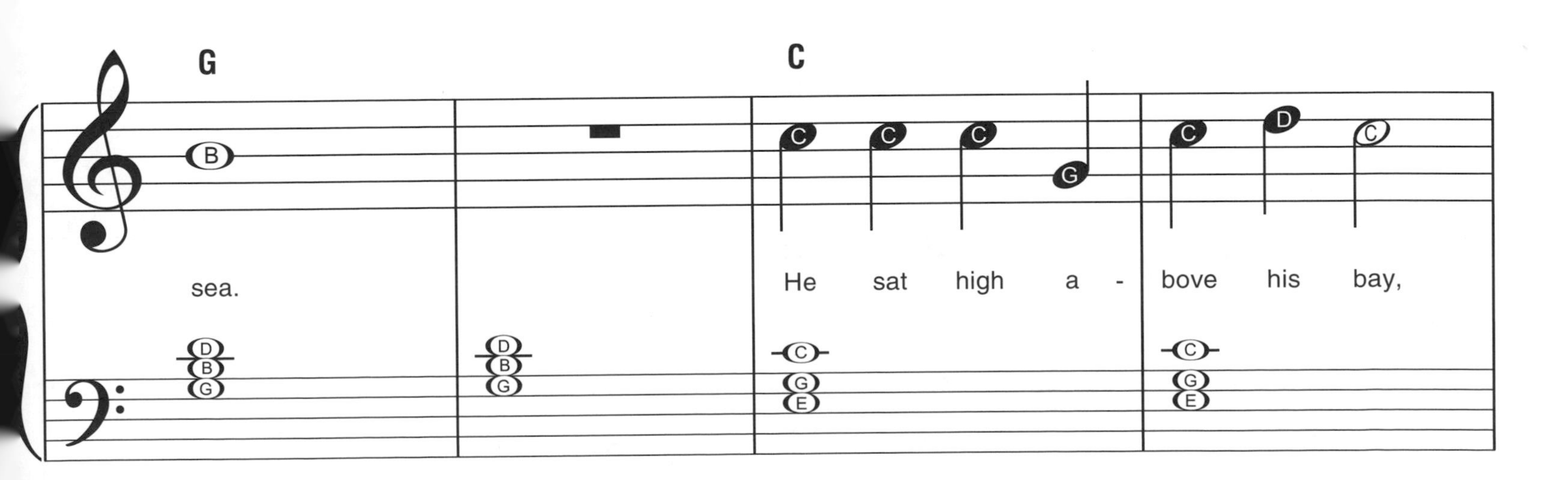

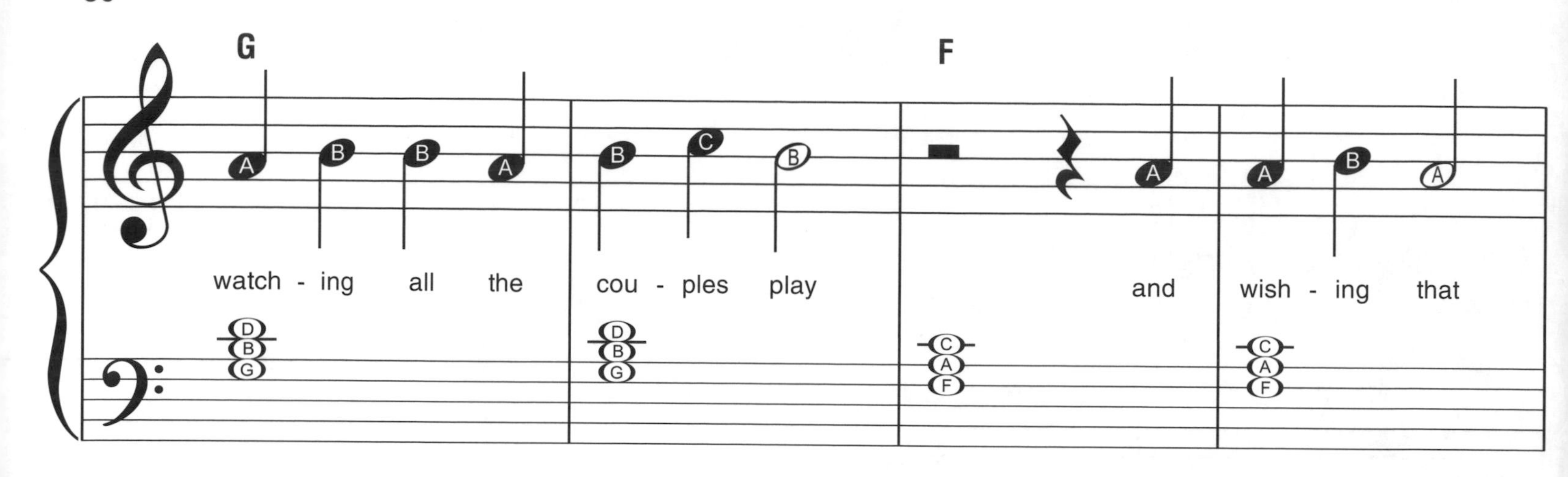
G
F
watch - ing all the
cou - ples play
and
wish - ing that

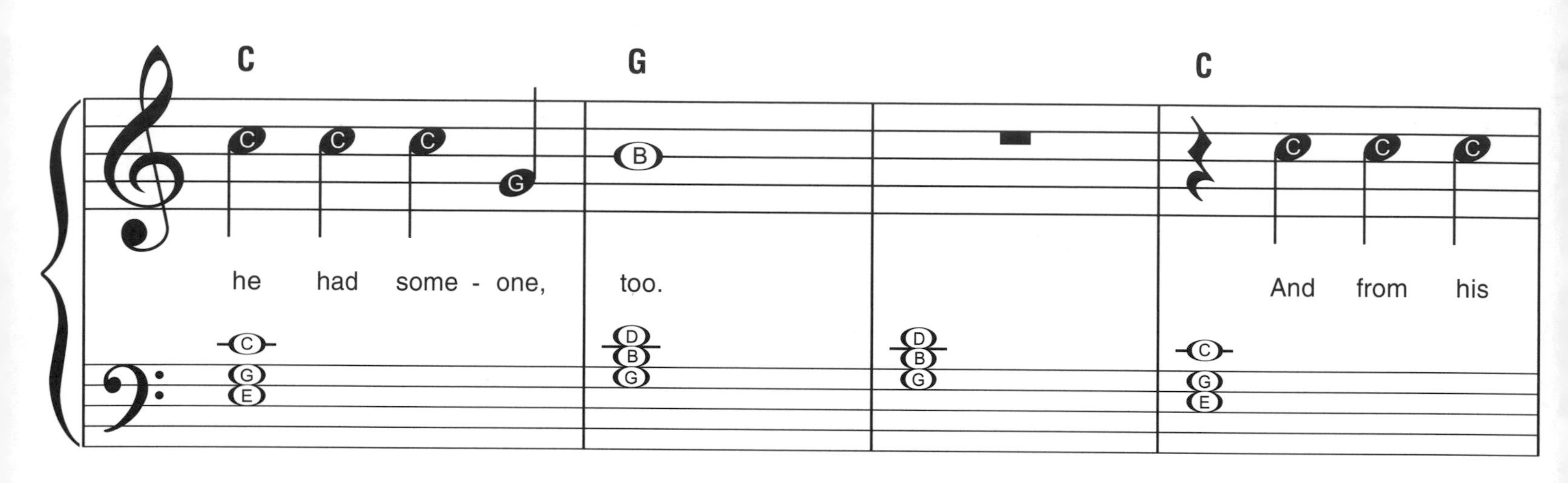
C
G
C
he had some - one,
too.
And from his

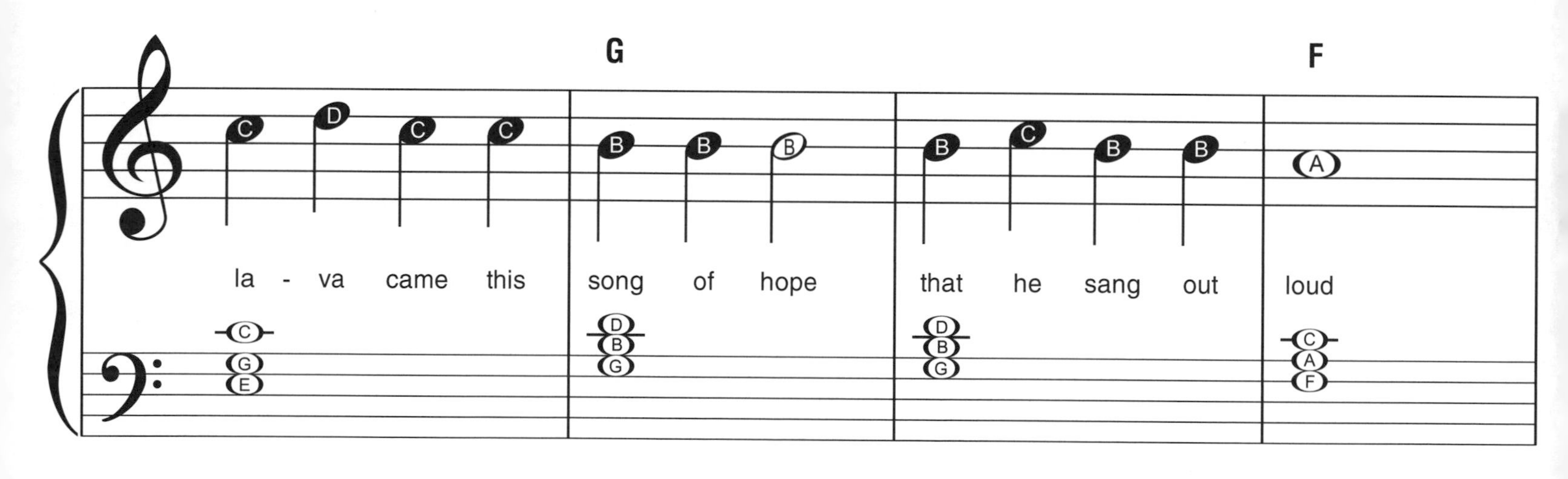
G
F
la - va came this
song of hope
that he sang out
loud

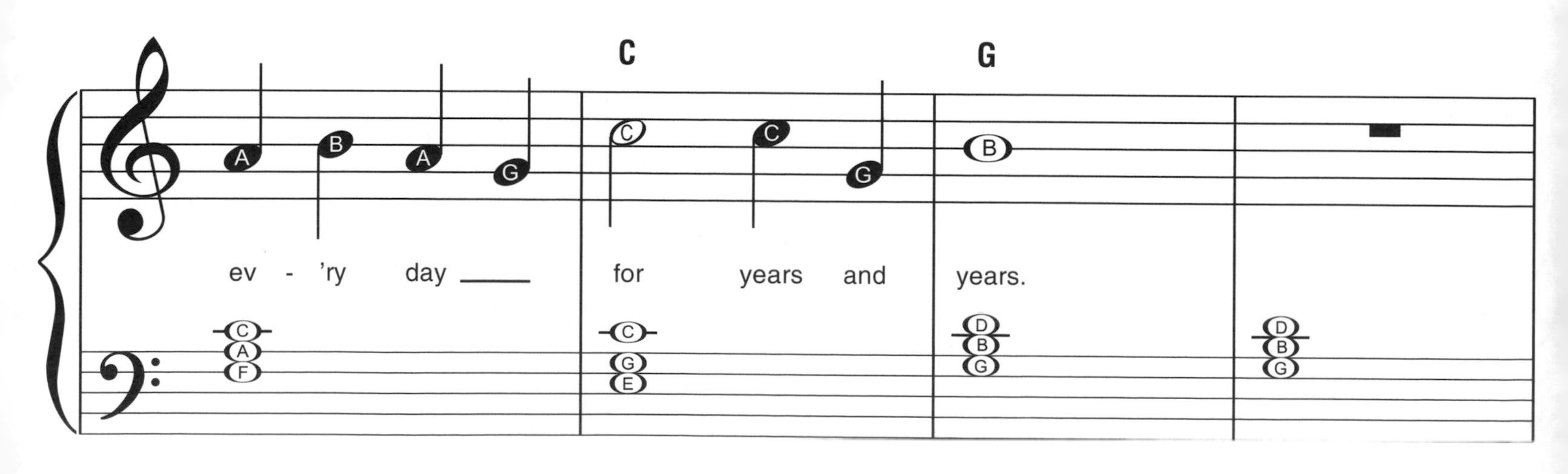
C
G
ev - 'ry day
for years and
years.

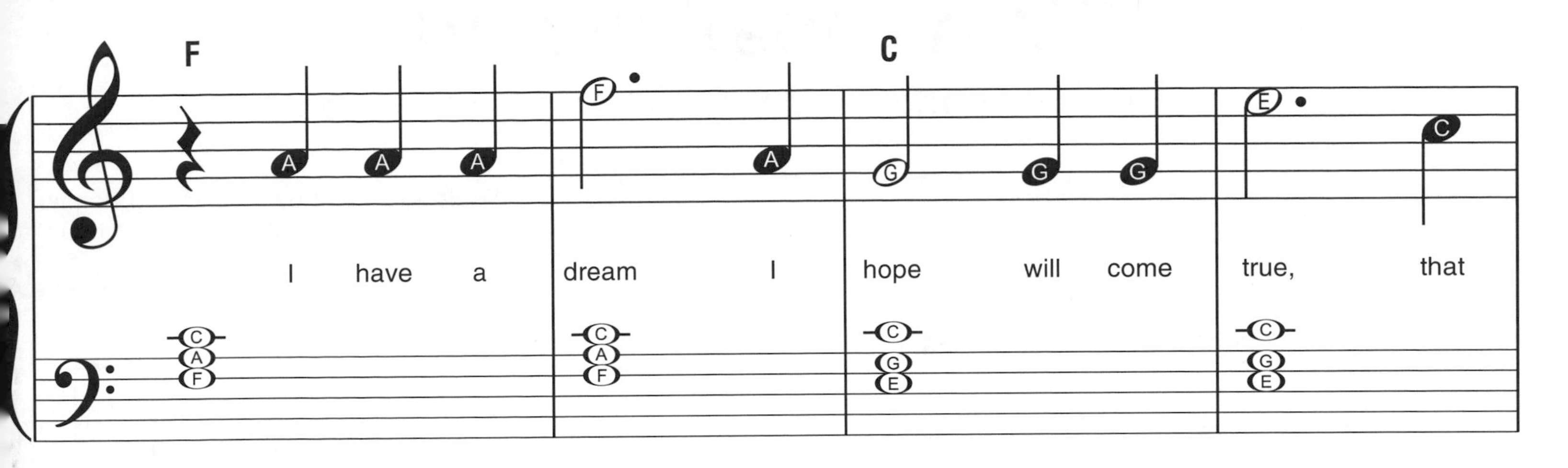
F
C
I have a dream I hope will come true, that

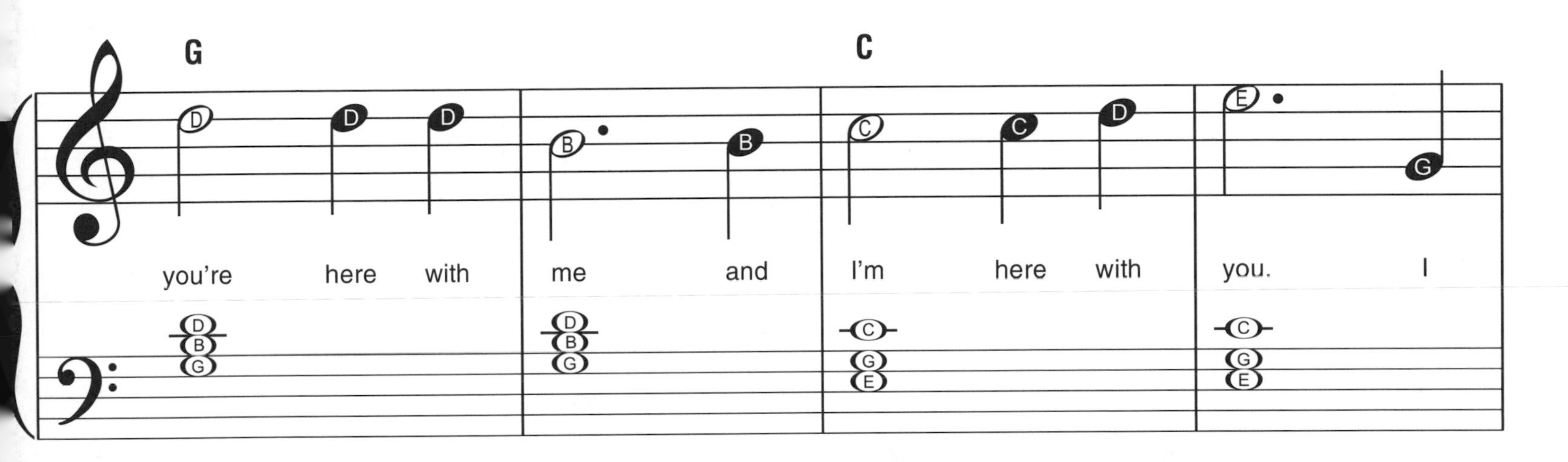
G
C
you're here with me and I'm here with you. I

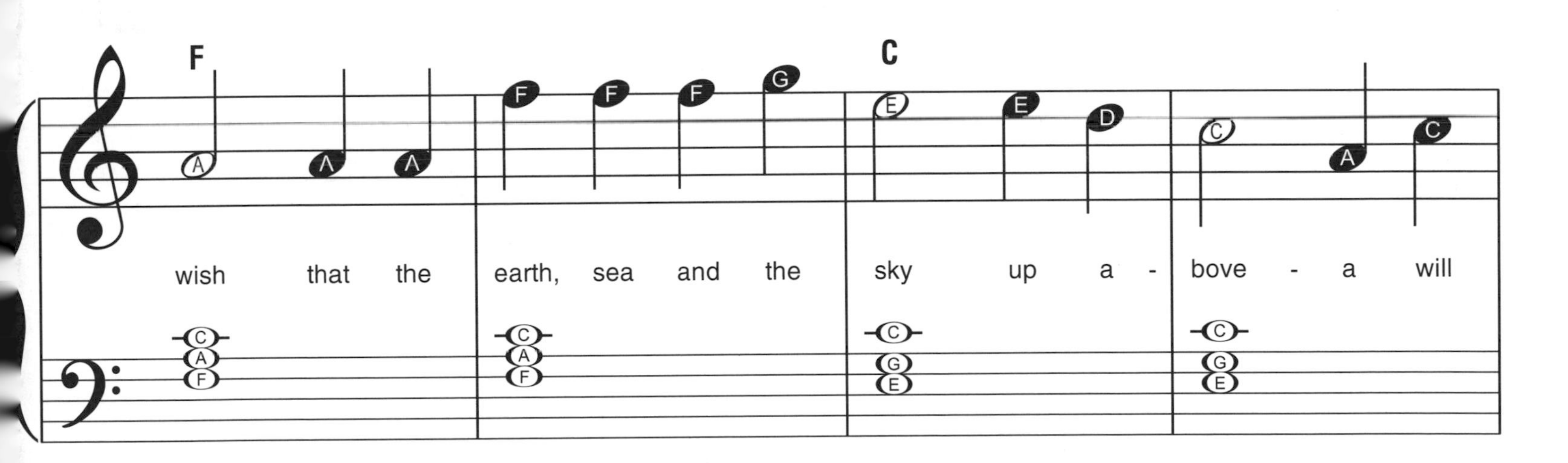
F
C
wish that the earth, sea and the sky up a - bove - a will

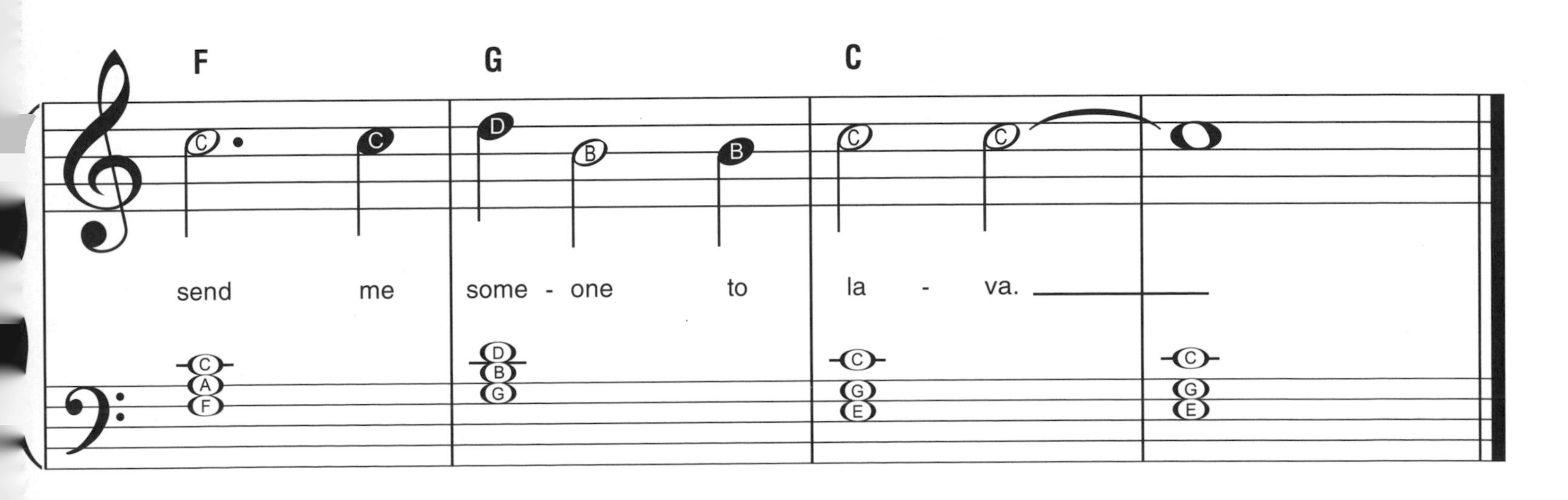
F
G
C
send me some - one to la - va.

It's a Small World

from Disney Parks' "it's a small world" attraction

Words and Music by Richard M. Sherman
and Robert B. Sherman

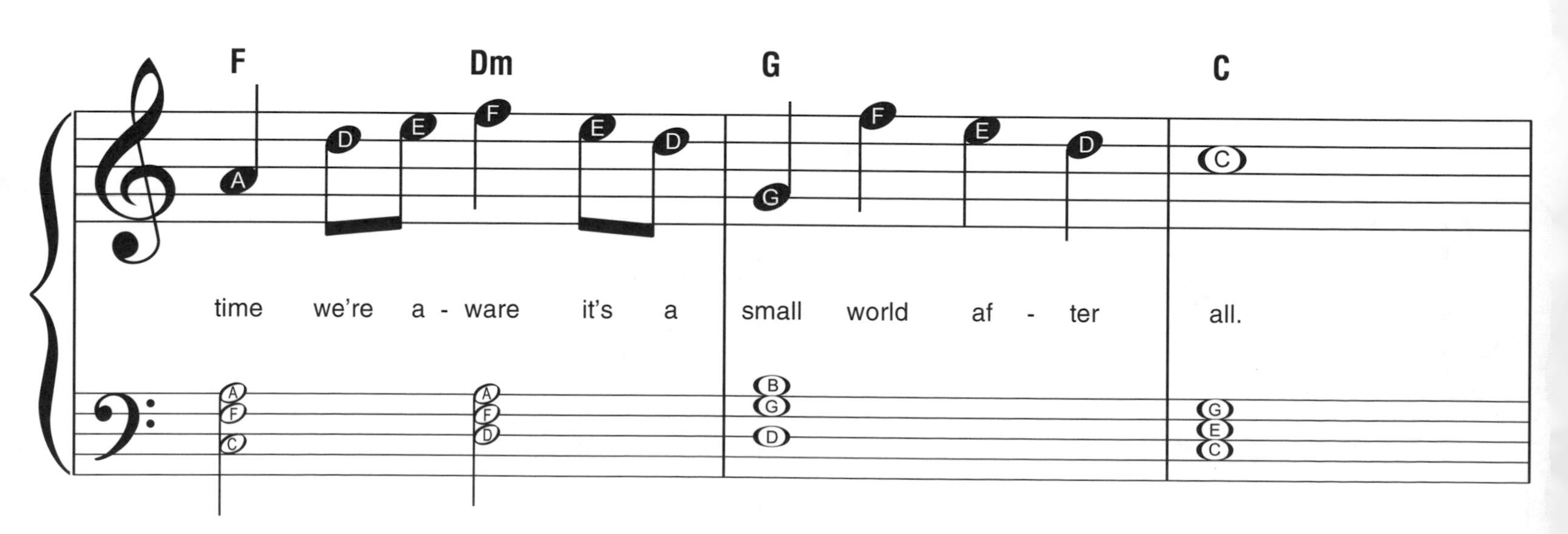

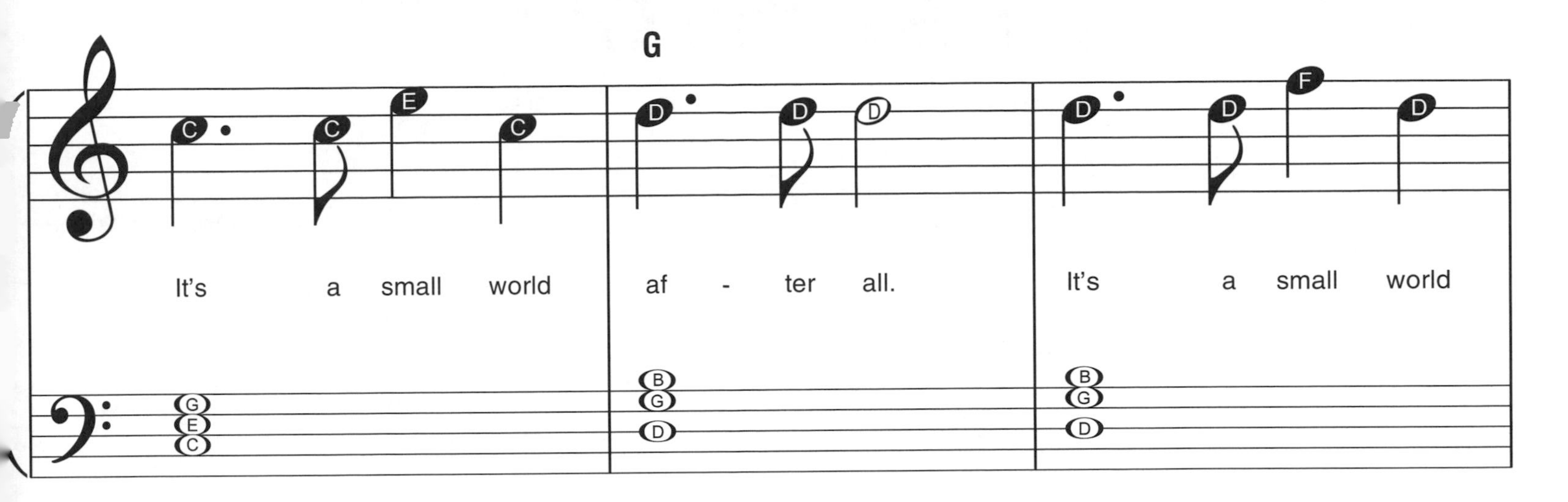
G
It's a small world af - ter all. It's a small world

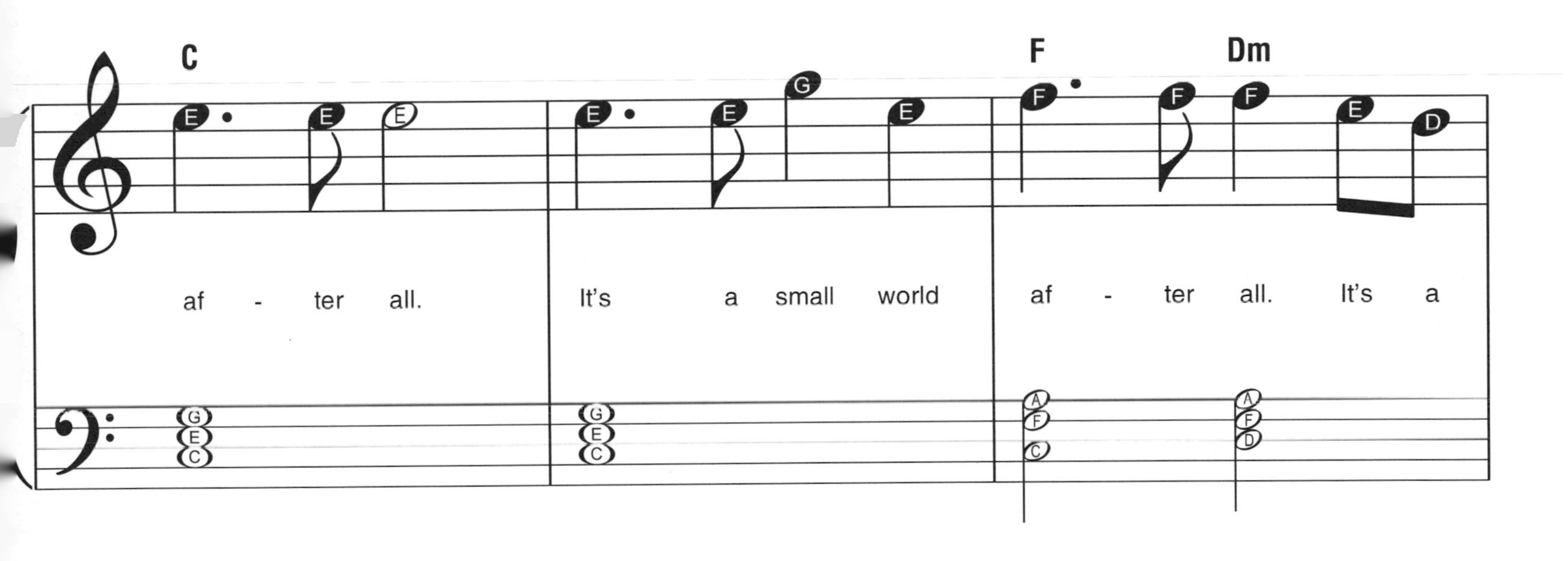
C
F
Dm
af - ter all. It's a small world af - ter all. It's a

1.
2.
G
C
C
small, small world. It's a world.

Kiss the Girl

from THE LITTLE MERMAID

Music by Alan Menken
Lyrics by Howard Ashman

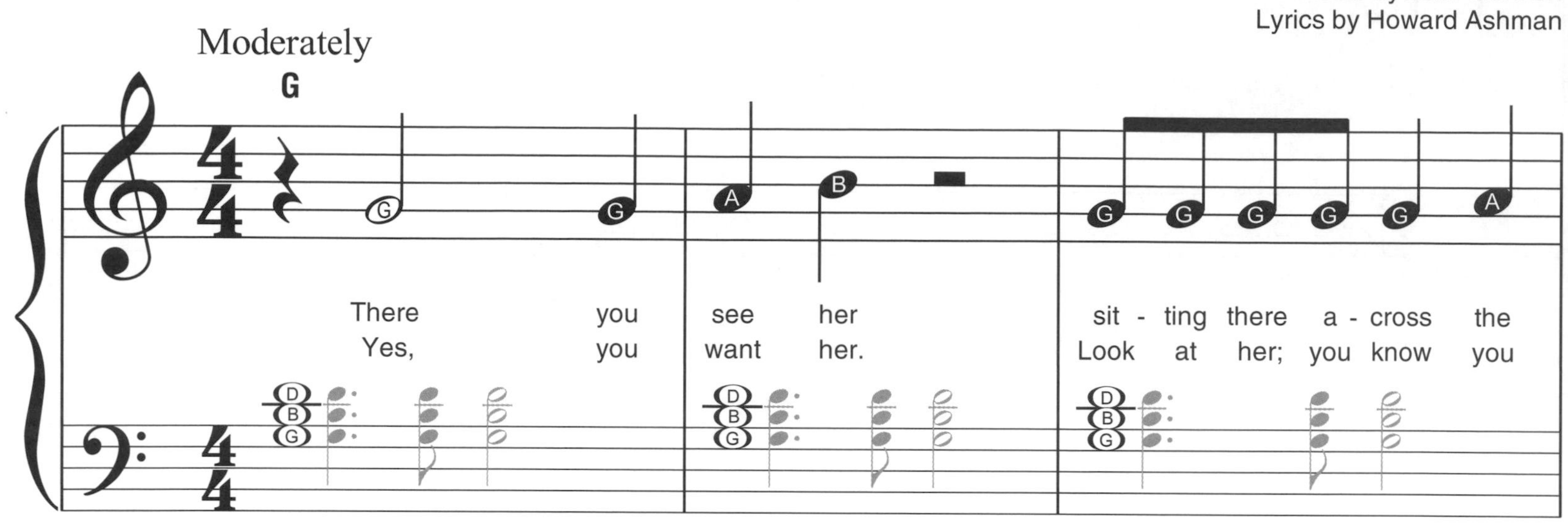

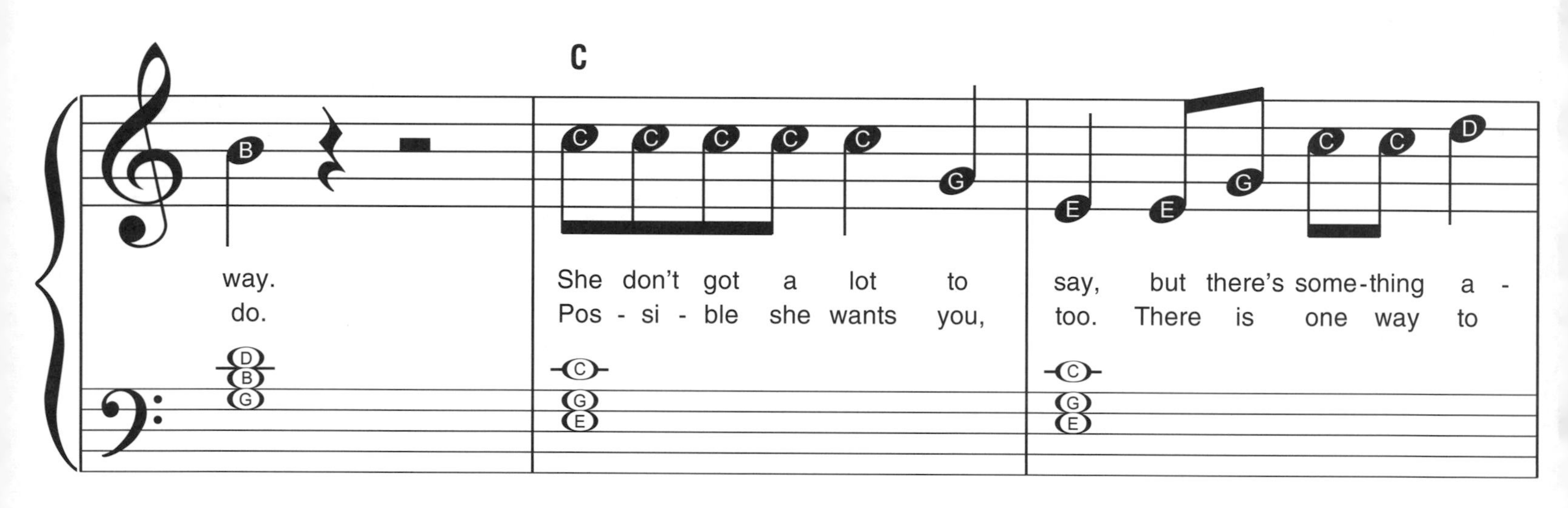

G
dy - ing to try. You wan - na
sin - gle word; go on and
kiss the girl.
kiss the girl.

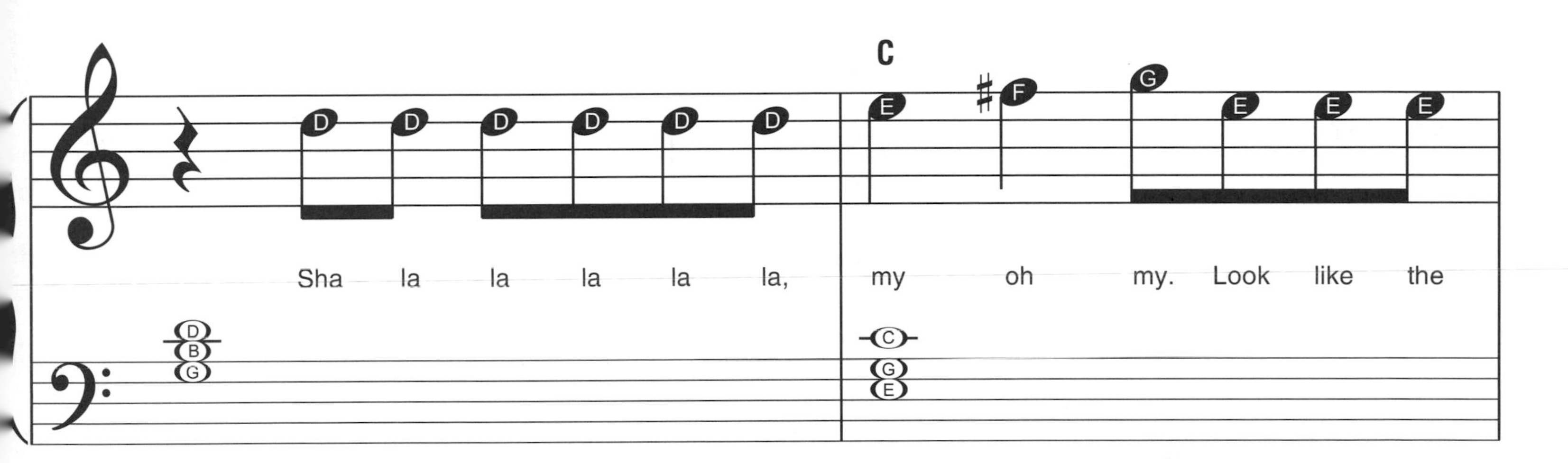
C
Sha la la la la la,
my oh my. Look like the

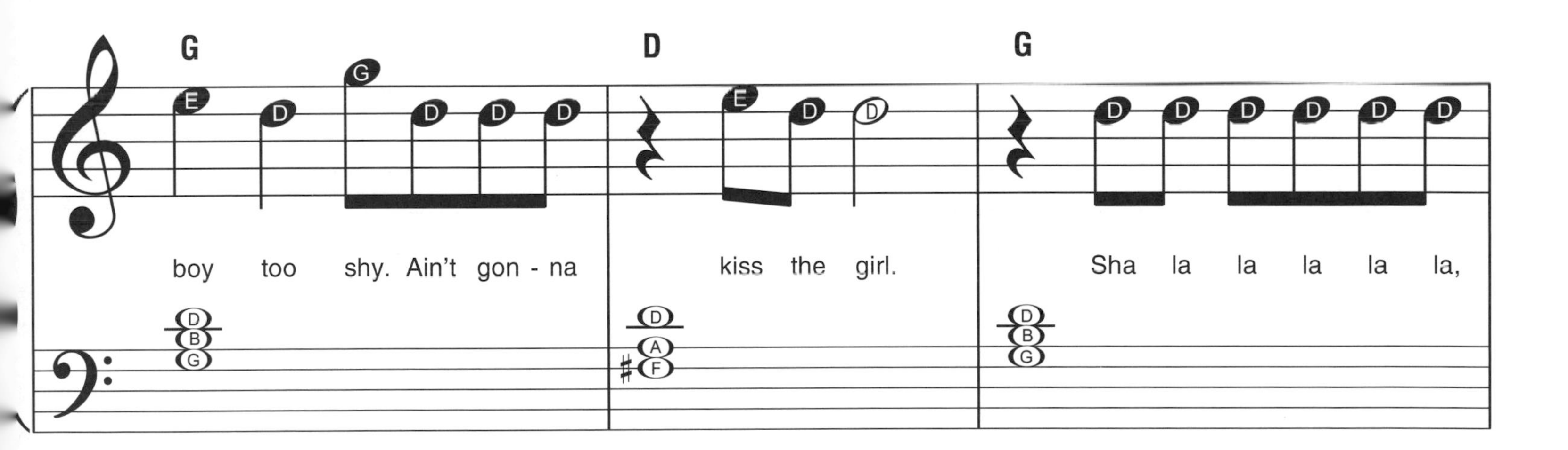
G
D
G
boy too shy. Ain't gon - na
kiss the girl.
Sha la la la la la,

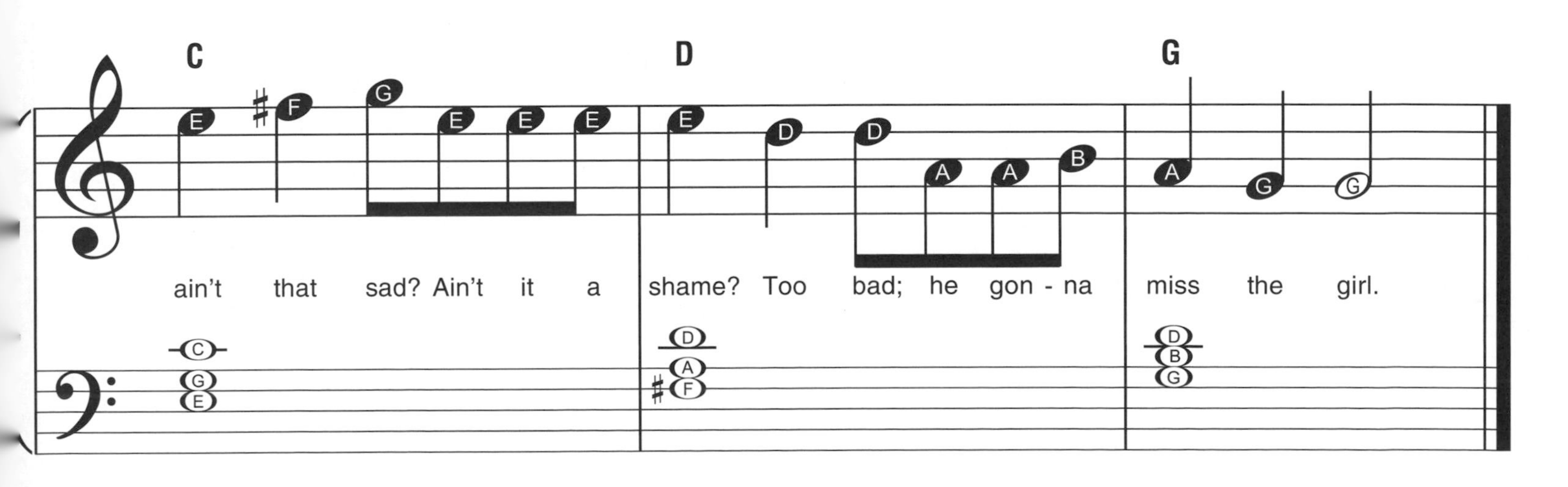
C
D
G
ain't that sad? Ain't it a
shame? Too bad; he gon - na
miss the girl.

Let's Go Fly a Kite

from MARY POPPINS

Words and Music by Richard M. Sherman
and Robert B. Sherman

Brightly

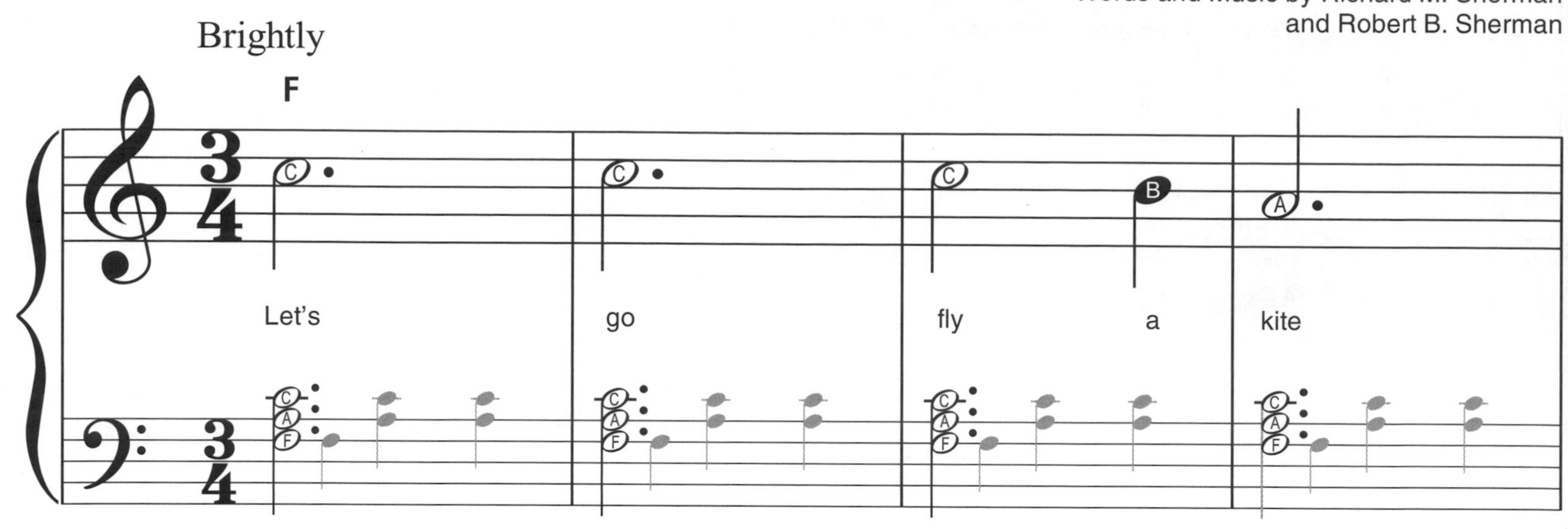

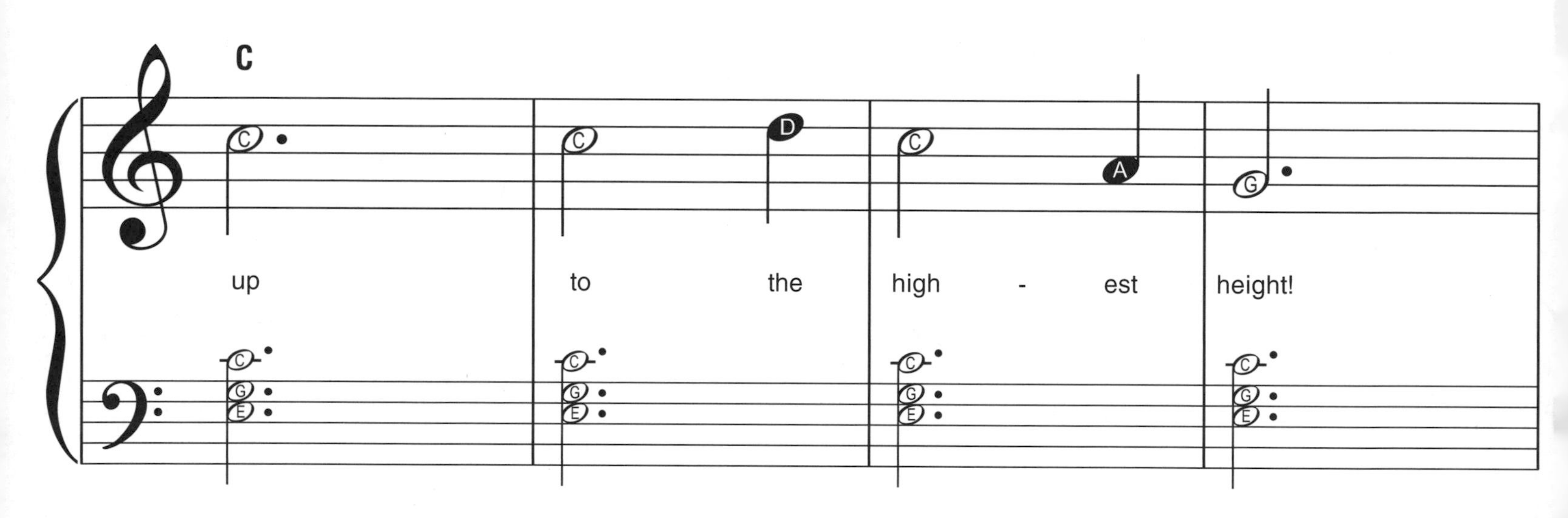

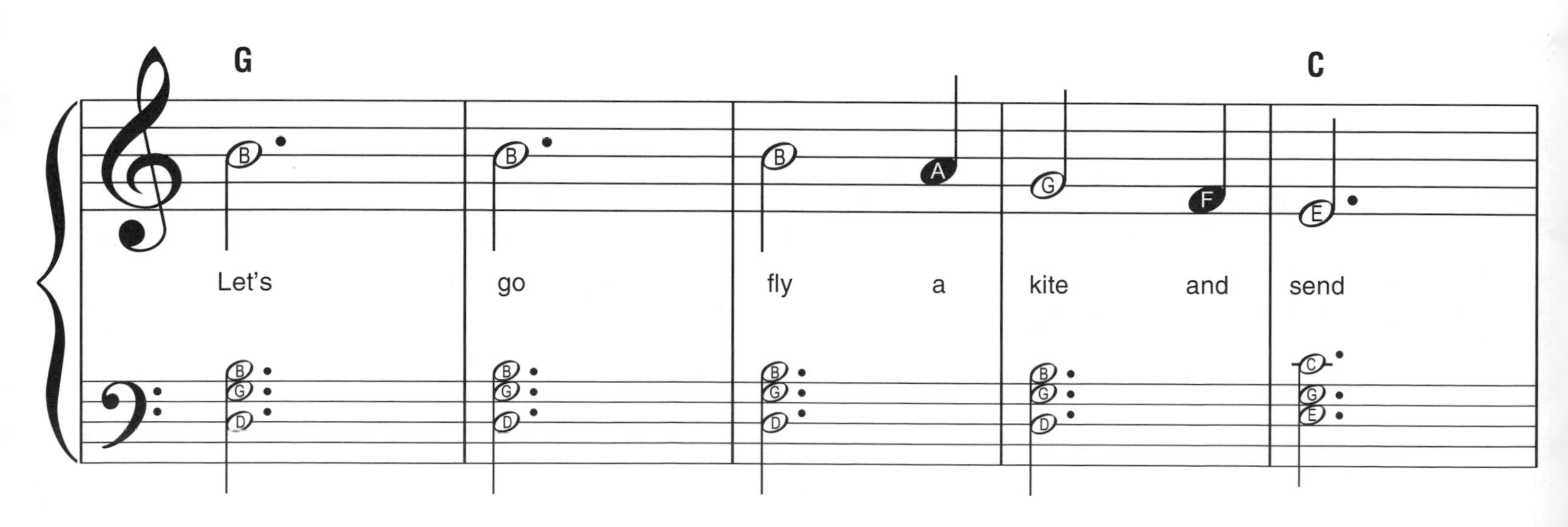

F
it soar - ing up through the
C
at - mos - phere, up where the air is
G
clear. Oh, let's go fly a
C F C
kite! Let's go fly a kite!

Mickey Mouse March

from THE MICKEY MOUSE CLUB

Words and Music by
Jimmie Dodd

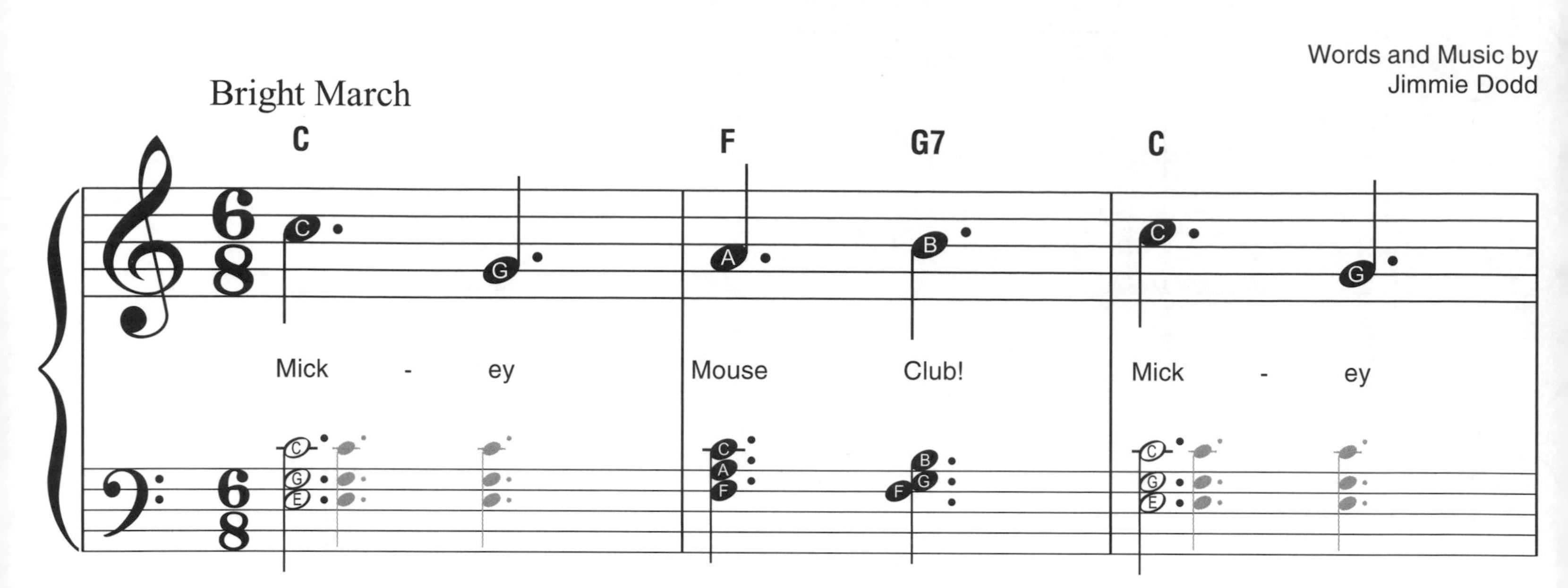

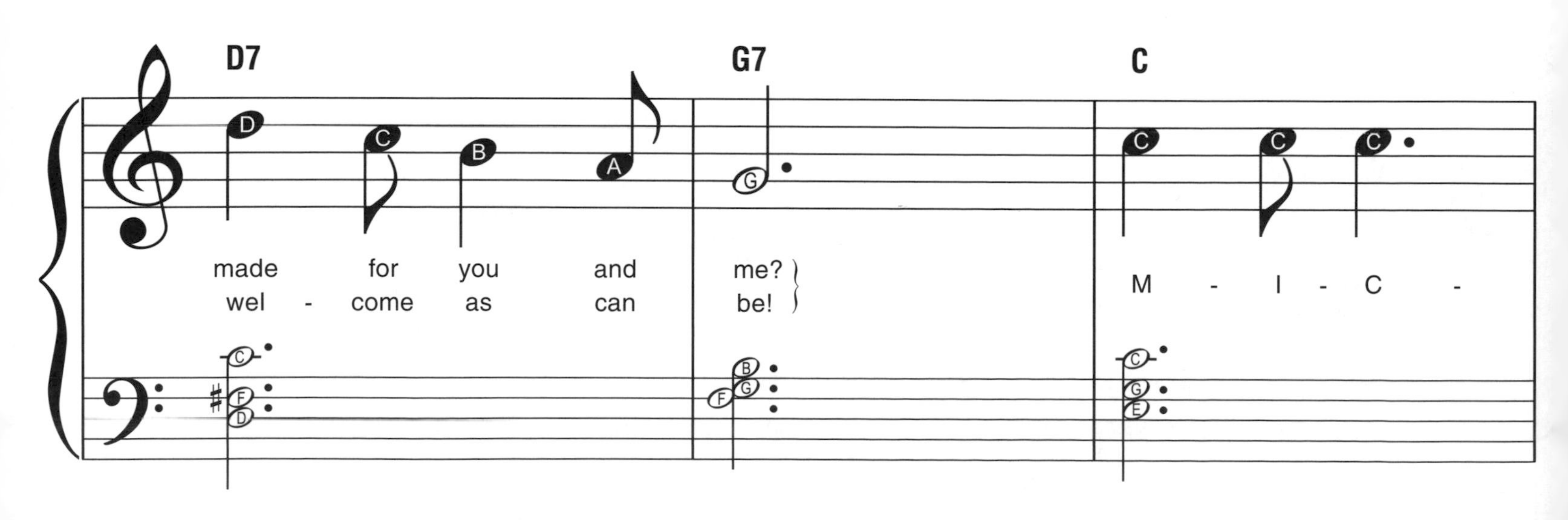

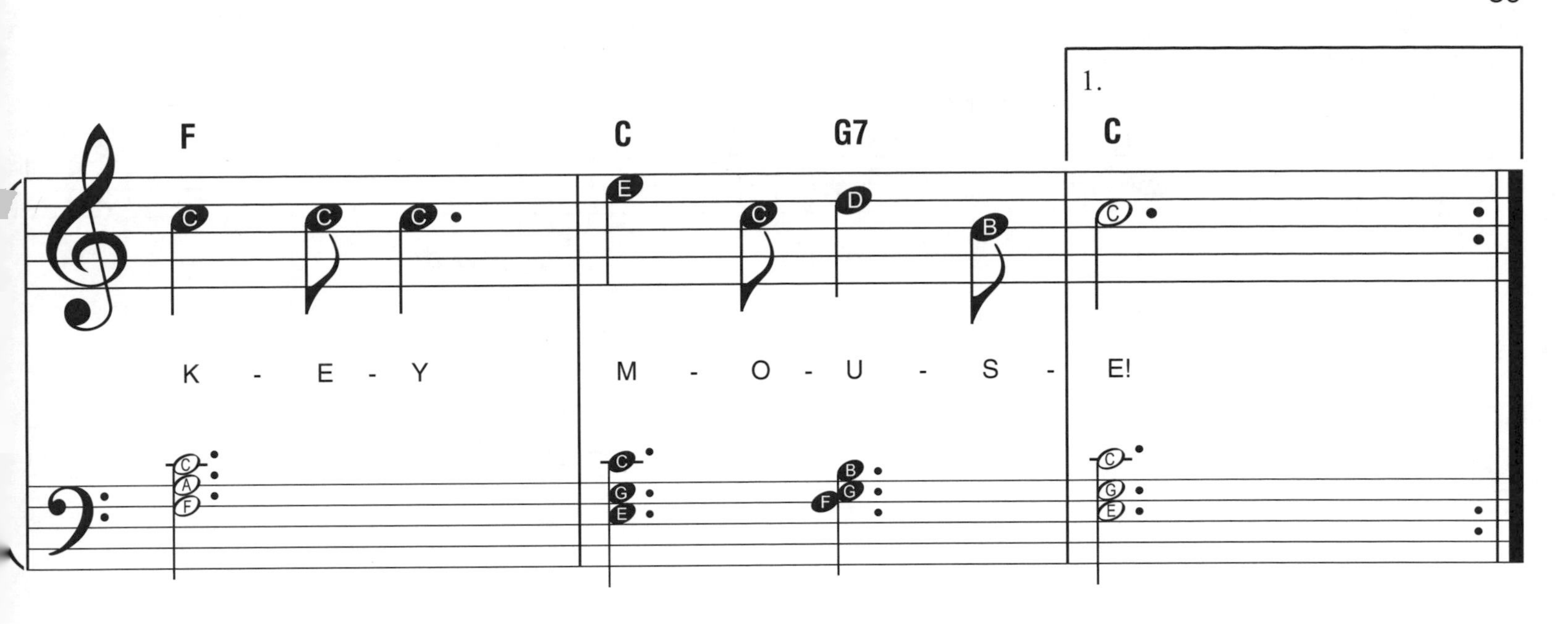
1.
F
C
G7
C
K - E - Y
M - O - U - S - E!

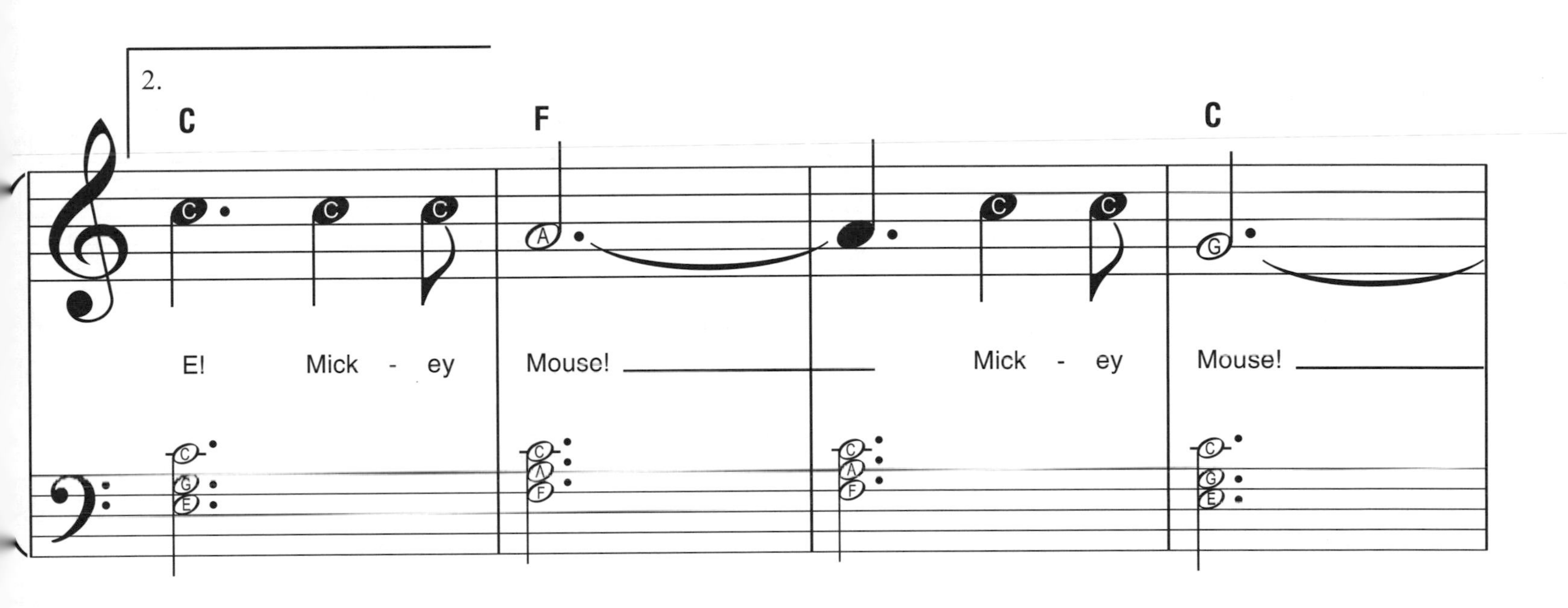
2.
C
F
C
E! Mick - ey
Mouse!
Mick - ey
Mouse!

D7
For - ev - er let us hold our ban - ner

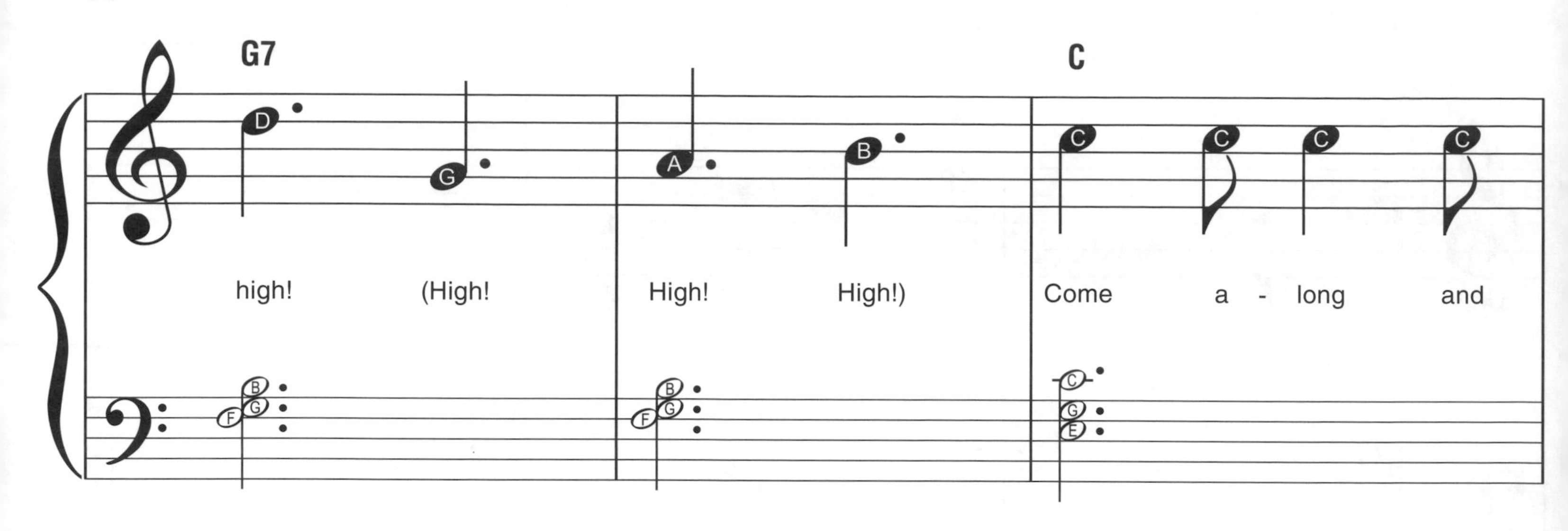
G7
C
D
G
A
B
C C C C
high! (High! High! High!) Come a - long and
B
G
F
B
G
F
C
G
E

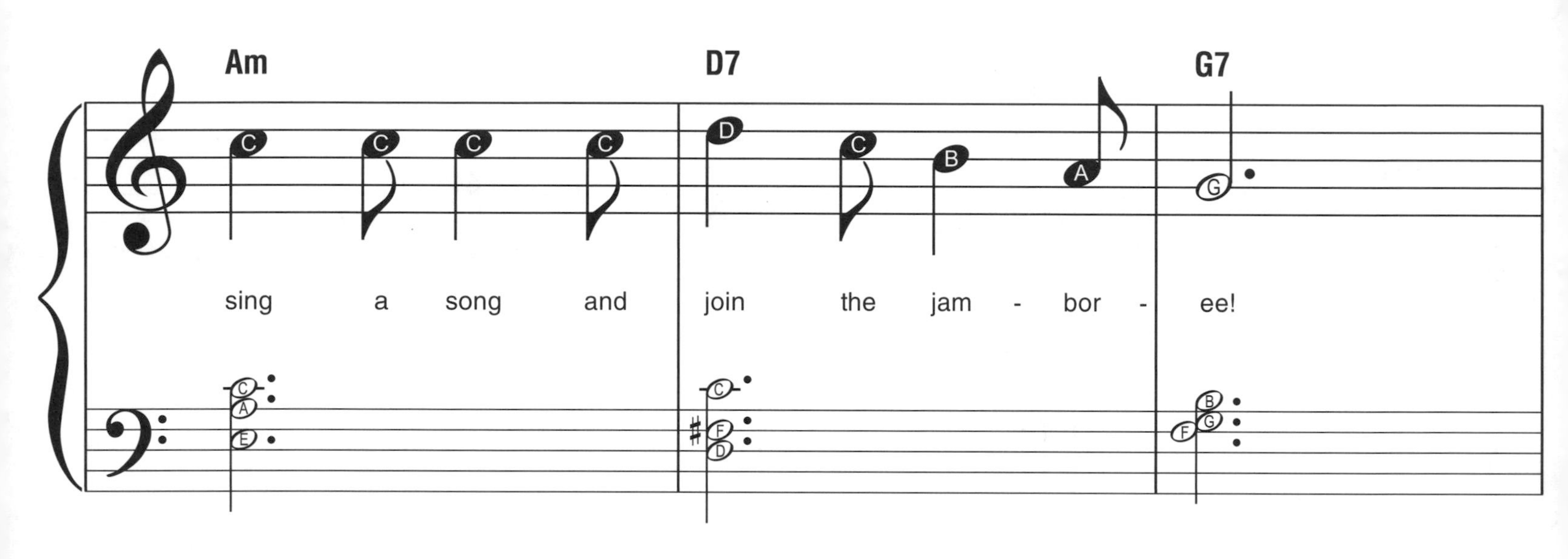
Am
D7
G7
C C C C
D
C
B
A
G
sing a song and join the jam - bor - ee!
C
A
E
C
F
D
B
G
F

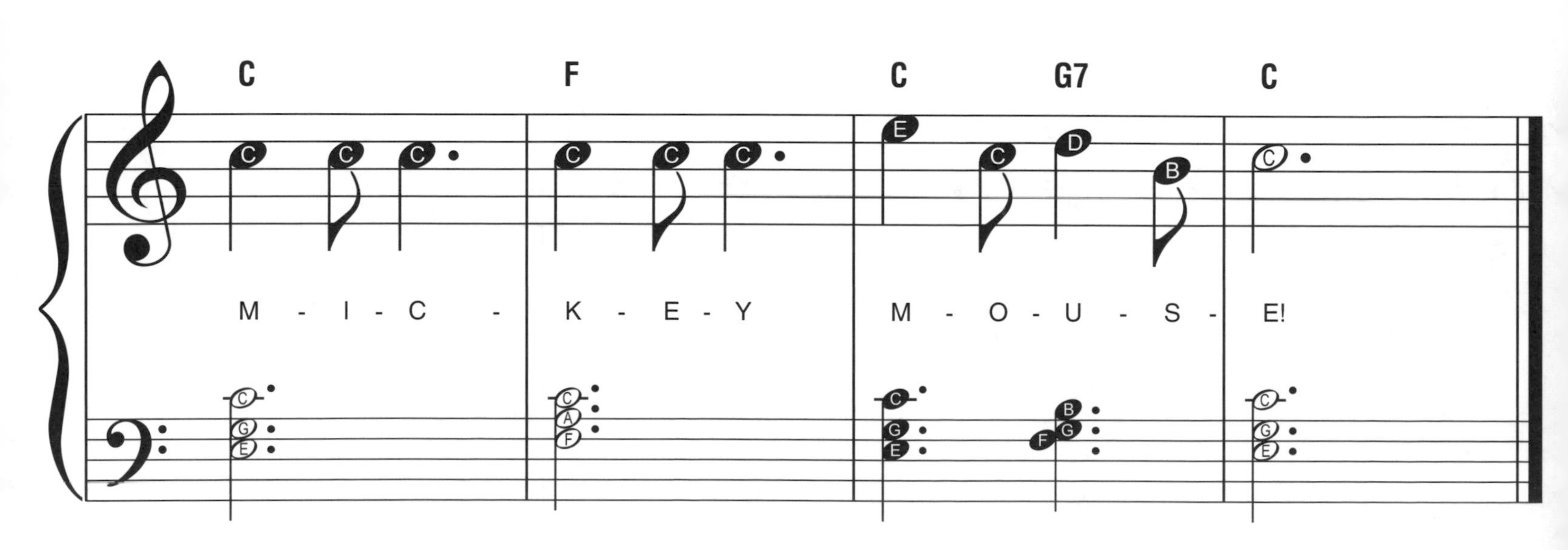
C
F
C
G7
C
C C C
C C C
E
C
D
B
C
M - I - C - K - E - Y M - O - U - S - E!
C
G
E
C
A
F
C
G
E
B
G
F
C
G
E

Let It Go
from FROZEN

Music and Lyrics by Kristen Anderson-Lopez
and Robert Lopez

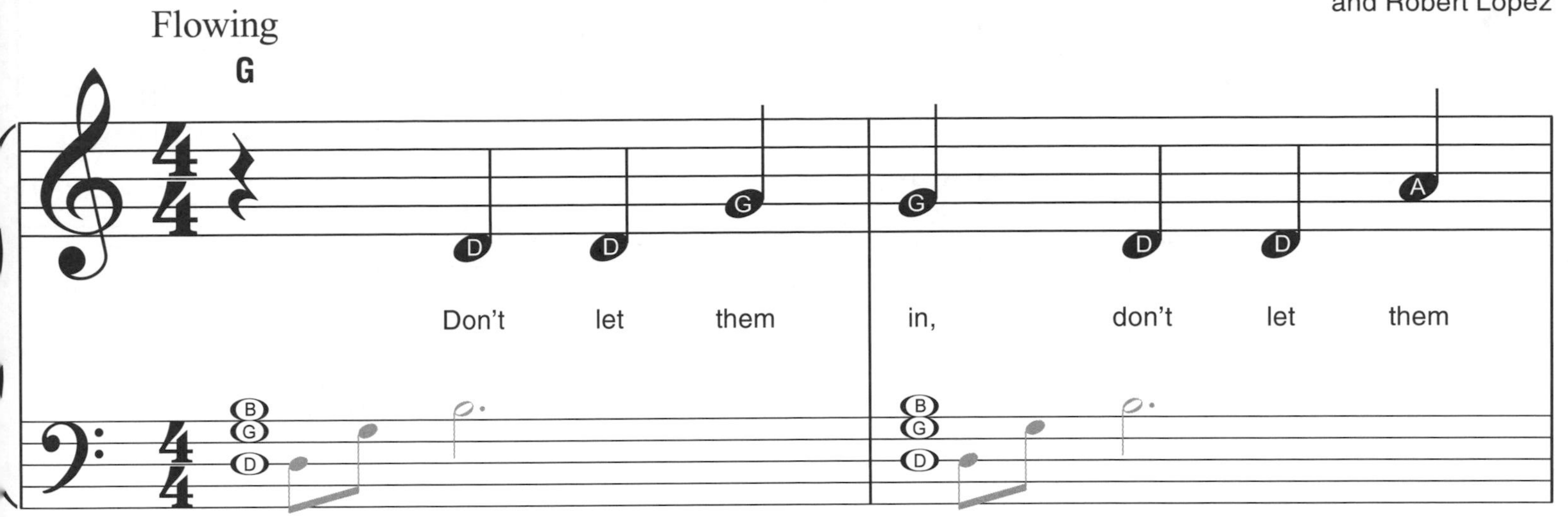

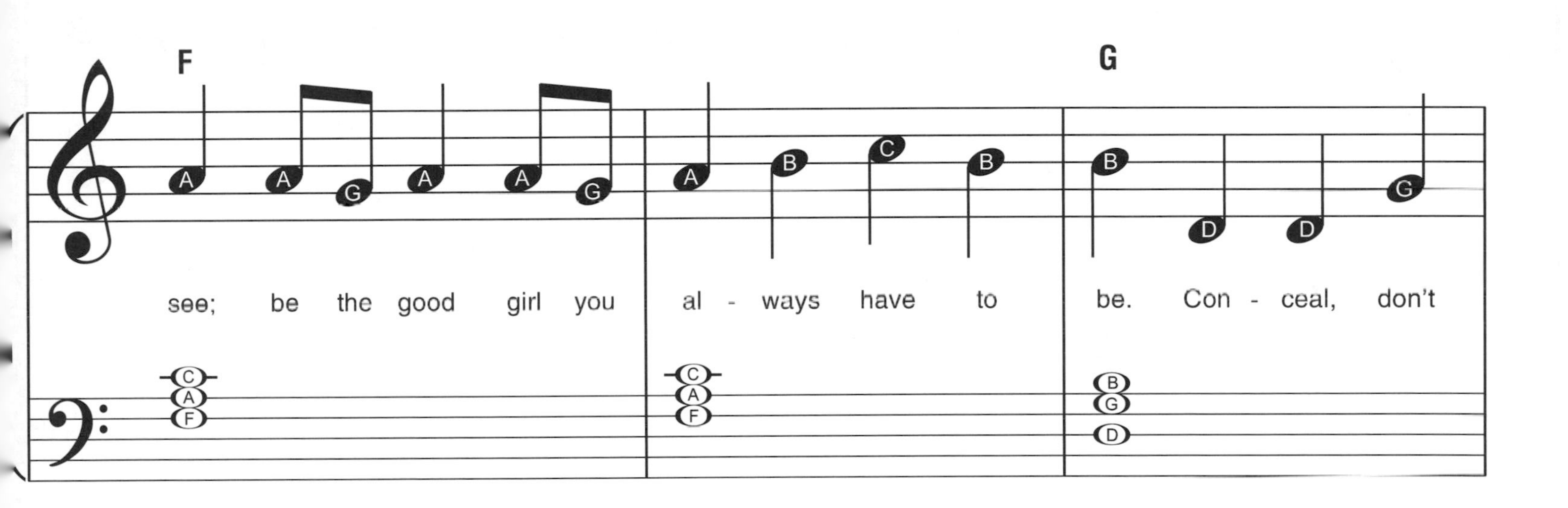

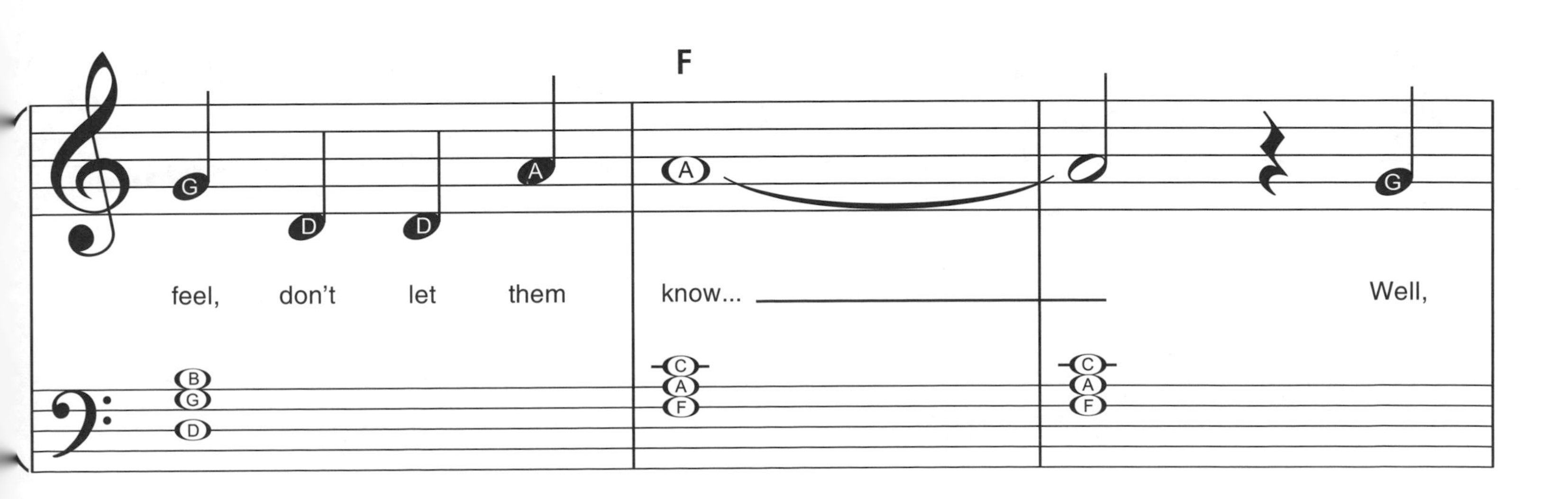

C
now they know. Let it go, let it

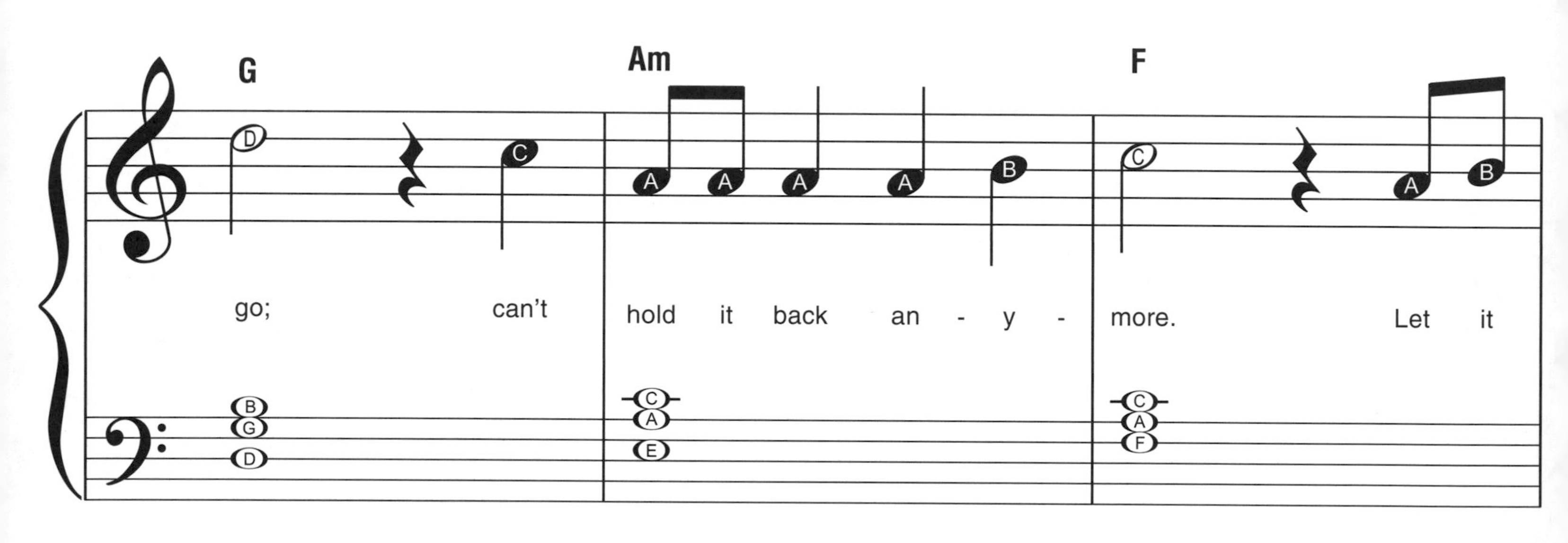
G
Am
F
go; can't hold it back an - y - more. Let it

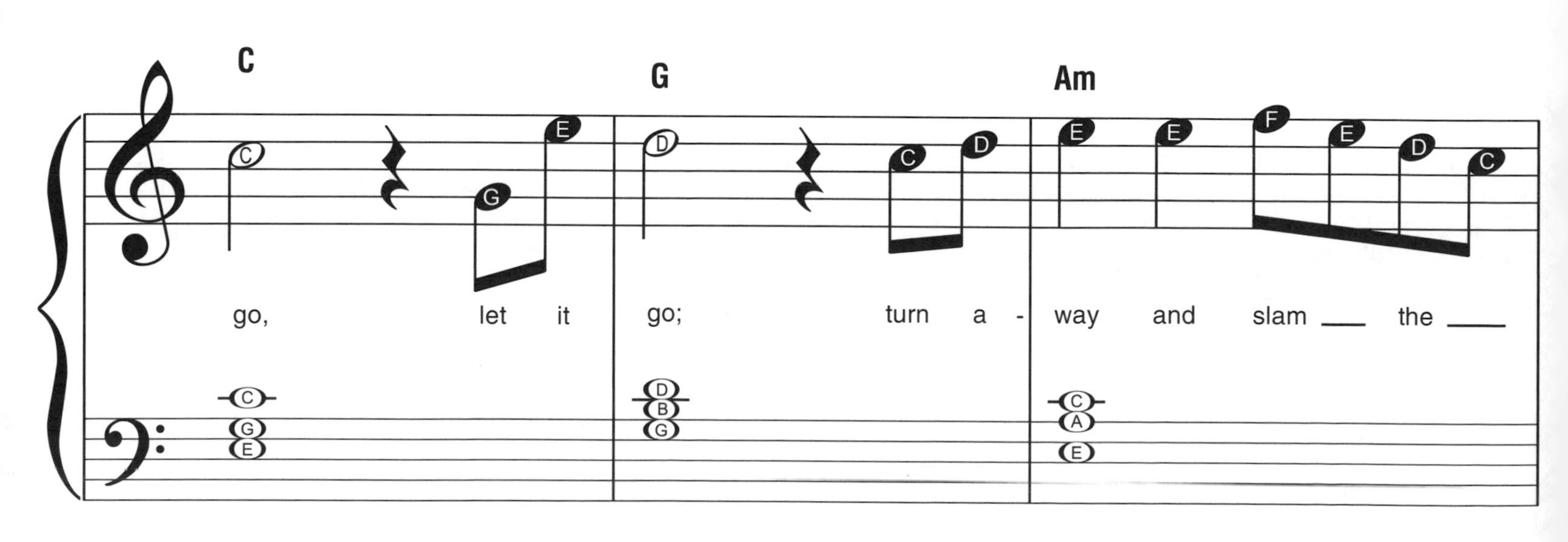
C
G
Am
go, let it go; turn a - way and slam the

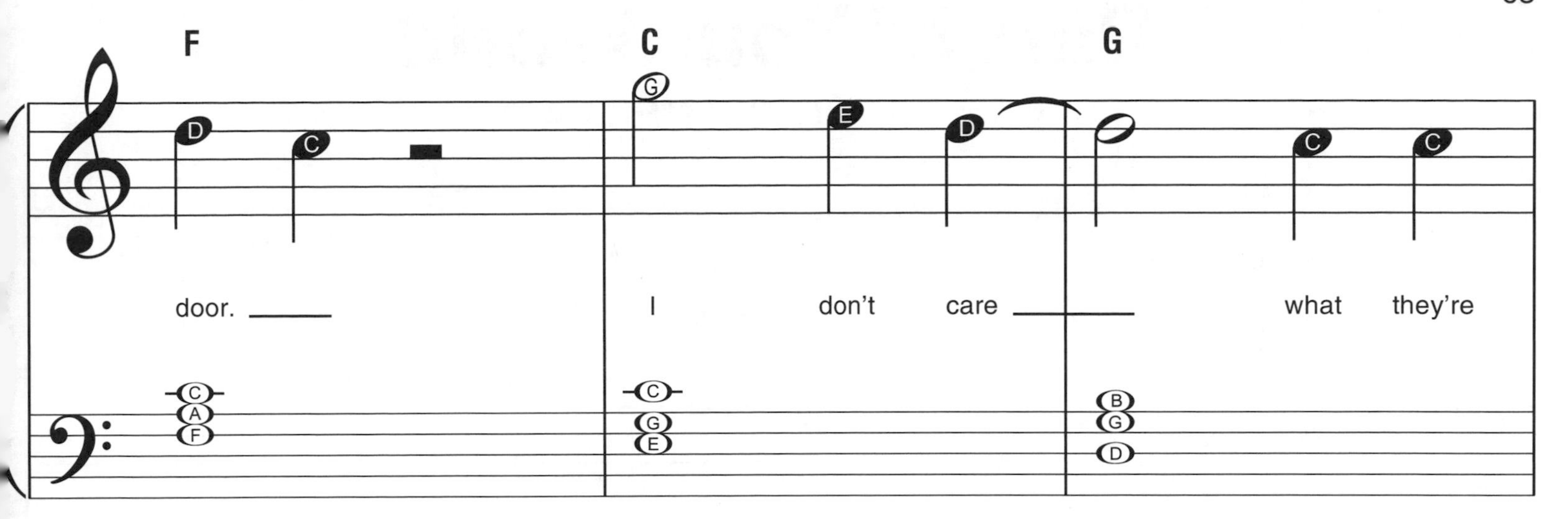
F
C
G
door.
I
don't
care
what
they're

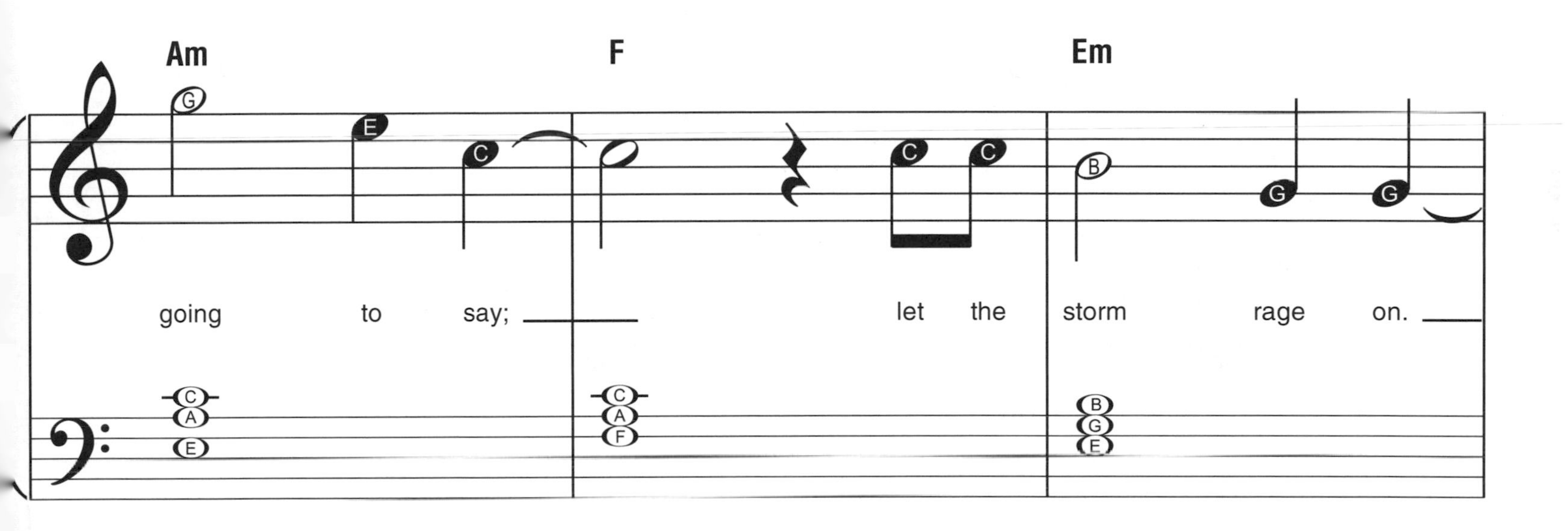
Am
F
Em
going
to
say;
let
the
storm
rage
on.

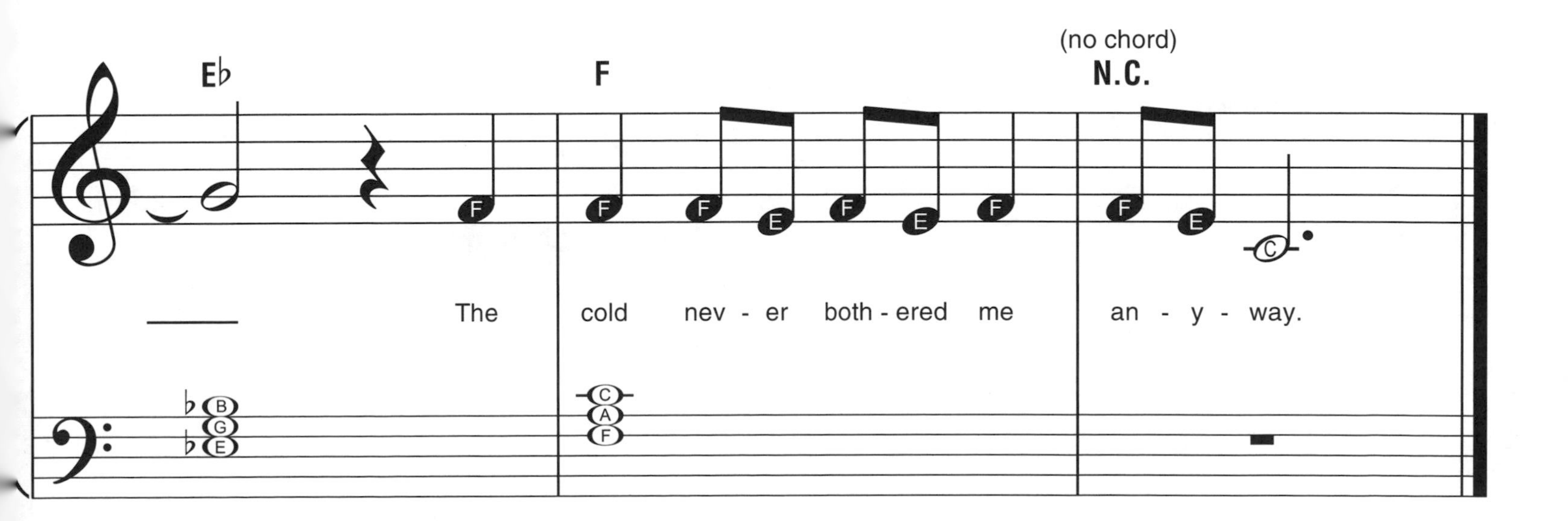
(no chord)
E♭
F
N.C.
The
cold
nev - er
both - ered
me
an - y - way.

Part of Your World

from THE LITTLE MERMAID

Music by Alan Menken
Lyrics by Howard Ashman

Moderately

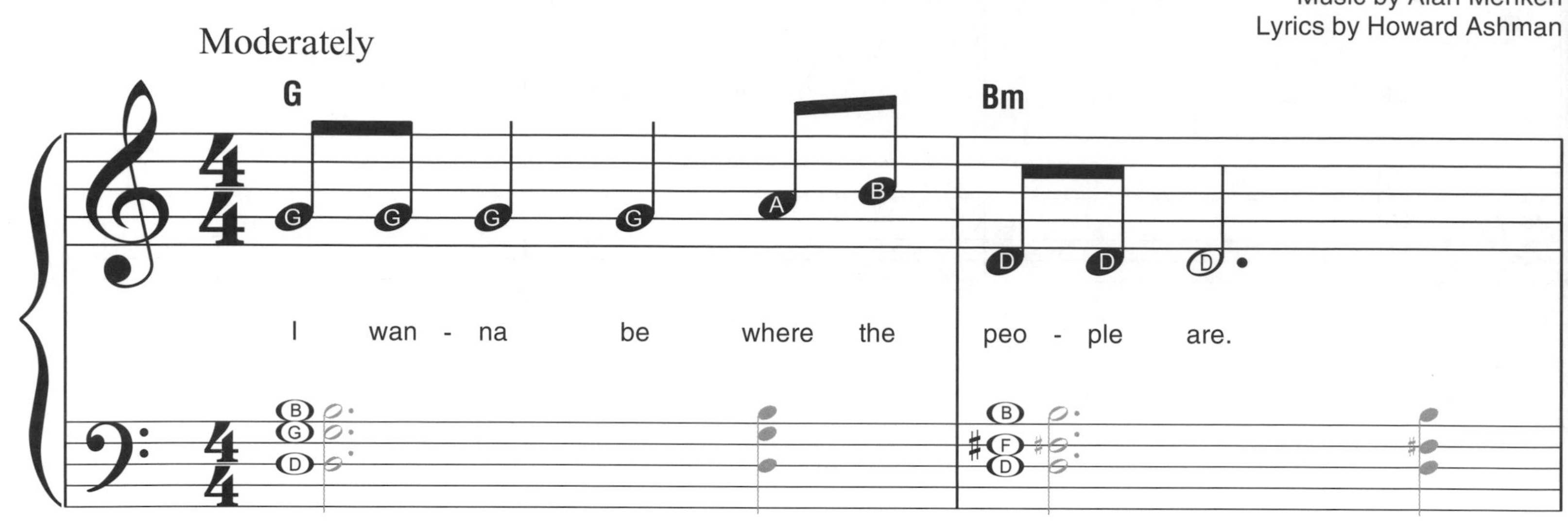

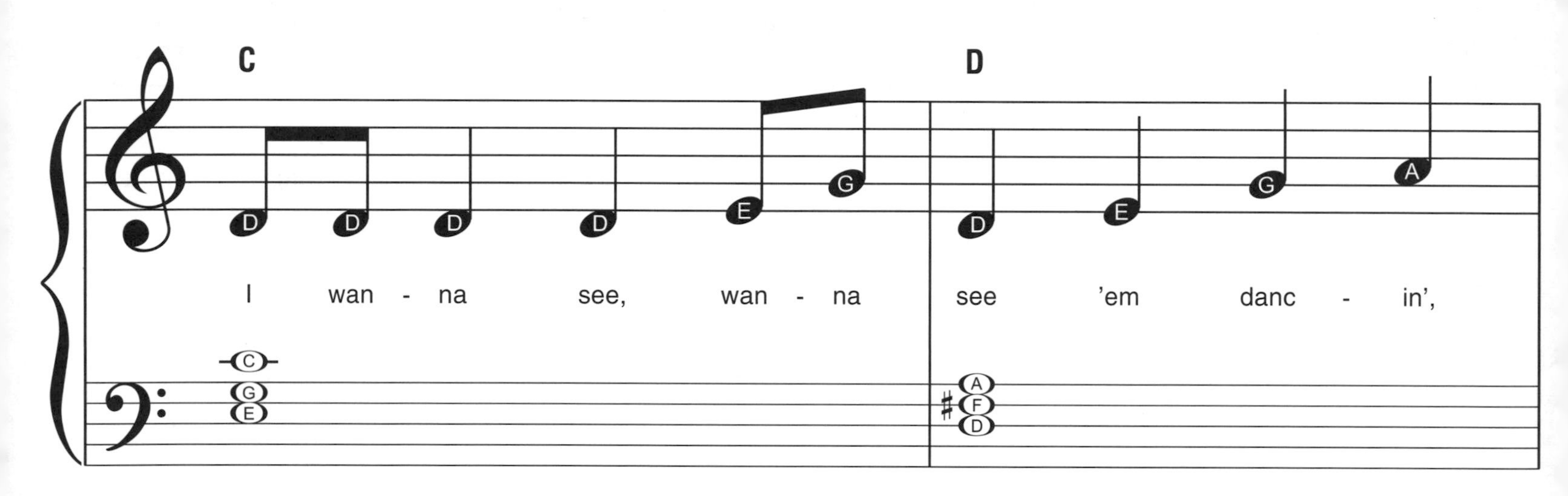

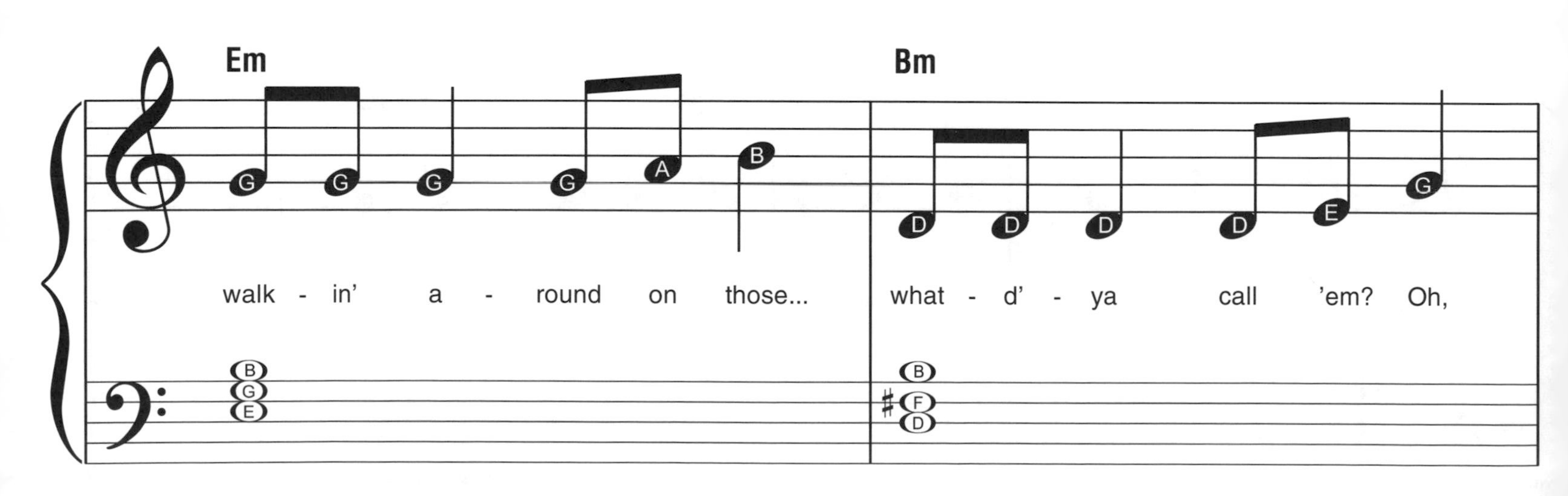

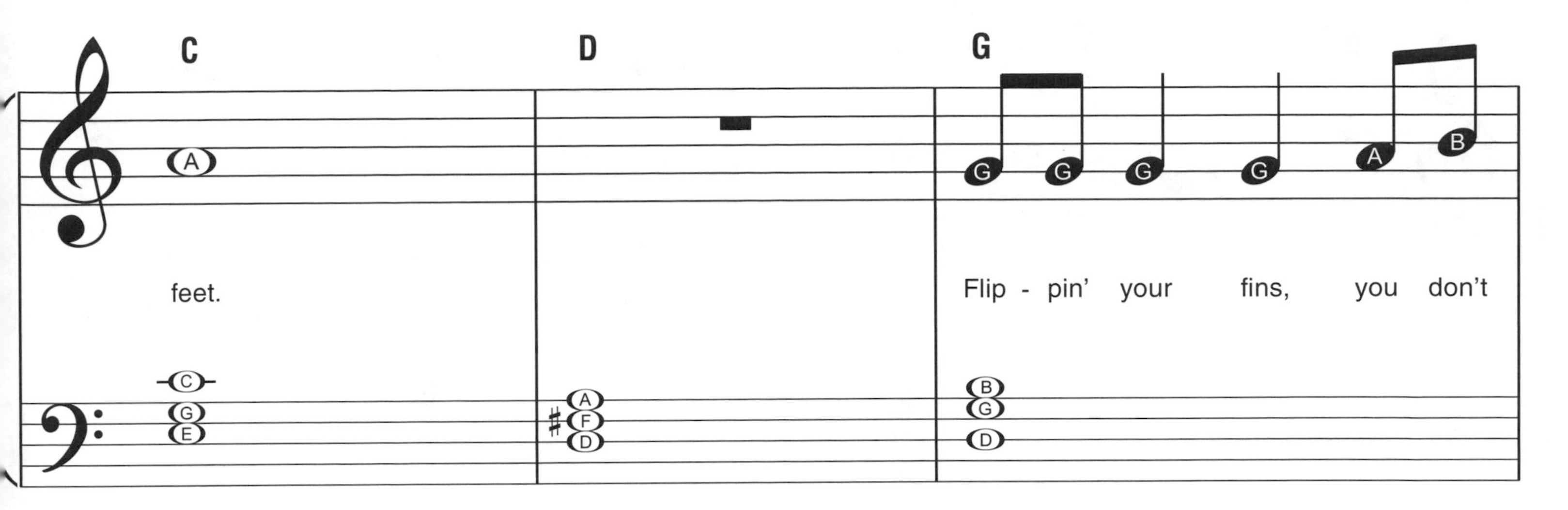
C
D
G
feet.
Flip - pin' your fins, you don't

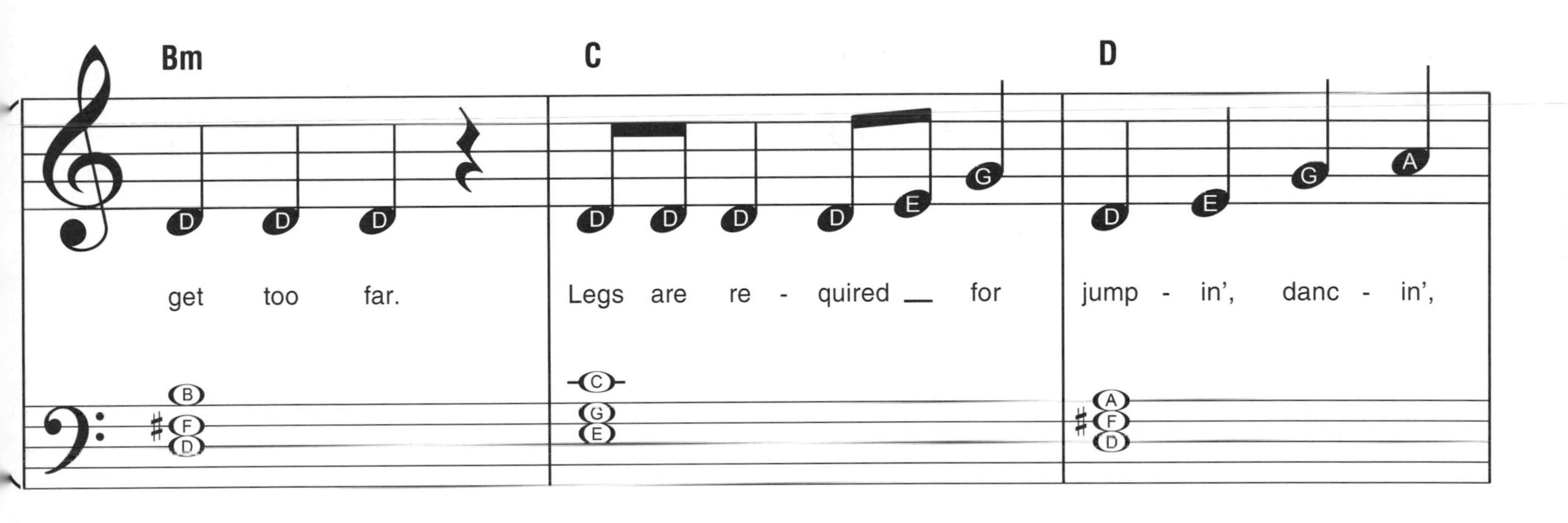
Bm
C
D
get too far.
Legs are re - quired __ for
jump - in', danc - in',

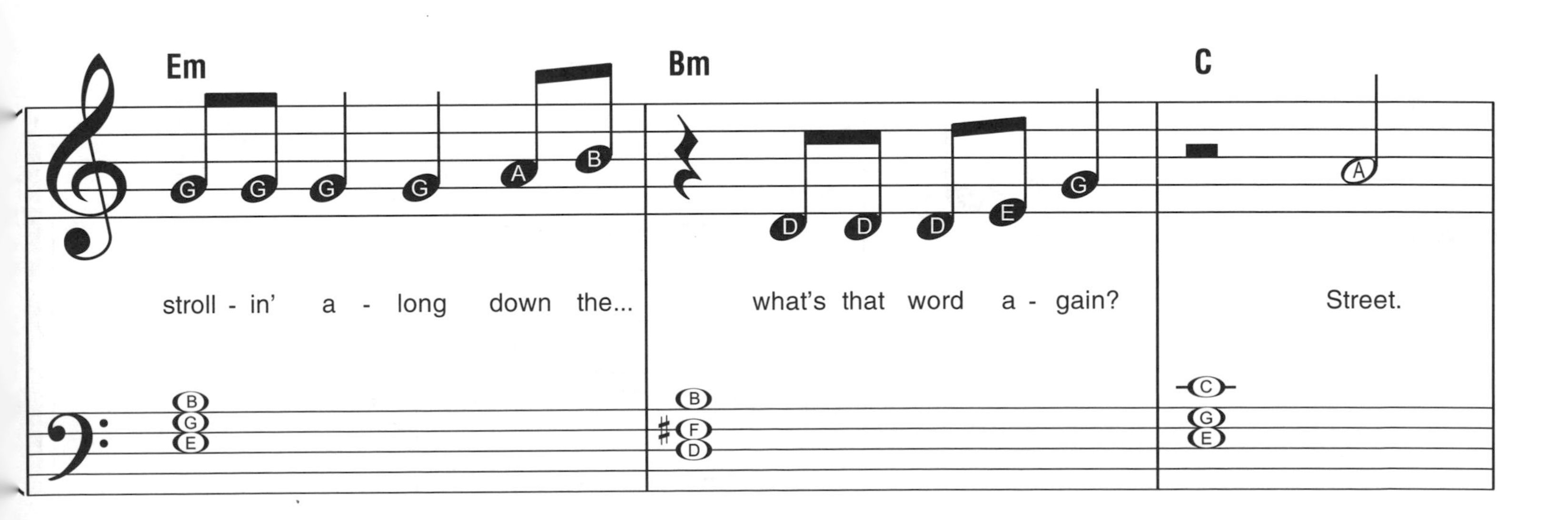
Em
Bm
C
stroll - in' a - long down the...
what's that word a - gain?
Street.

D
G
G7
Up where they
walk, up where they
run, up where they

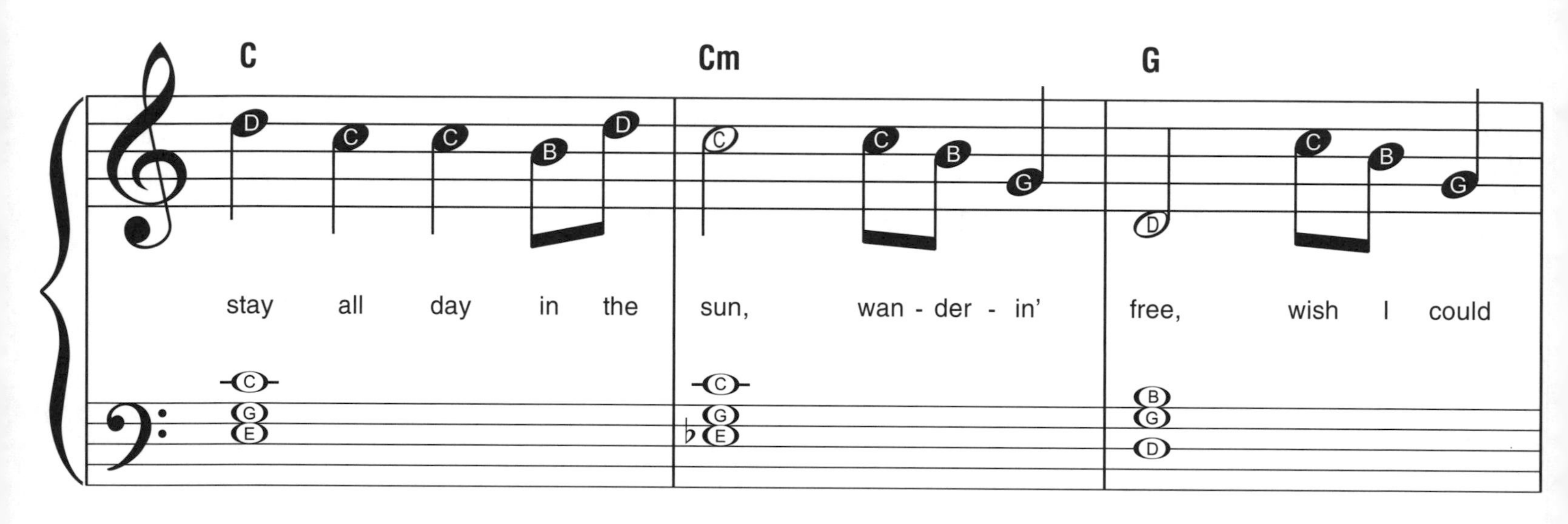
C
Cm
G
stay all day in the
sun, wan - der - in'
free, wish I could

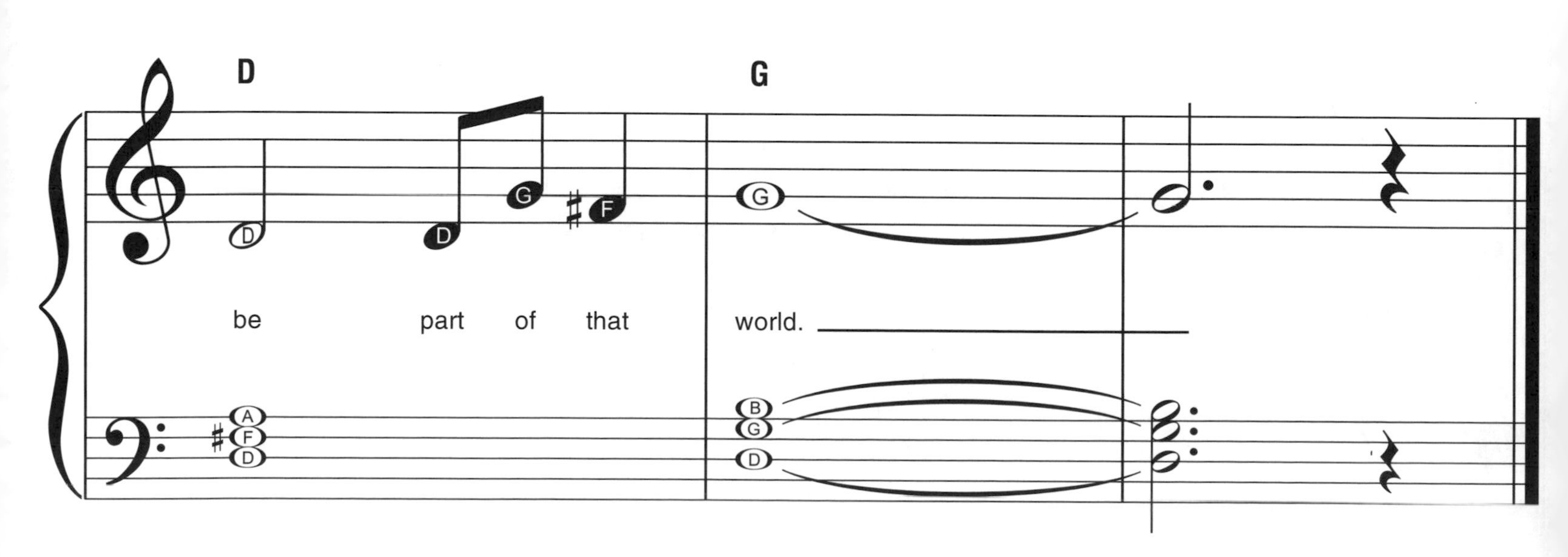
D
G
be part of that
world.

Reflection

from MULAN

Music by Matthew Wilder
Lyrics by David Zippel

Moderately

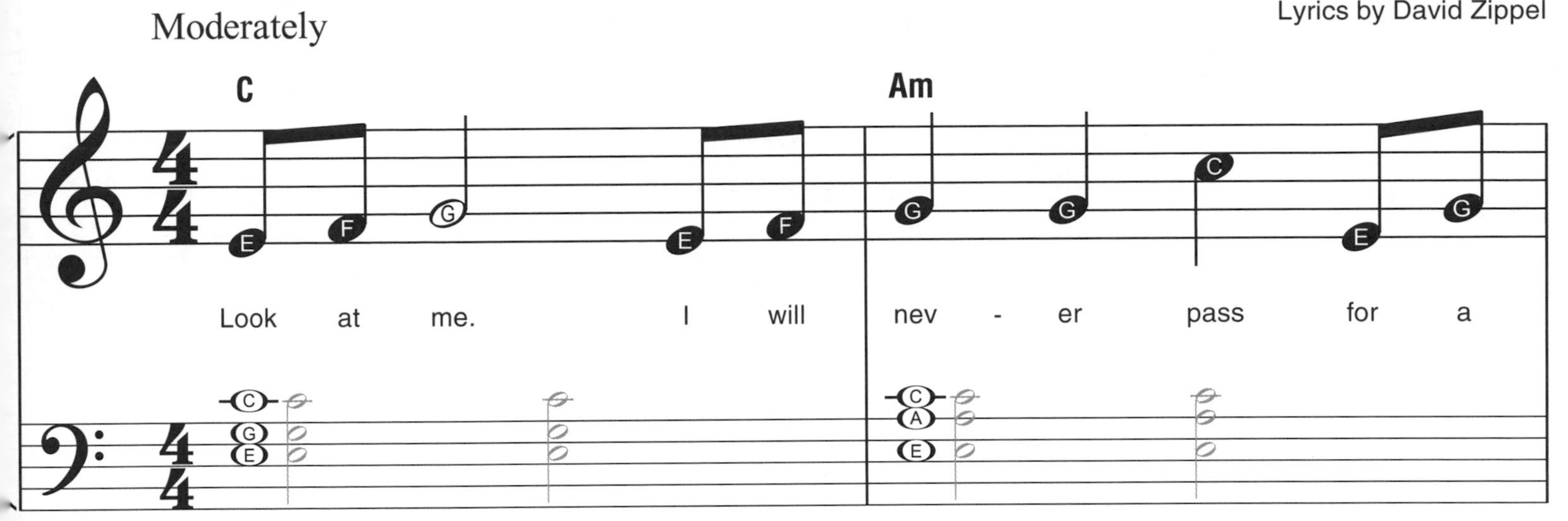

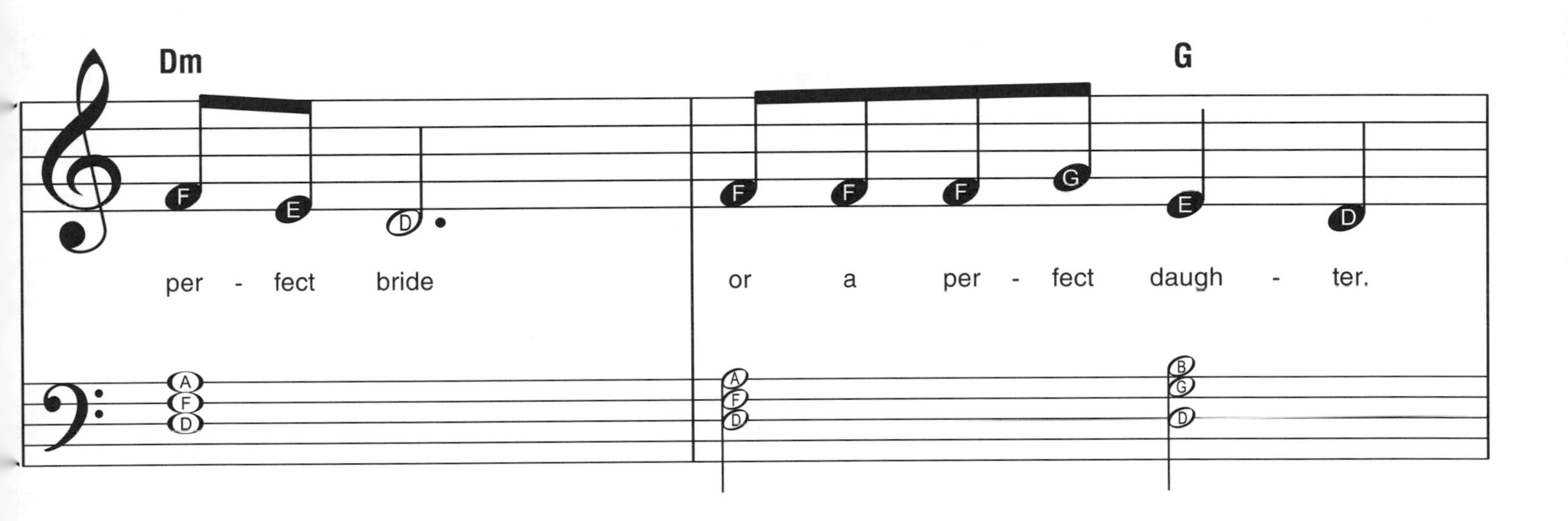

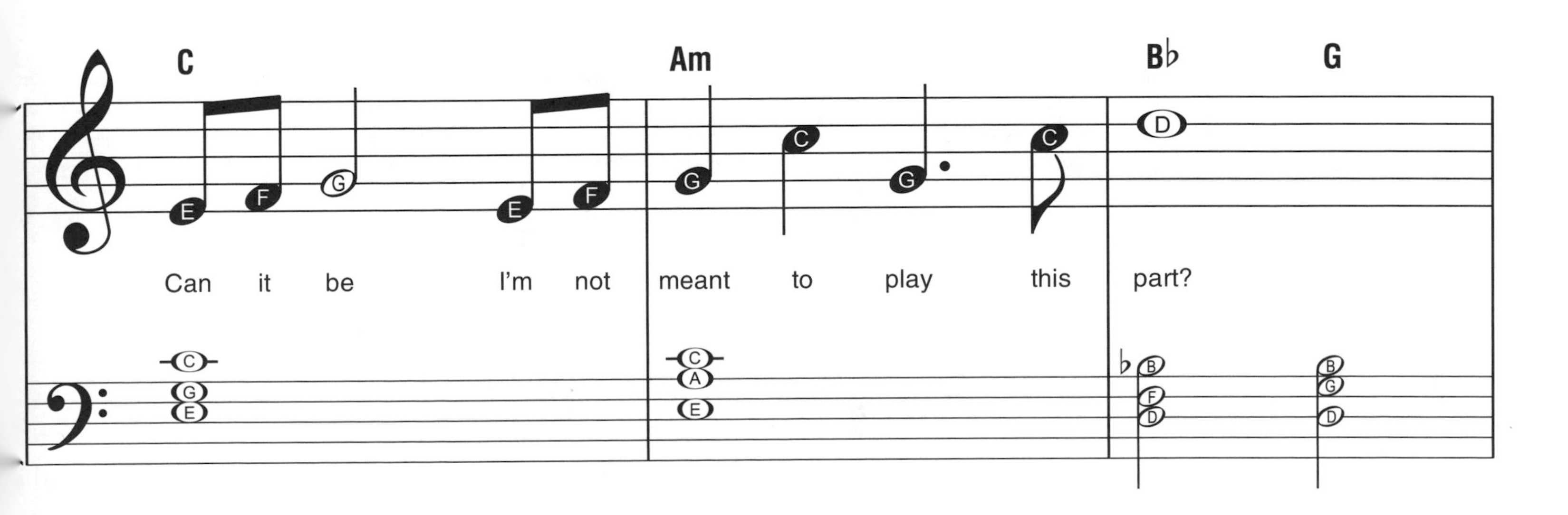

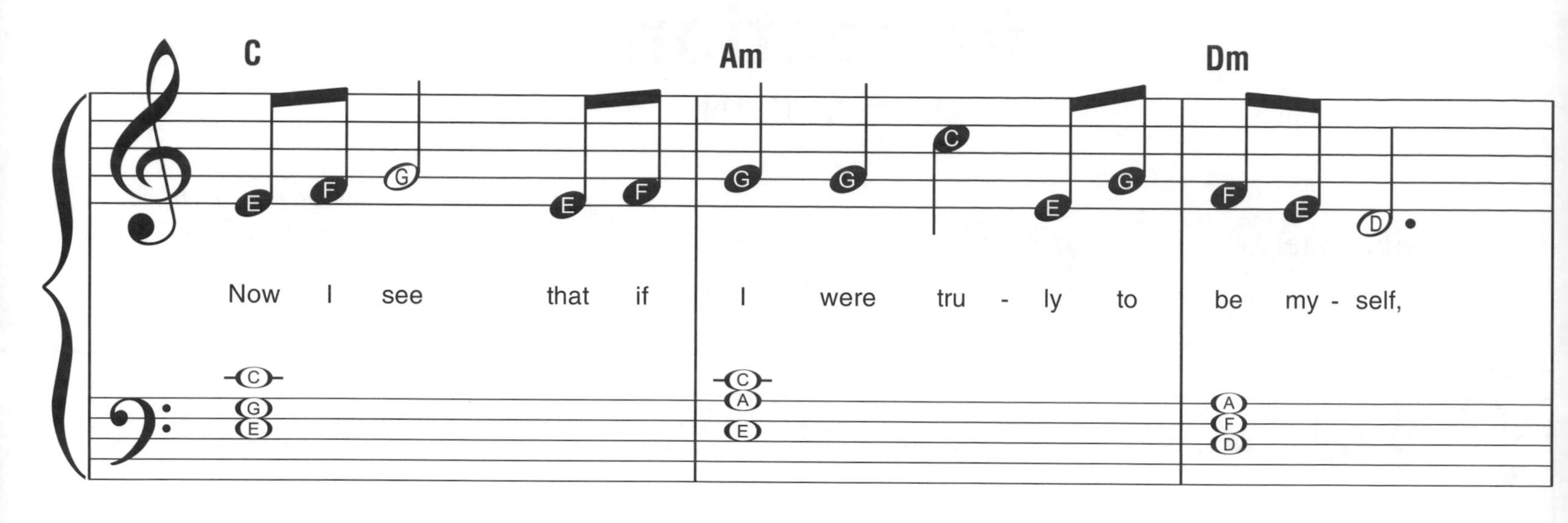
C
Am
Dm
Now I see that if I were tru - ly to be my - self,

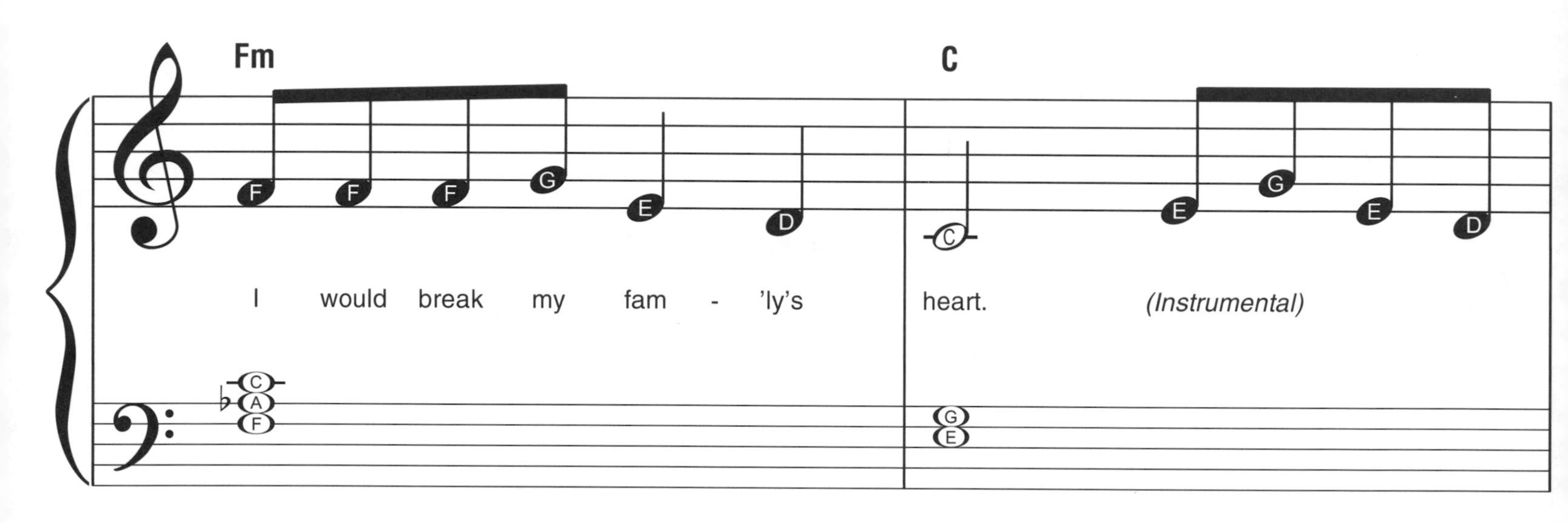
Fm
C
I would break my fam - 'ly's heart.
(Instrumental)

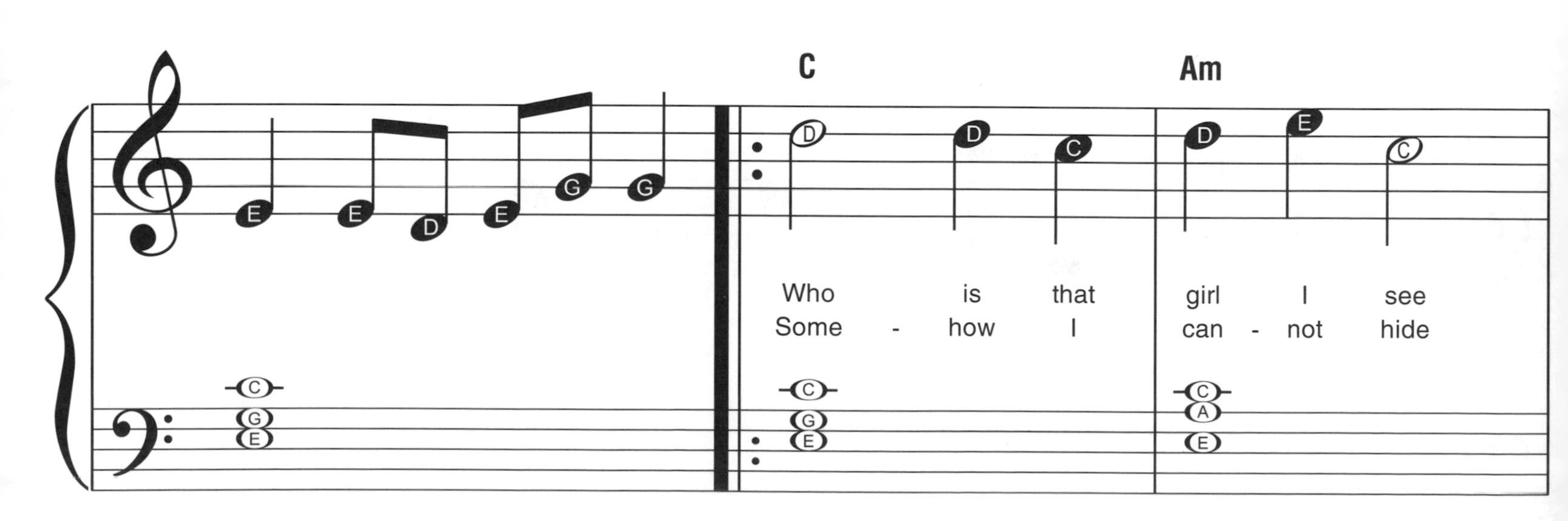
C
Am
Who is that girl I see
Some - how I can - not hide

F
Fm
C
B
C
A
G
C
F
E
G
C
E
star - ing straight
who I am,
back at me?
though I've tried.
Why is my re -
When will my re -
C
A
F
C
A
F
C
G
E

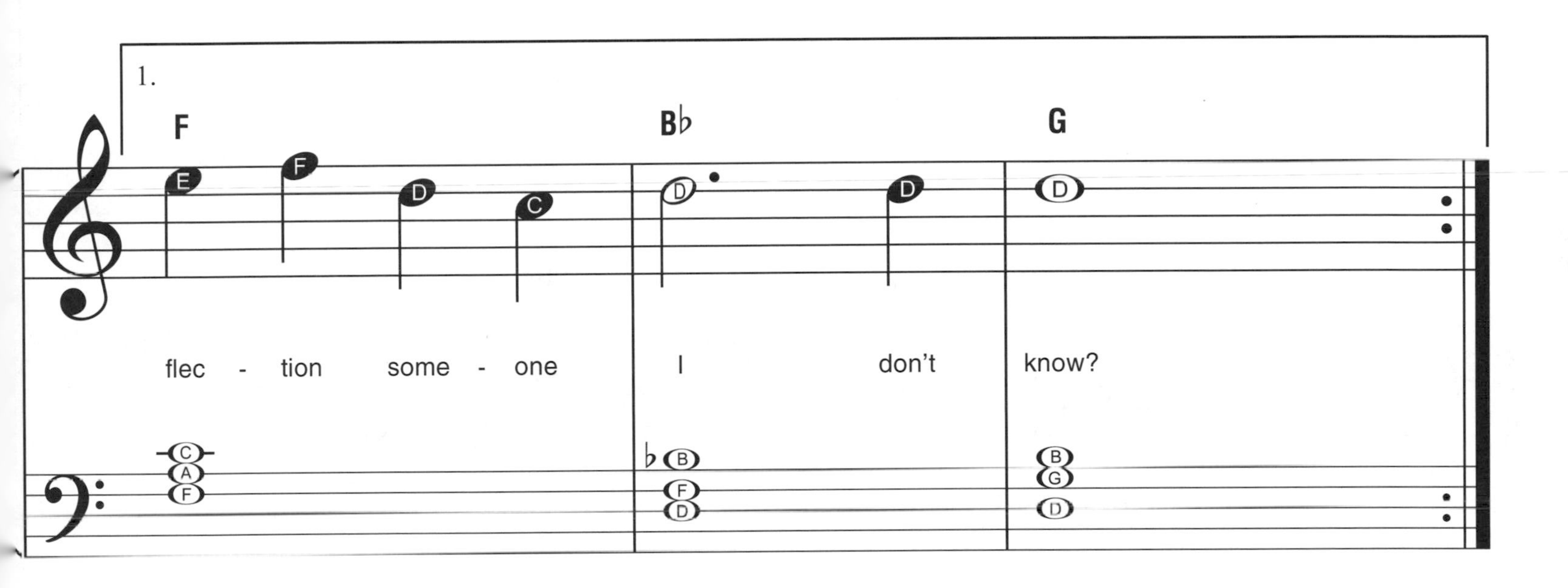
1.
F
B♭
G
E
F
D
C
D
D
D
flec - tion some - one
I don't
know?
C
A
F
B
F
D
B
G
D

2.
F
Fm
C
E
F
D
D
E
C
B
C
flec - tion show
who I am in -
side?
C
A
F
C
A
F
C
G
E

Remember Me
(Ernesto de la Cruz)
from COCO

Words and Music by Kristen Anderson-Lopez
and Robert Lopez

Moderately fast

C Fm

Re - mem - ber me, though I have to say good - bye. Re - mem - ber

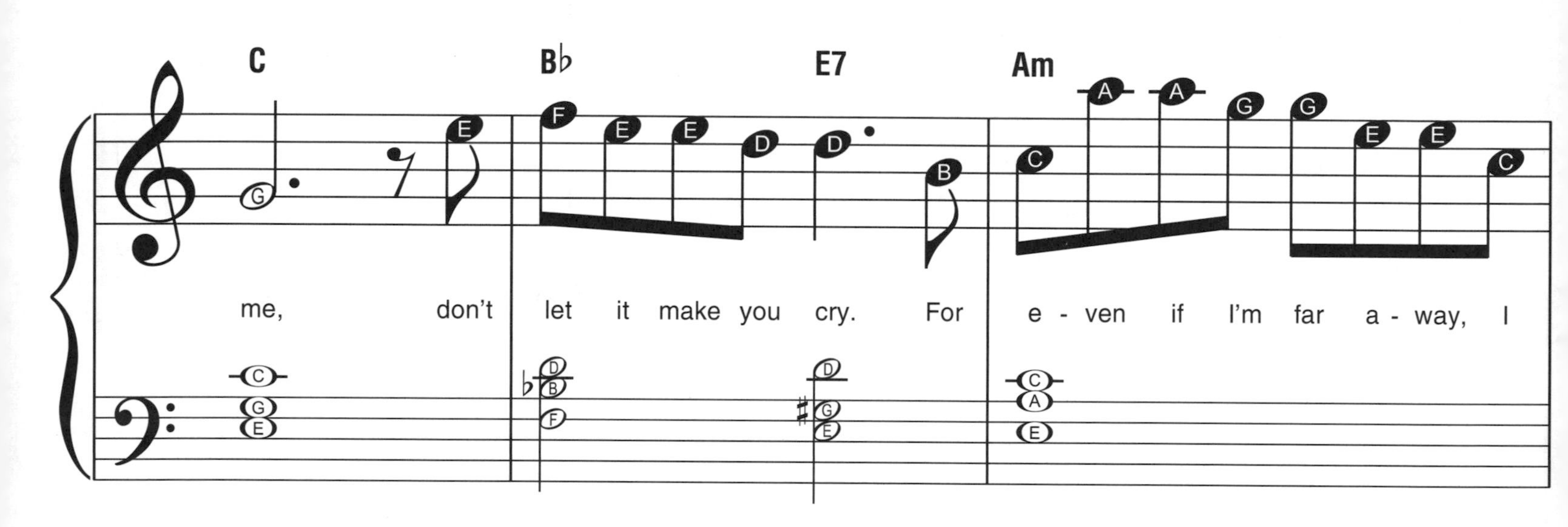

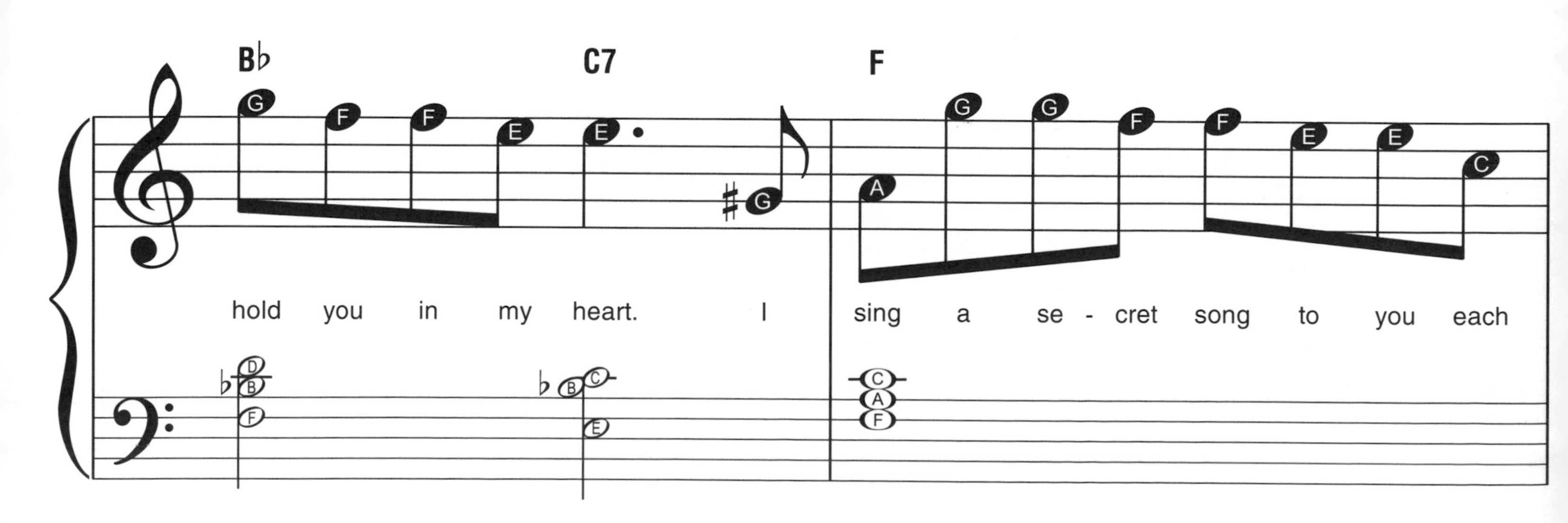

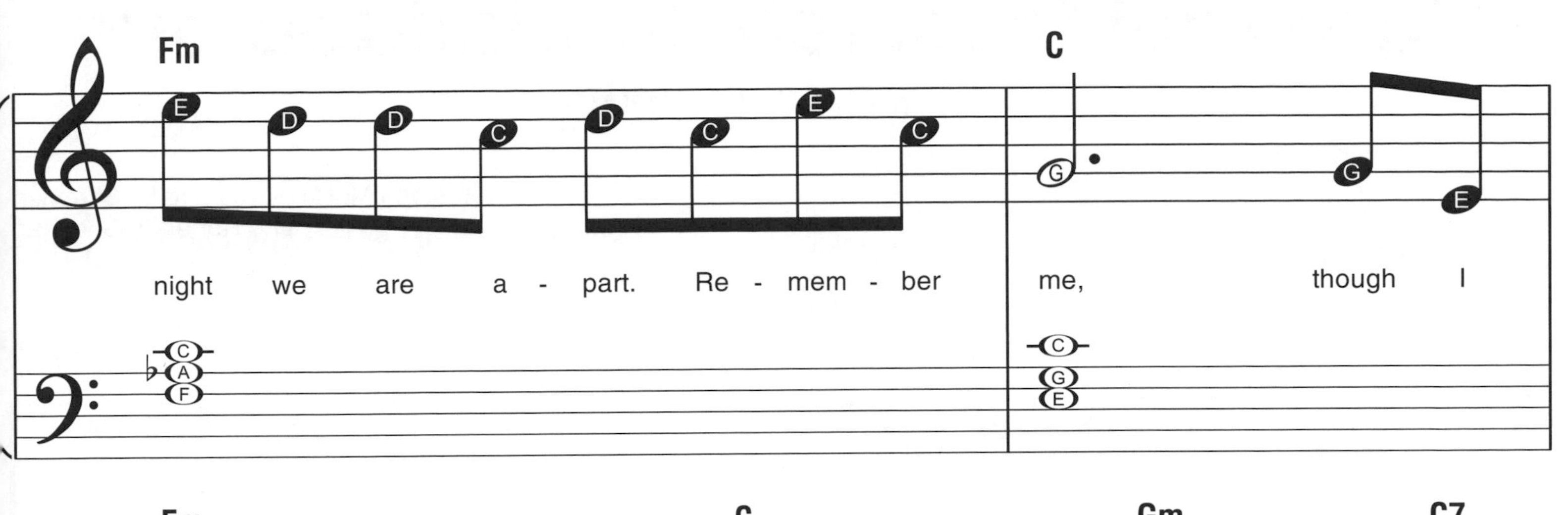
Fm
C
night we are a - part. Re - mem - ber
me, though I

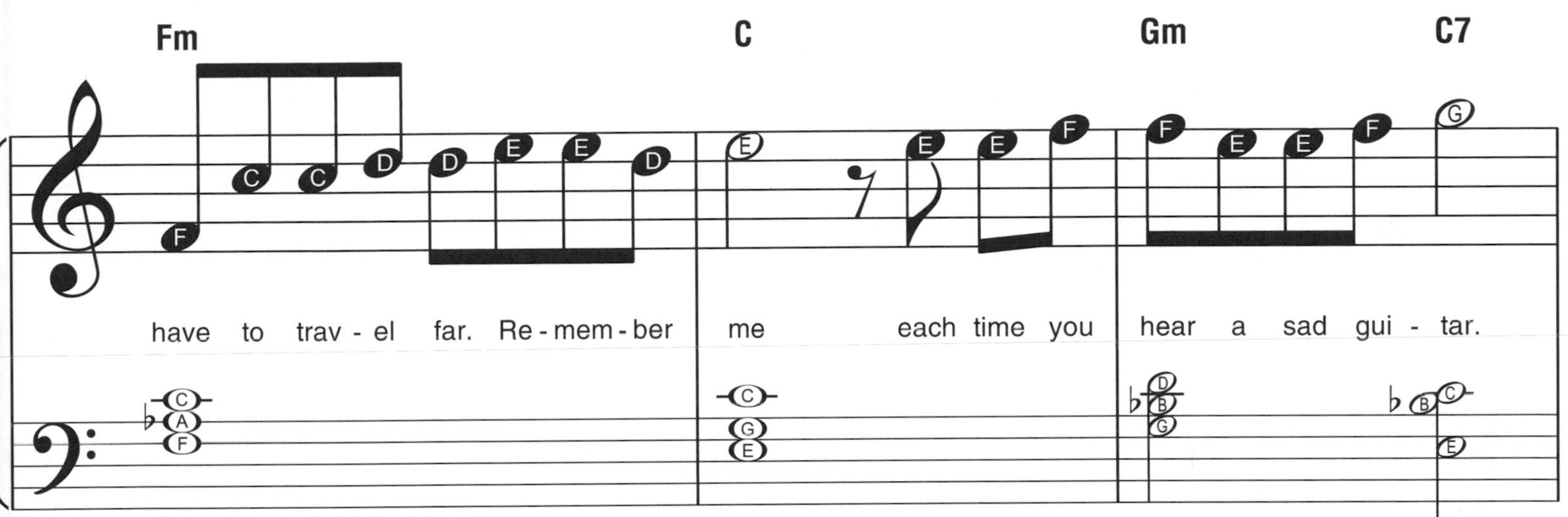
Fm
C
Gm
C7
have to trav - el far. Re - mem - ber
me each time you
hear a sad gui - tar.

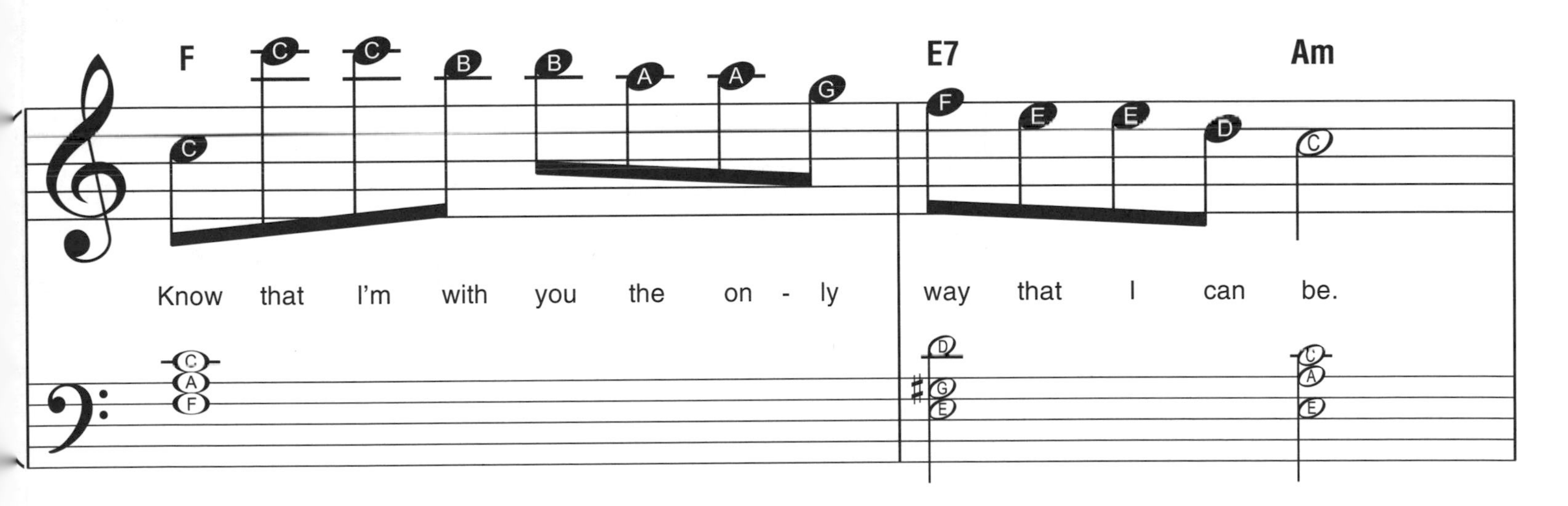
F
E7
Am
Know that I'm with you the on - ly
way that I can be.

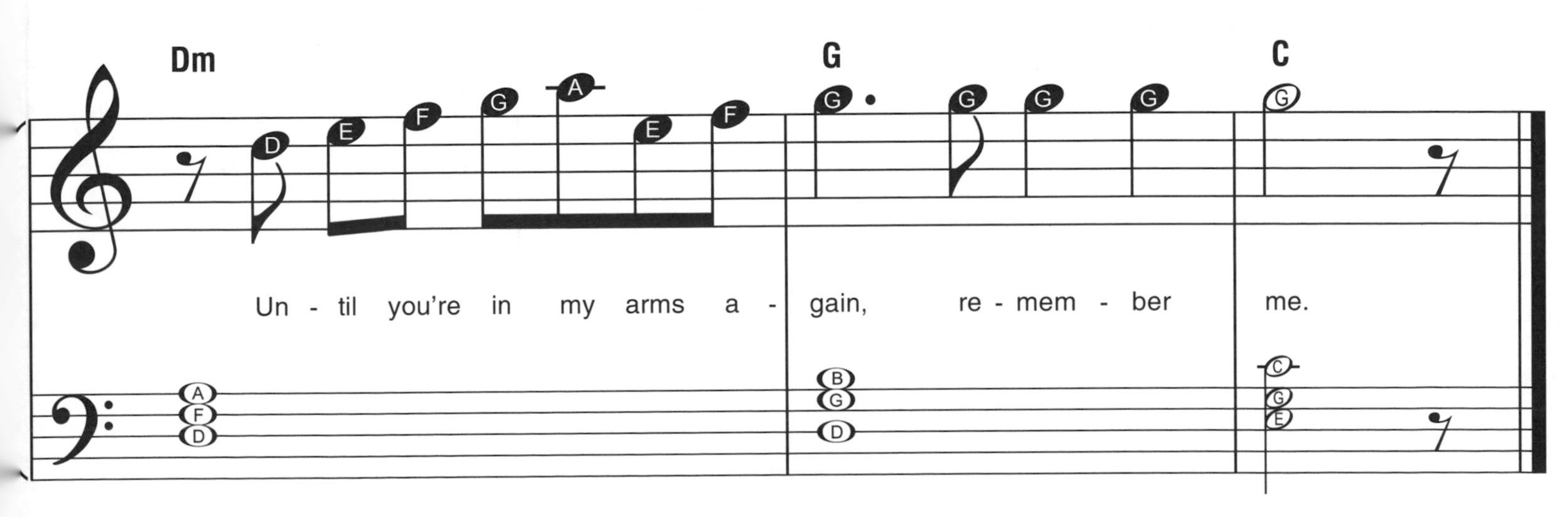
Dm
G
C
Un - til you're in my arms a -
gain, re - mem - ber
me.

Supercalifragilisticexpialidocious

from MARY POPPINS

Words and Music by Richard M. Sherman
and Robert B. Sherman

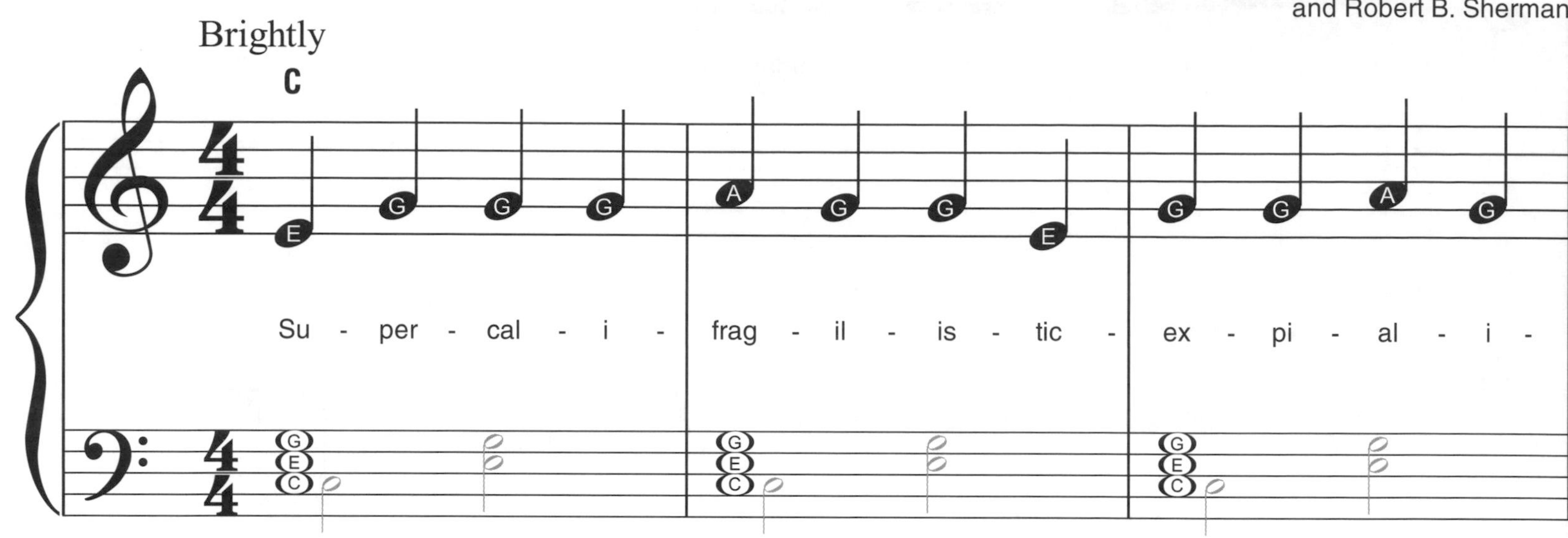

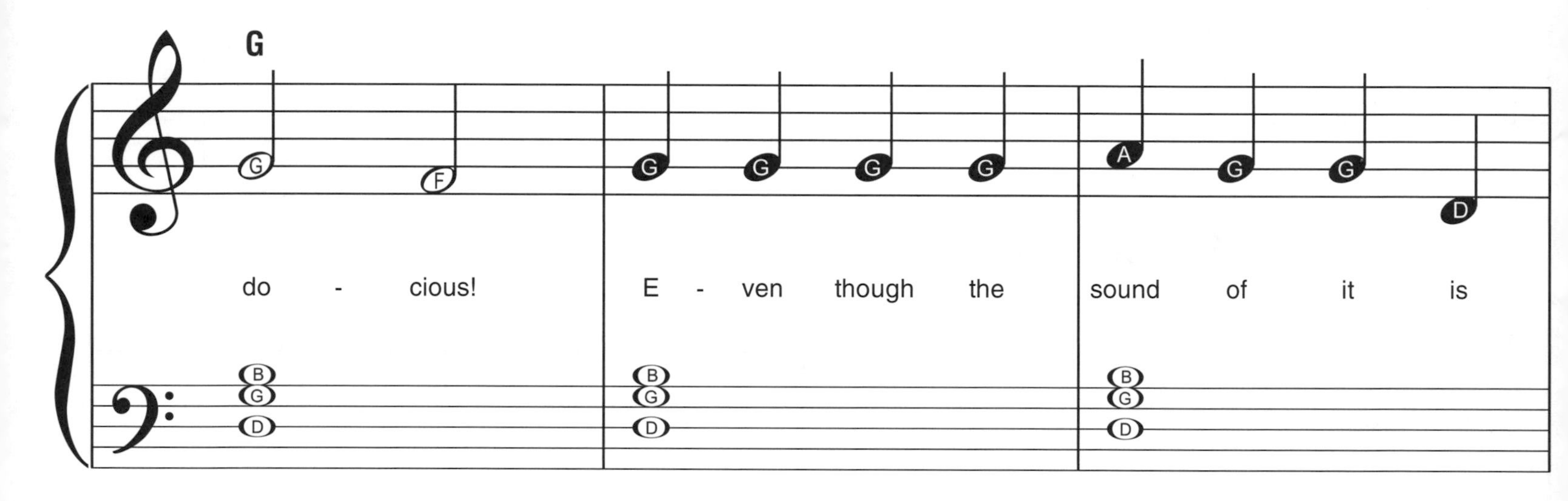

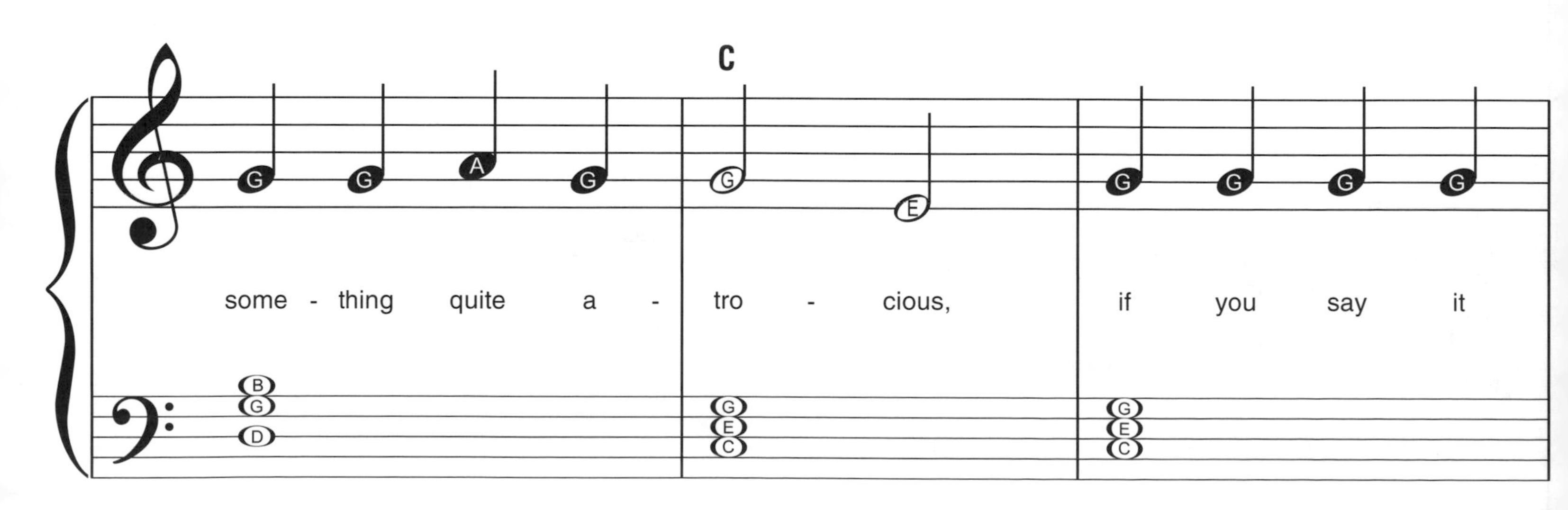

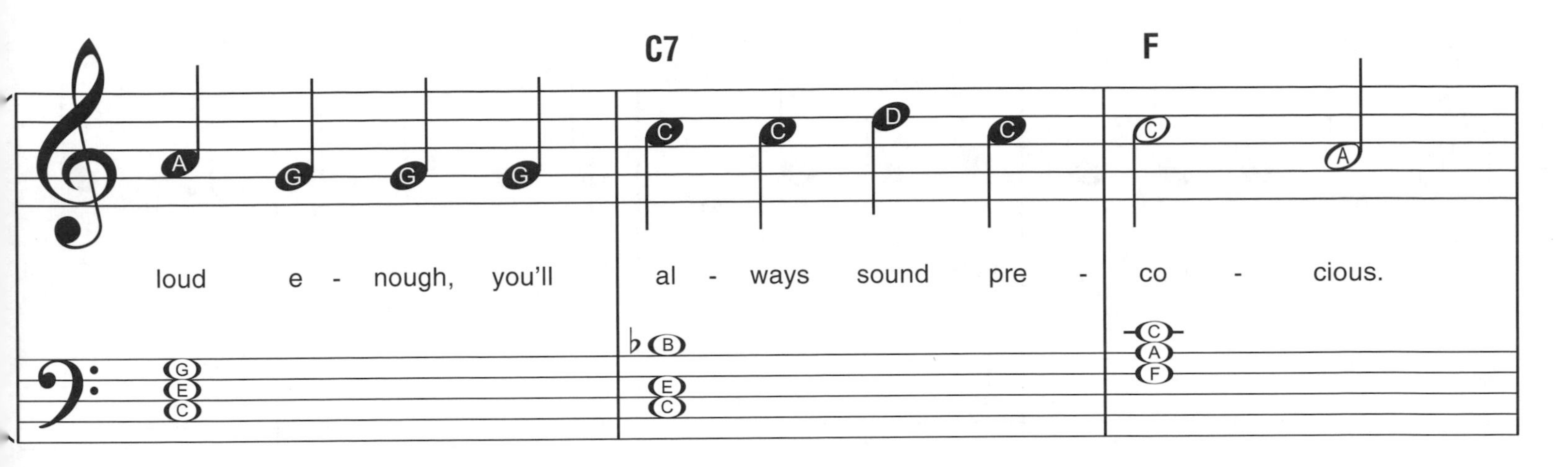
C7
F
loud e - nough, you'll al - ways sound pre - co - cious.

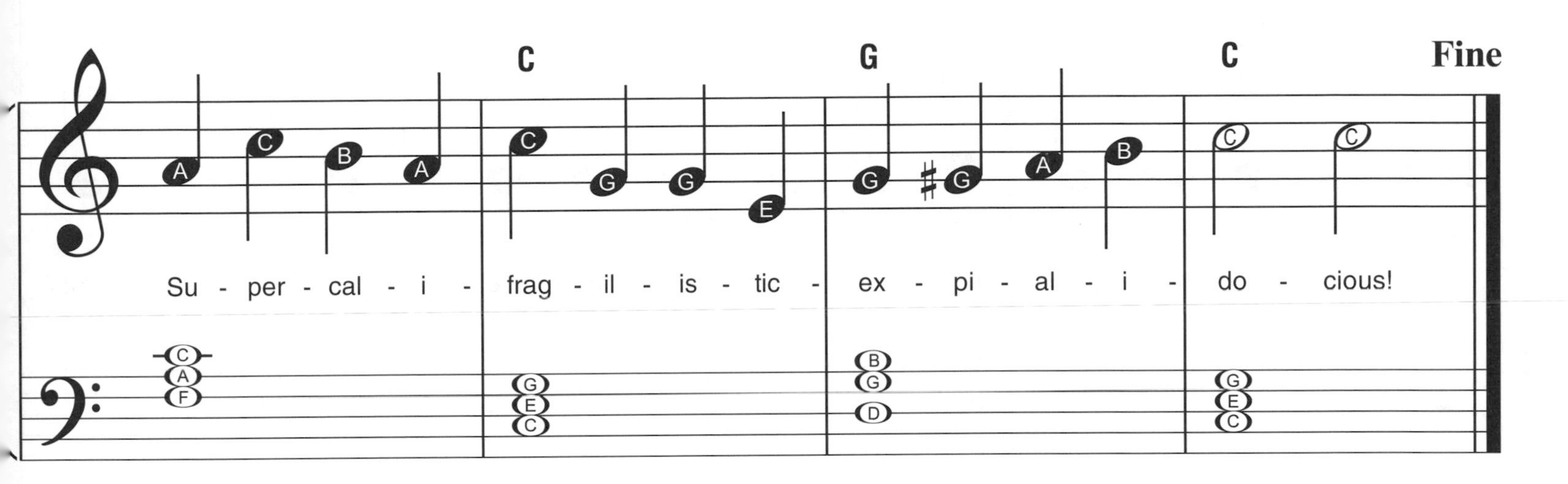
C
G
C
Fine
Su - per - cal - i - frag - il - is - tic - ex - pi - al - i - do - cious!

G
Um did - dle did - dle did - dle um did - dle ay!

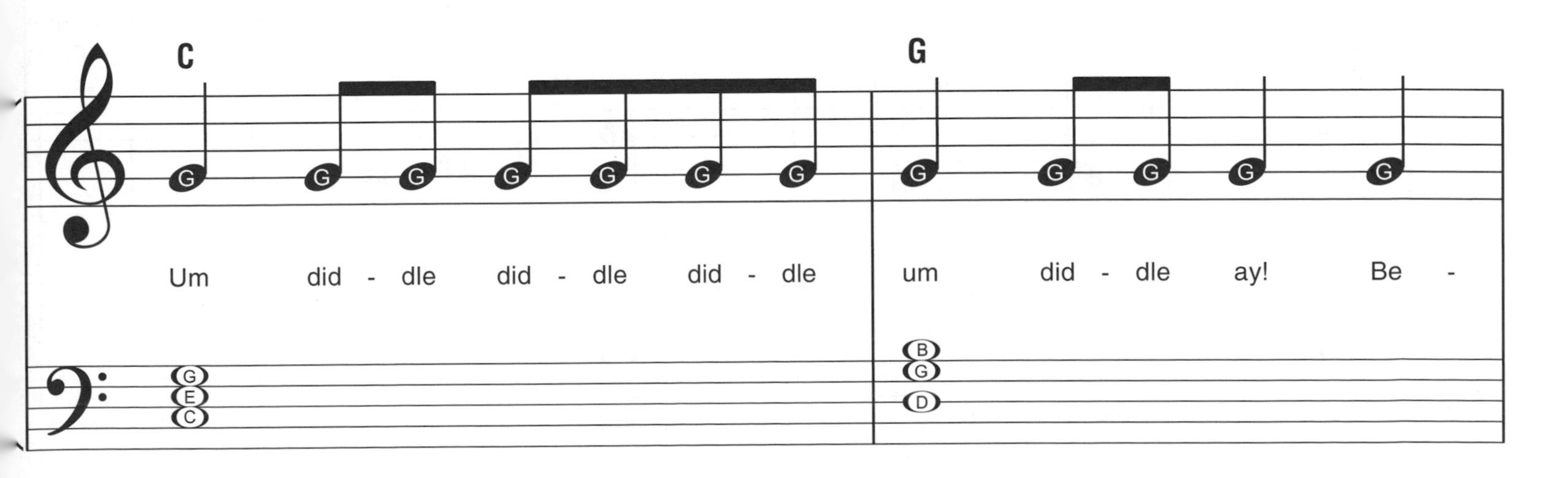
C
G
Um did - dle did - dle did - dle um did - dle ay! Be -

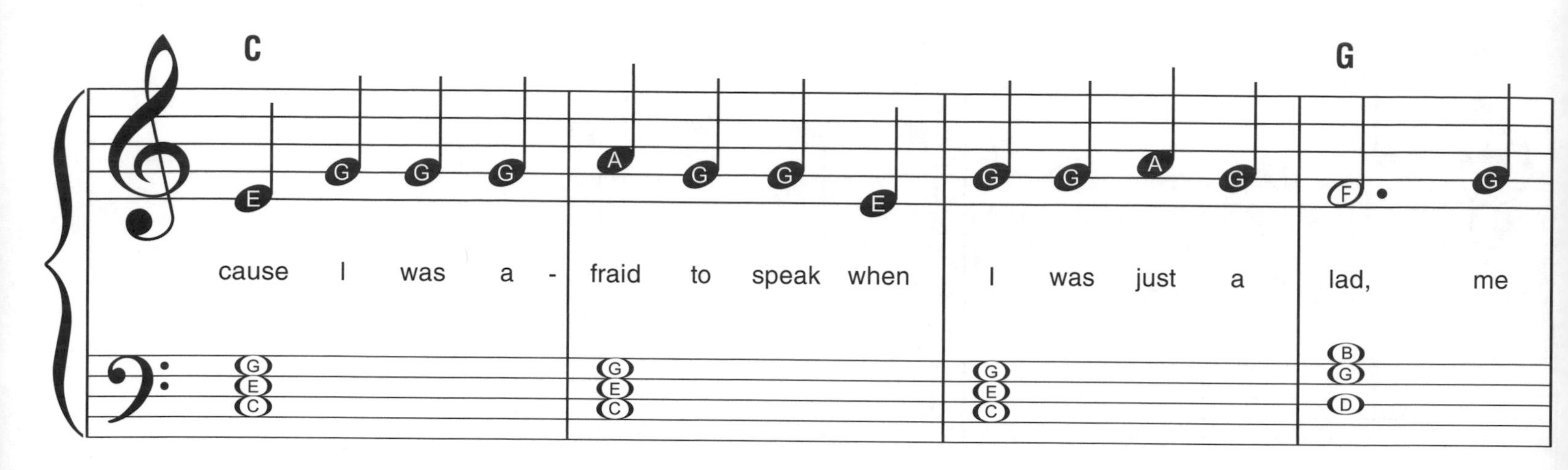

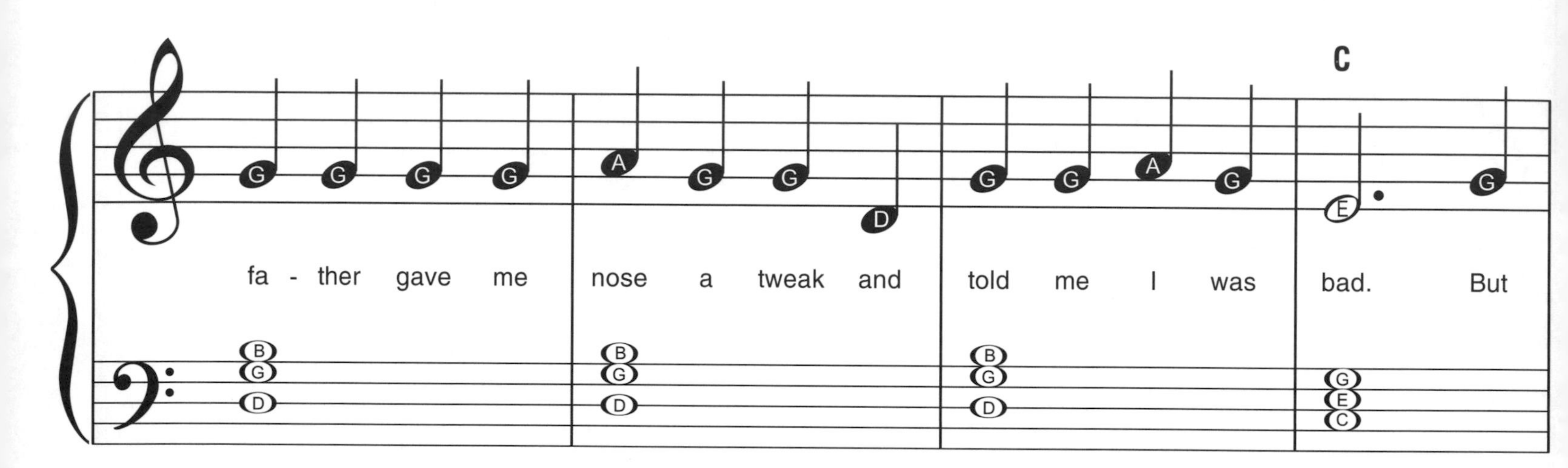

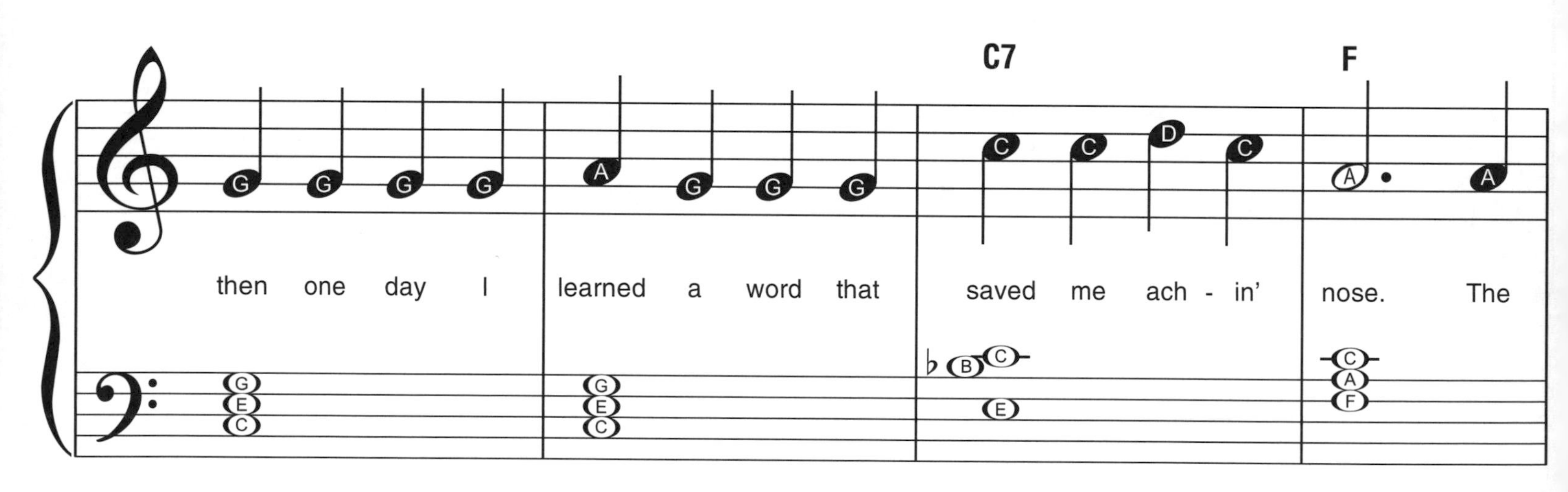

D.C. al Fine
(Return to beginning
and play to Fine)

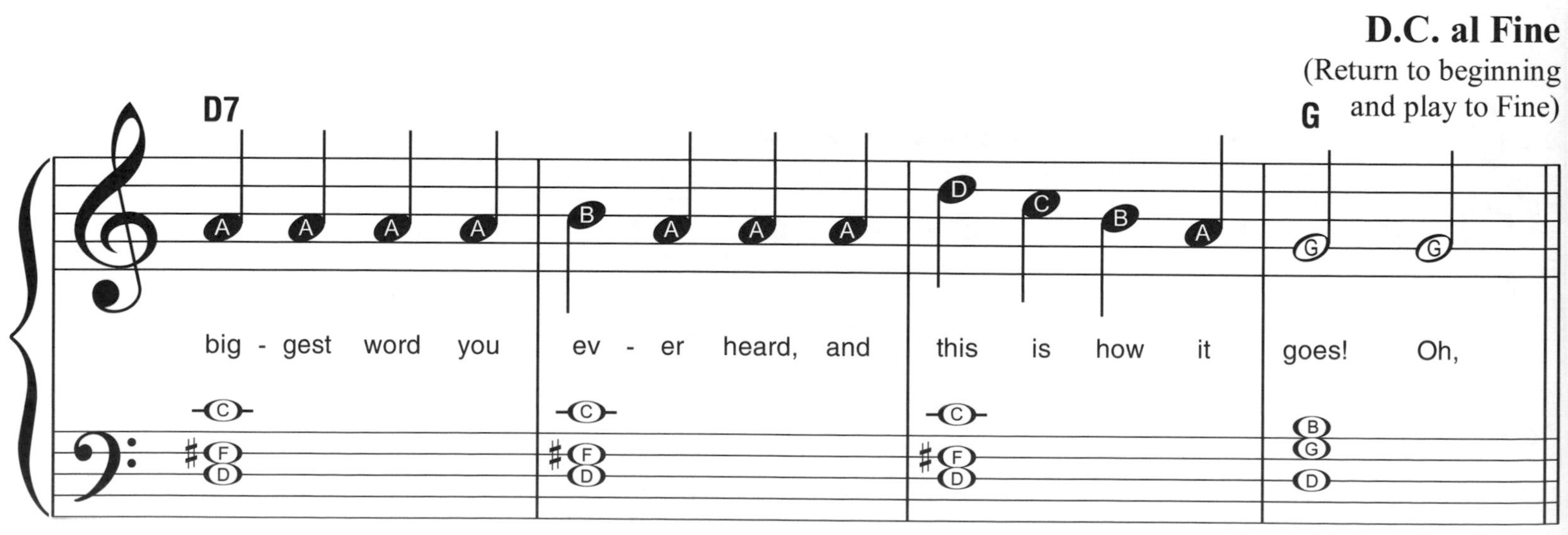

That's How You Know

from ENCHANTED

Music by Alan Menken
Lyrics by Stephen Schwartz

Moderately bright

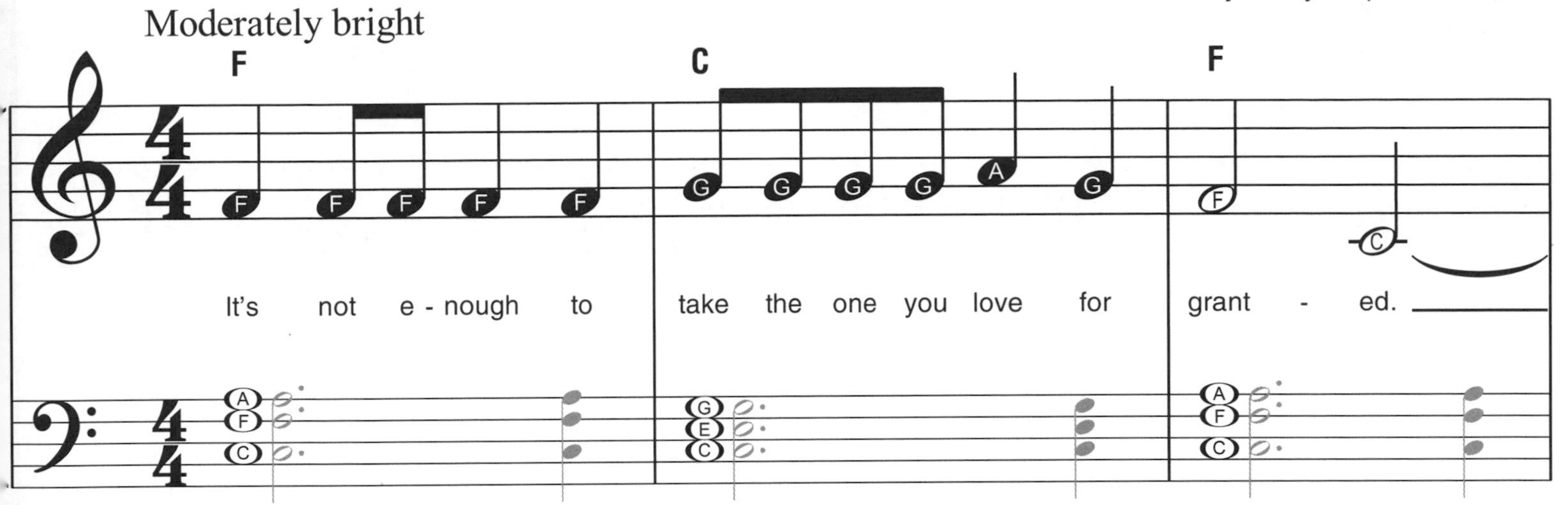

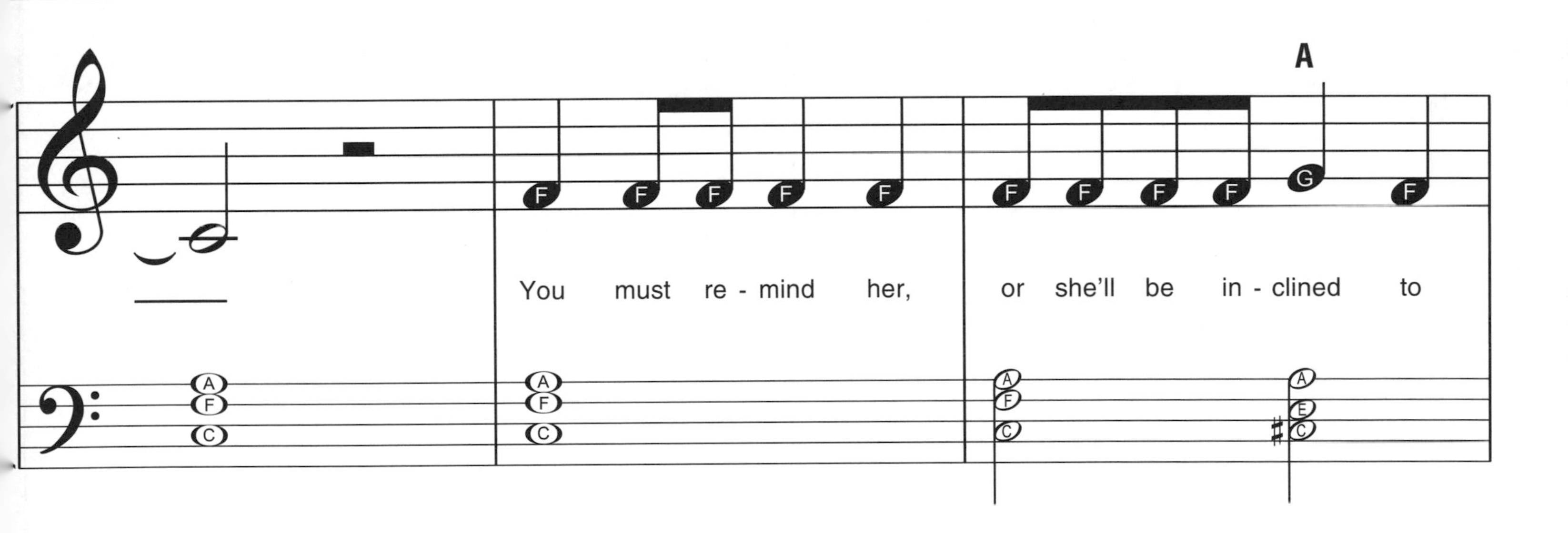

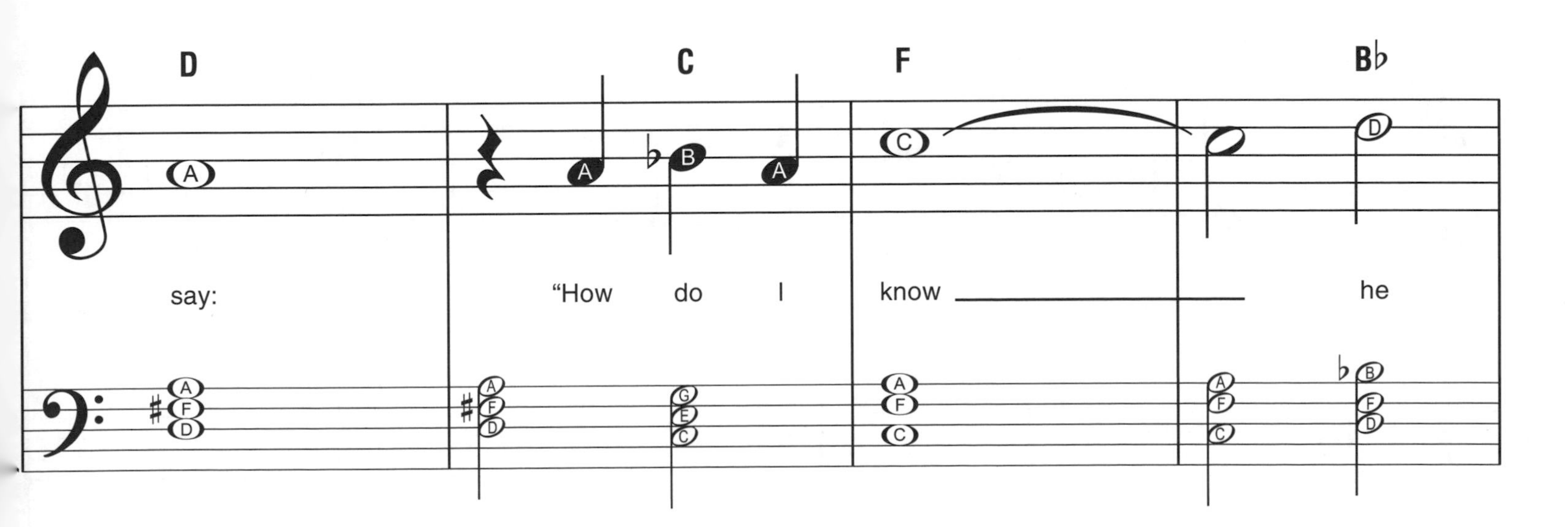

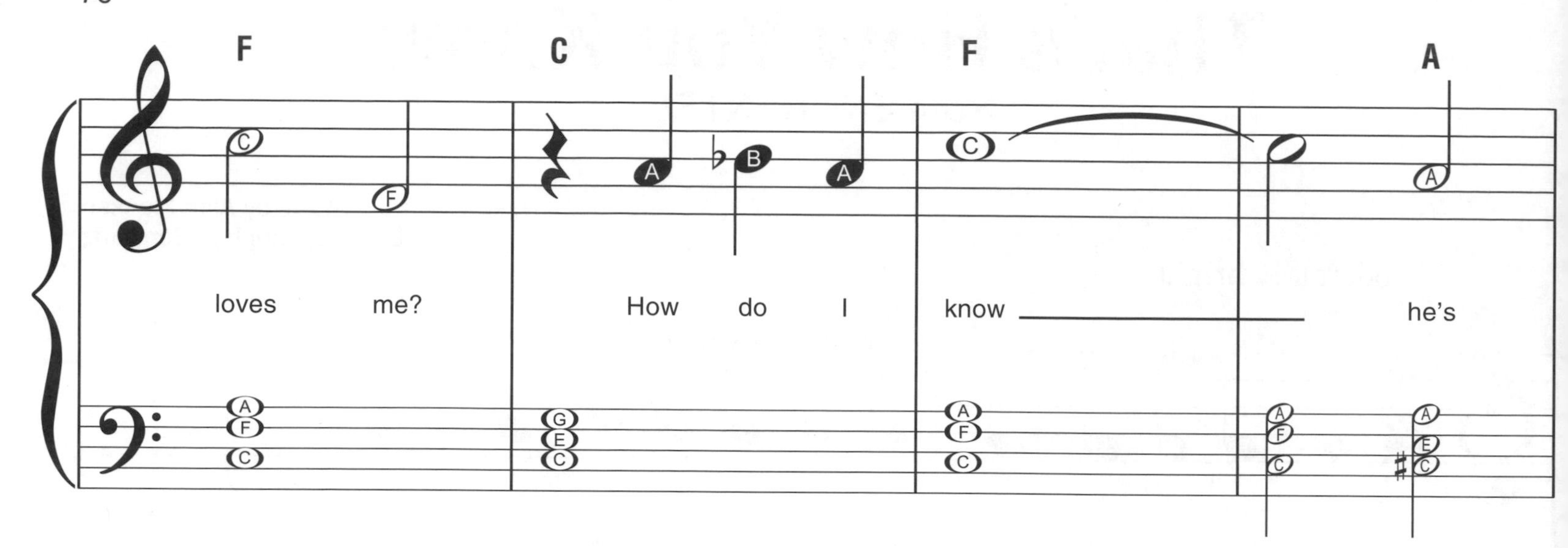
F
C
F
A
loves me? How do I know he's

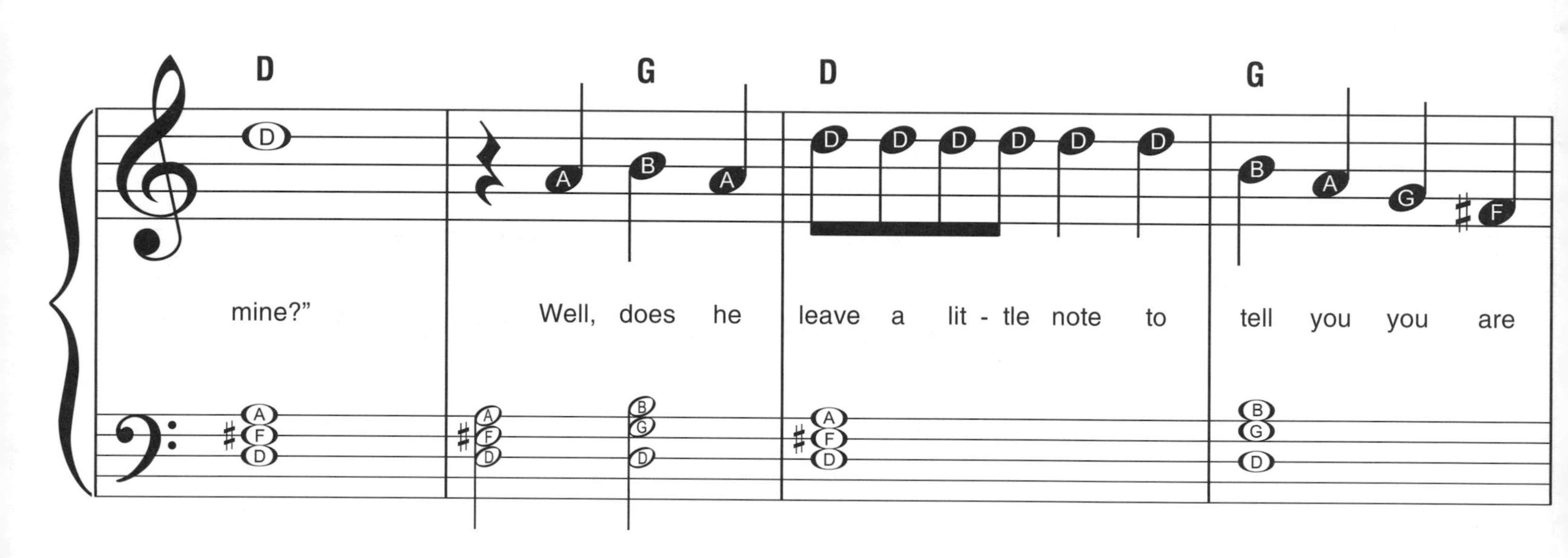
D
G
D
G
mine?" Well, does he leave a lit - tle note to tell you you are

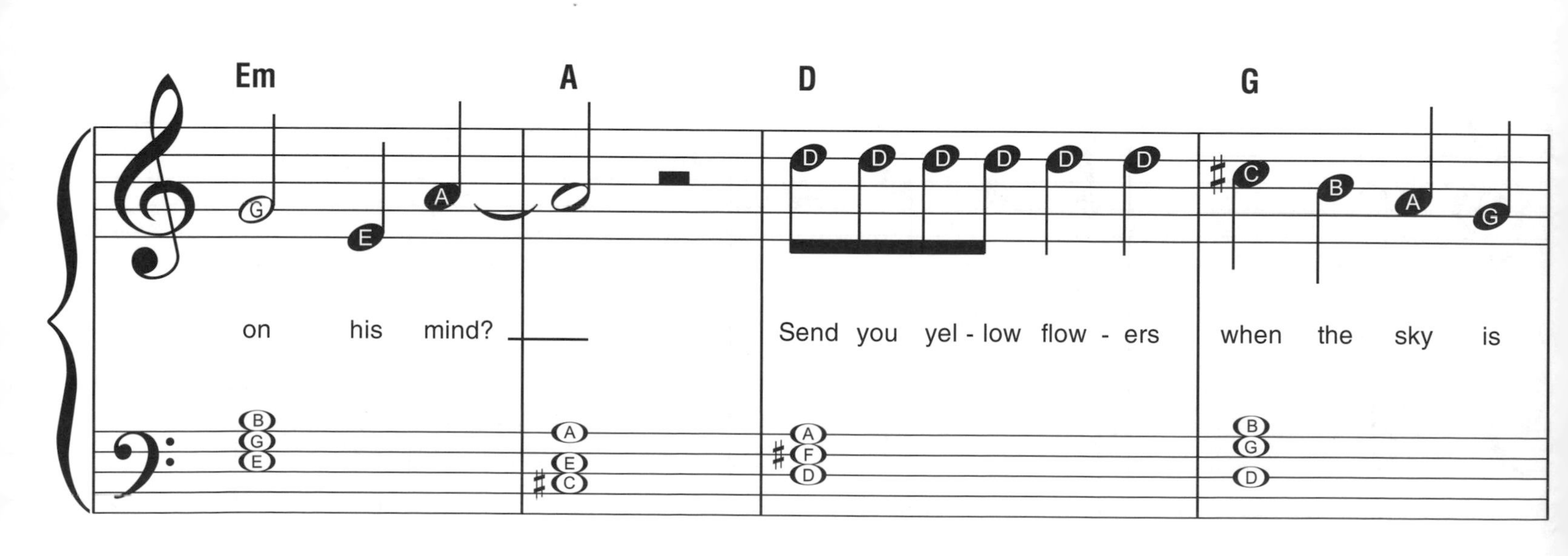
Em
A
D
G
on his mind? Send you yel - low flow - ers when the sky is

Em
A
F♯m
Bm
gray? Hey.
He'll find a new way to
show you a

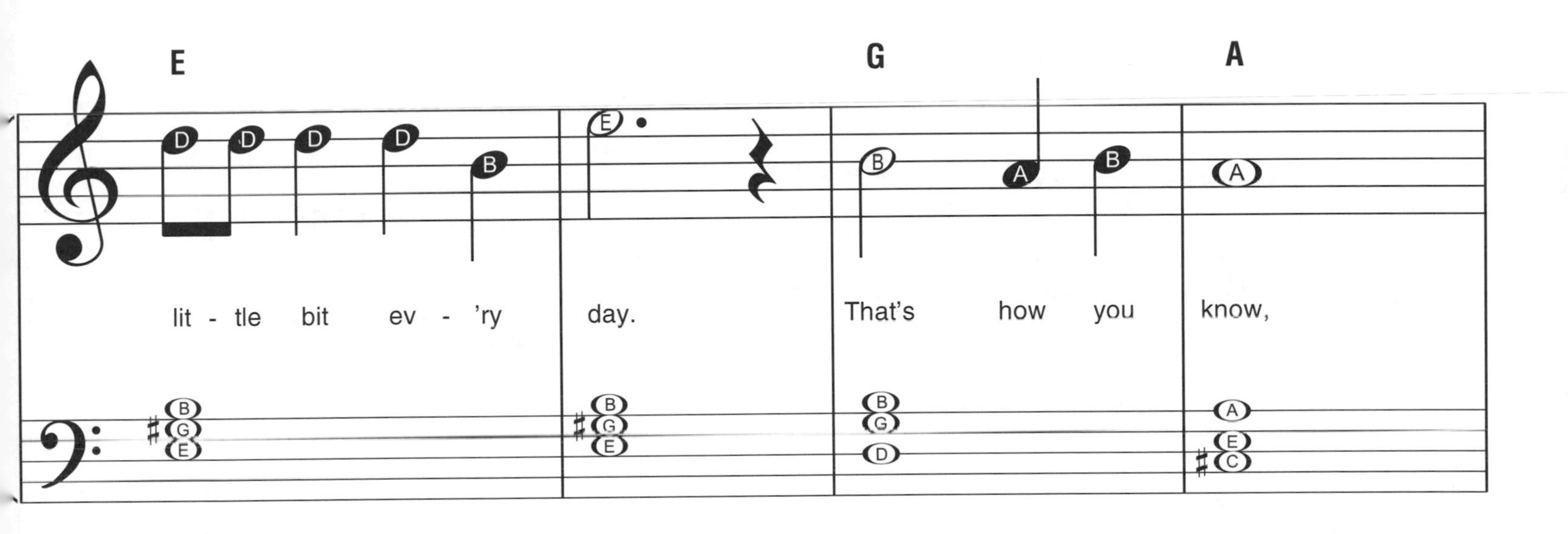
E
G
A
lit - tle bit ev - 'ry
day.
That's how you
know,

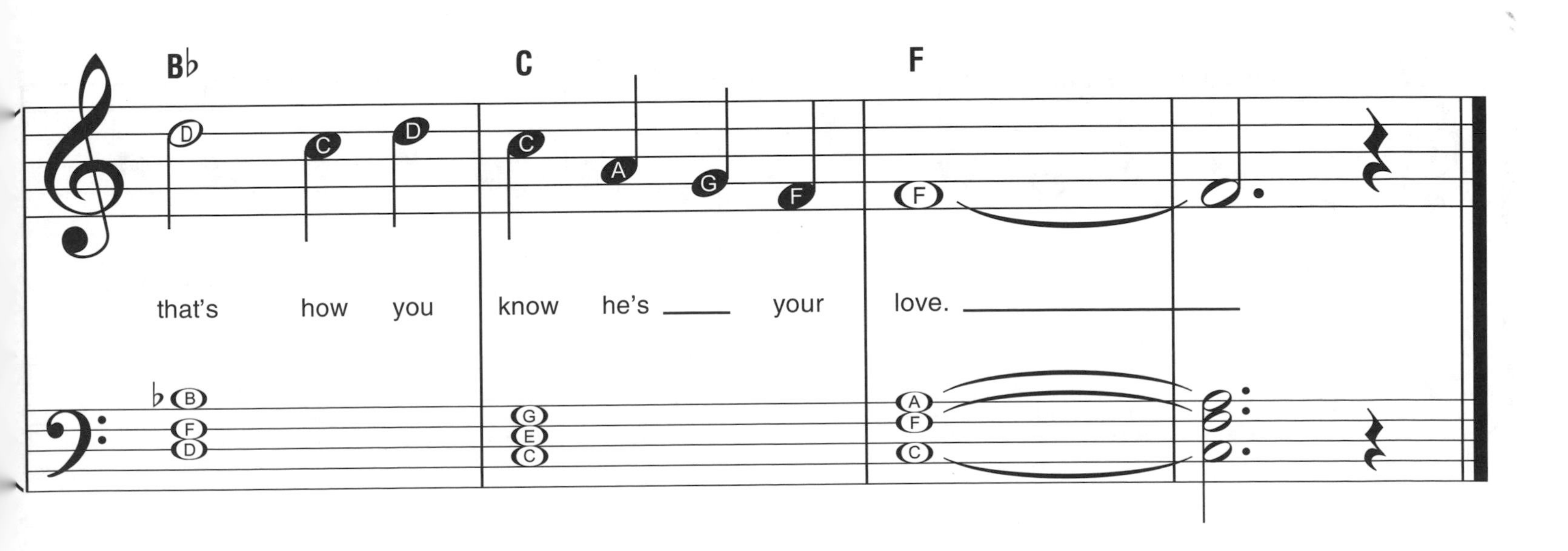
B♭
C
F
that's how you
know he's your
love.

When She Loved Me

from TOY STORY 2

Music and Lyrics by
Randy Newman

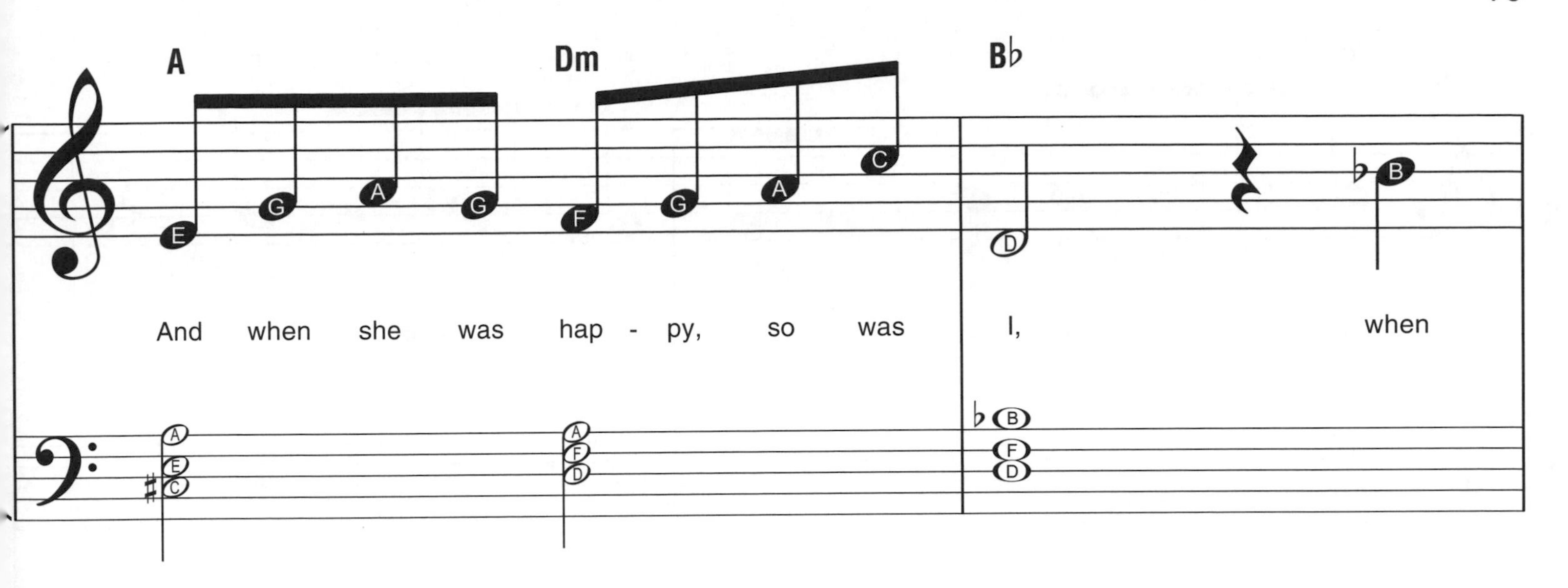
A
Dm
B♭
And when she was hap - py, so was I, when

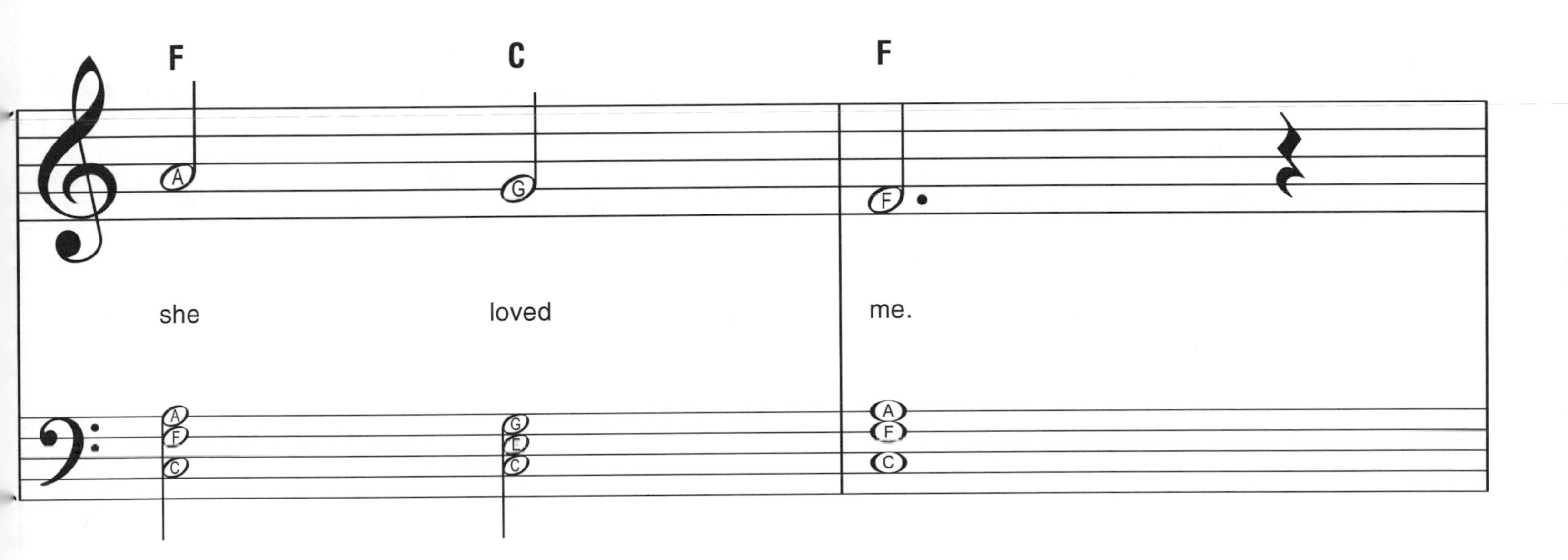
F
C
F
she loved me.

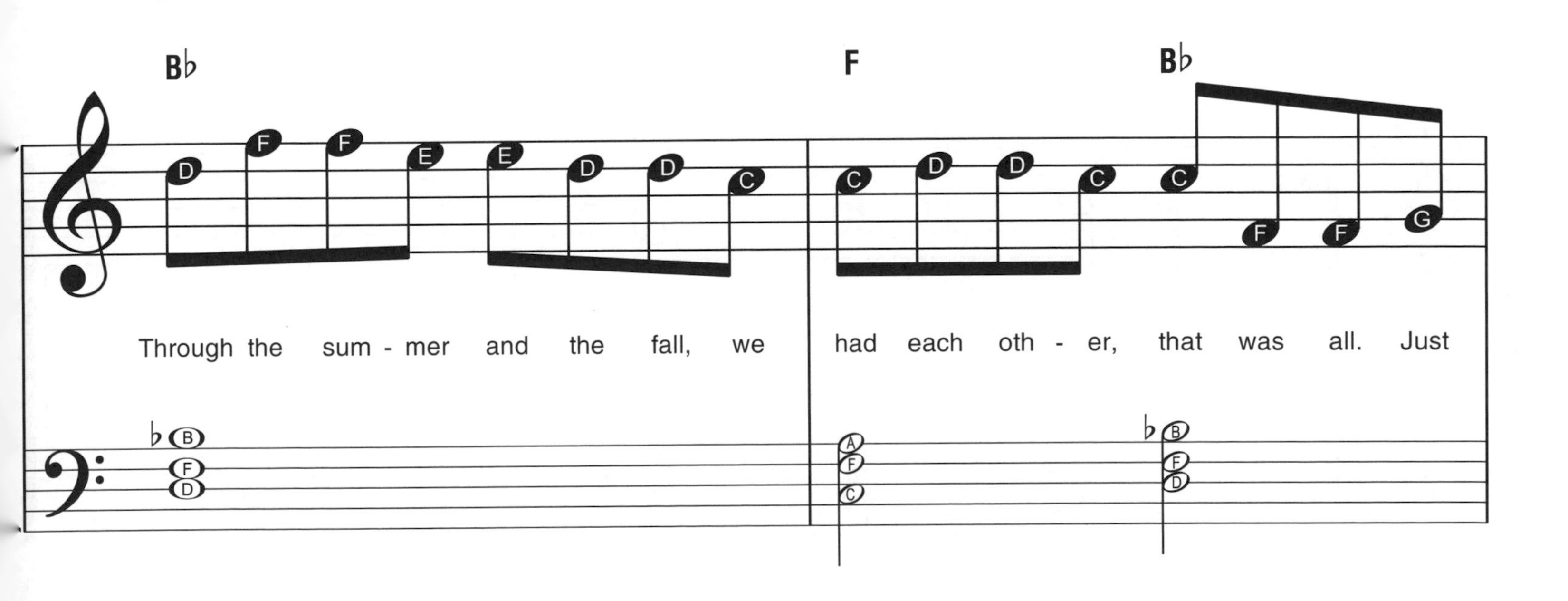
B♭
F
B♭
Through the sum - mer and the fall, we had each oth - er, that was all. Just

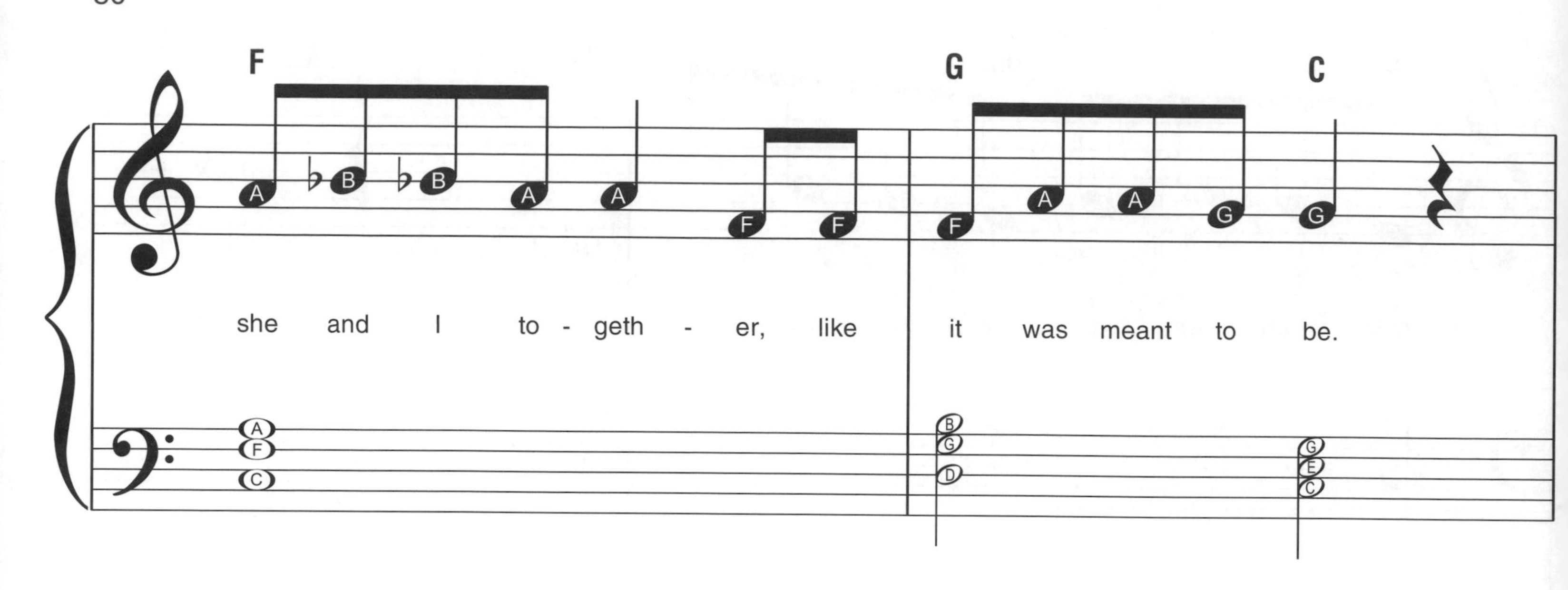
F
G
C
she and I to - geth - er, like
it was meant to be.

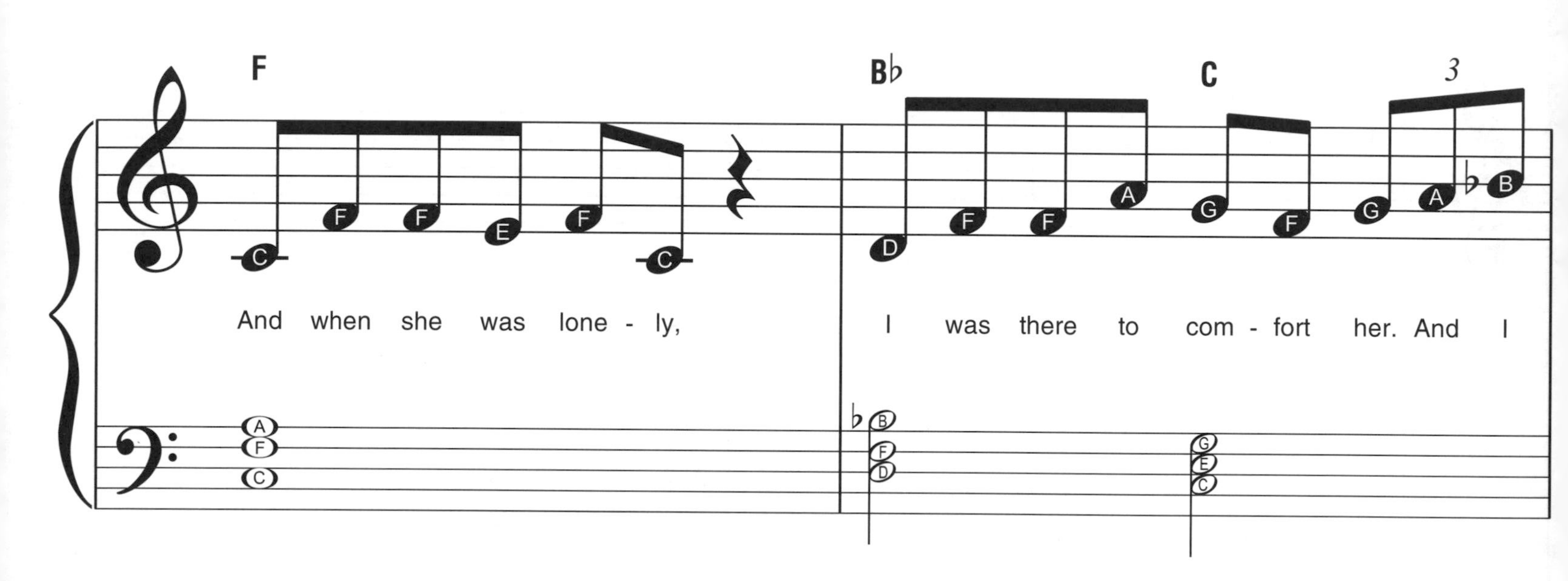
F
B♭
C
3
And when she was lone - ly,
I was there to com - fort her. And I

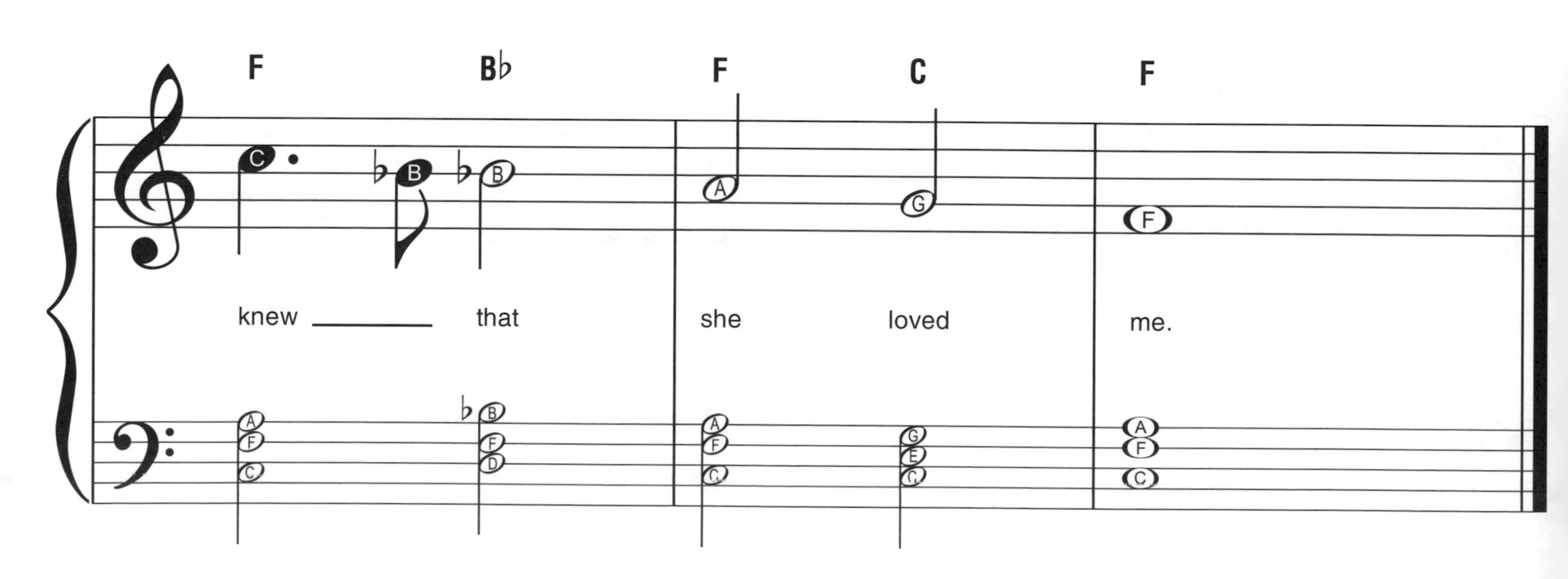
F
B♭
F
C
F
knew ______ that
she loved
me.

A Whole New World

from ALADDIN

Music by Alan Menken
Lyrics by Tim Rice

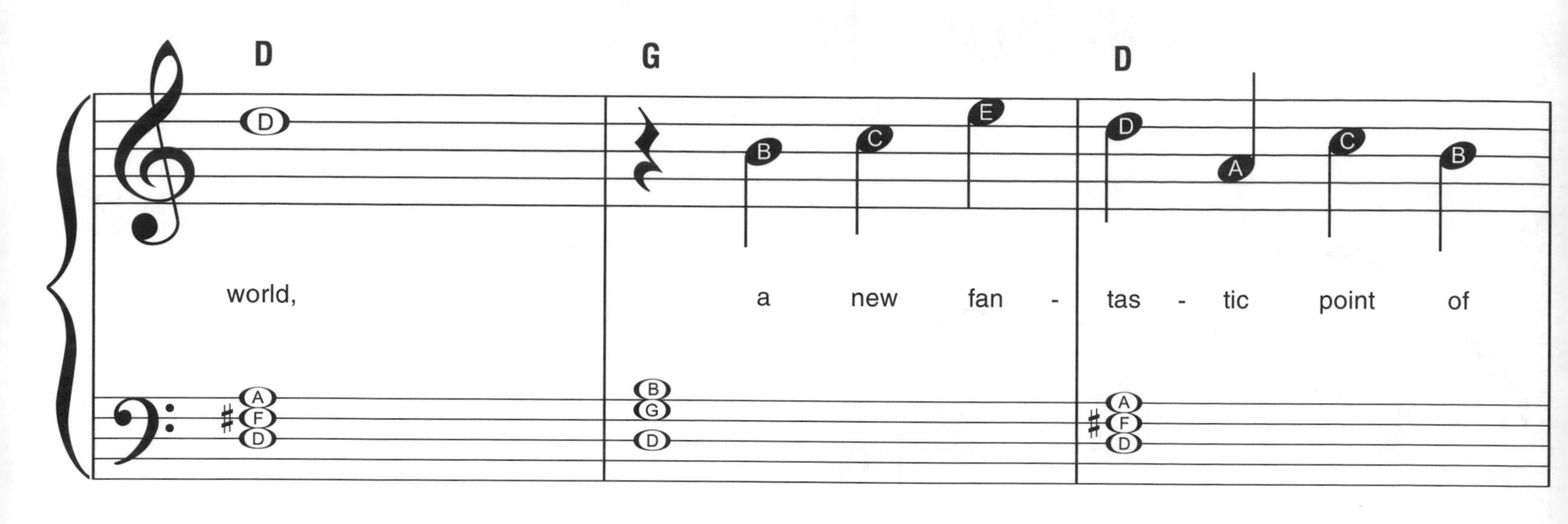
D
G
D
world,
a new fan - tas - tic point of

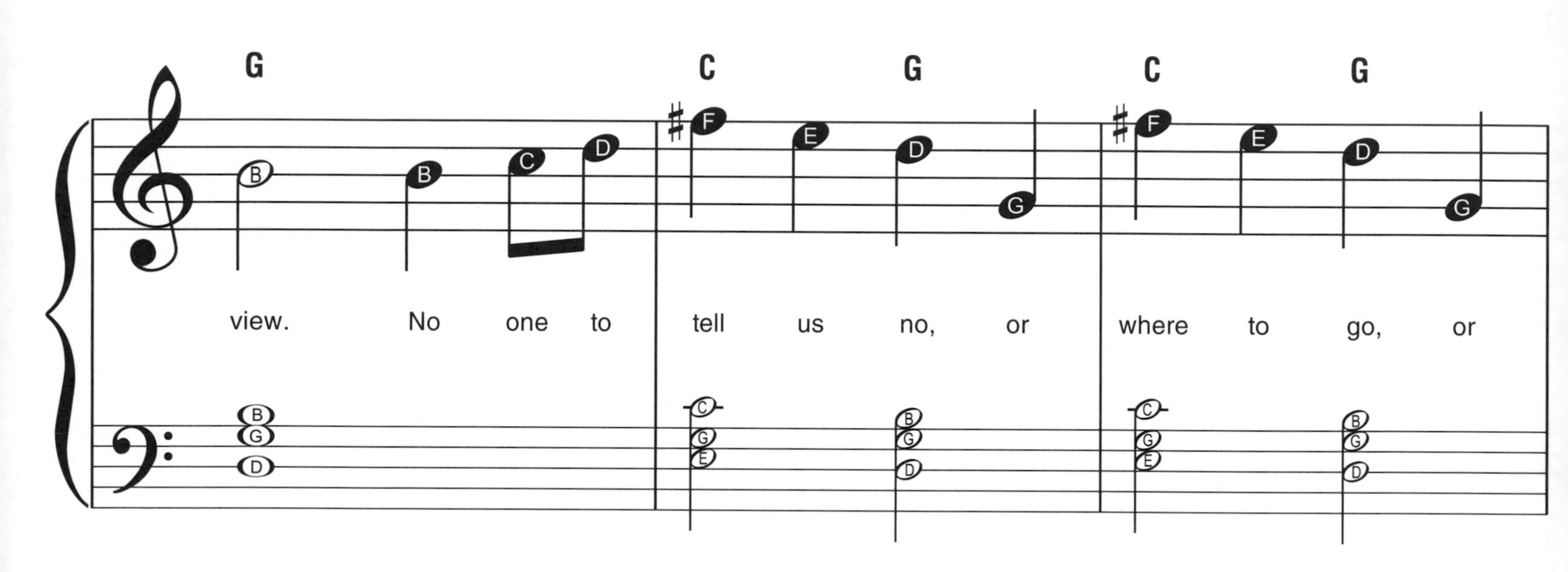
G
C
G
C
G
view. No one to tell us no, or where to go, or

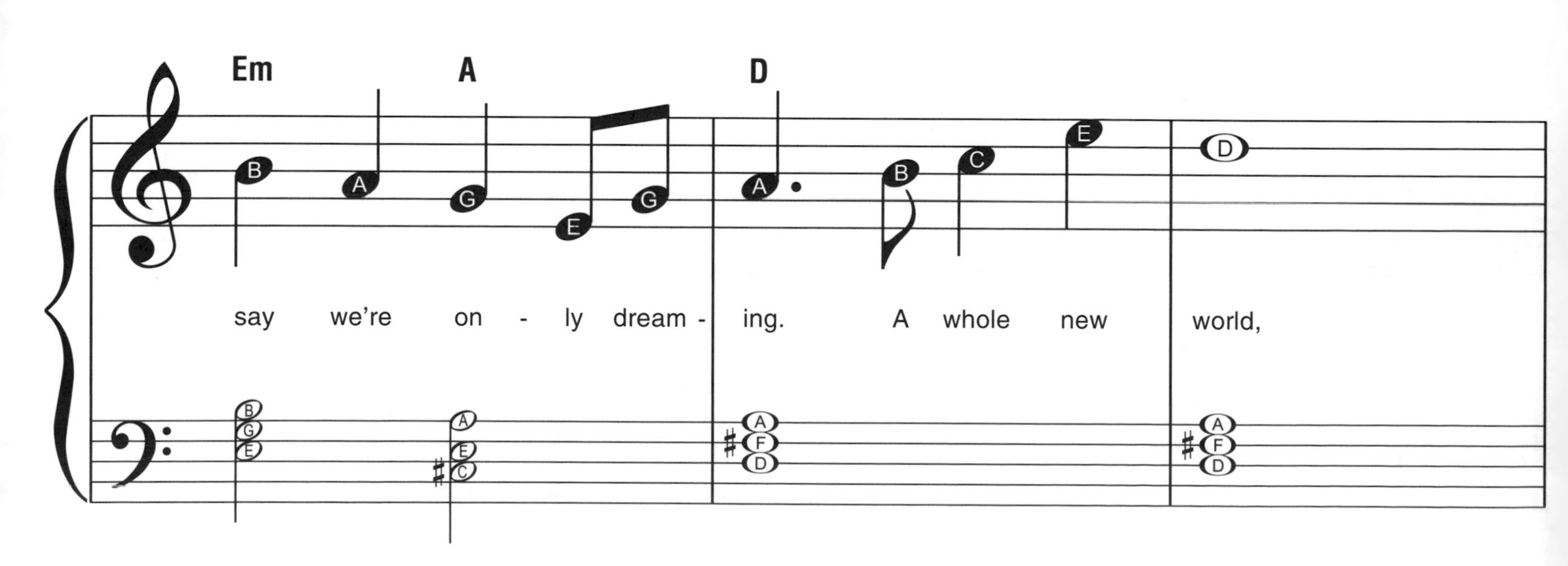
Em
A
D
say we're on - ly dream - ing. A whole new world,

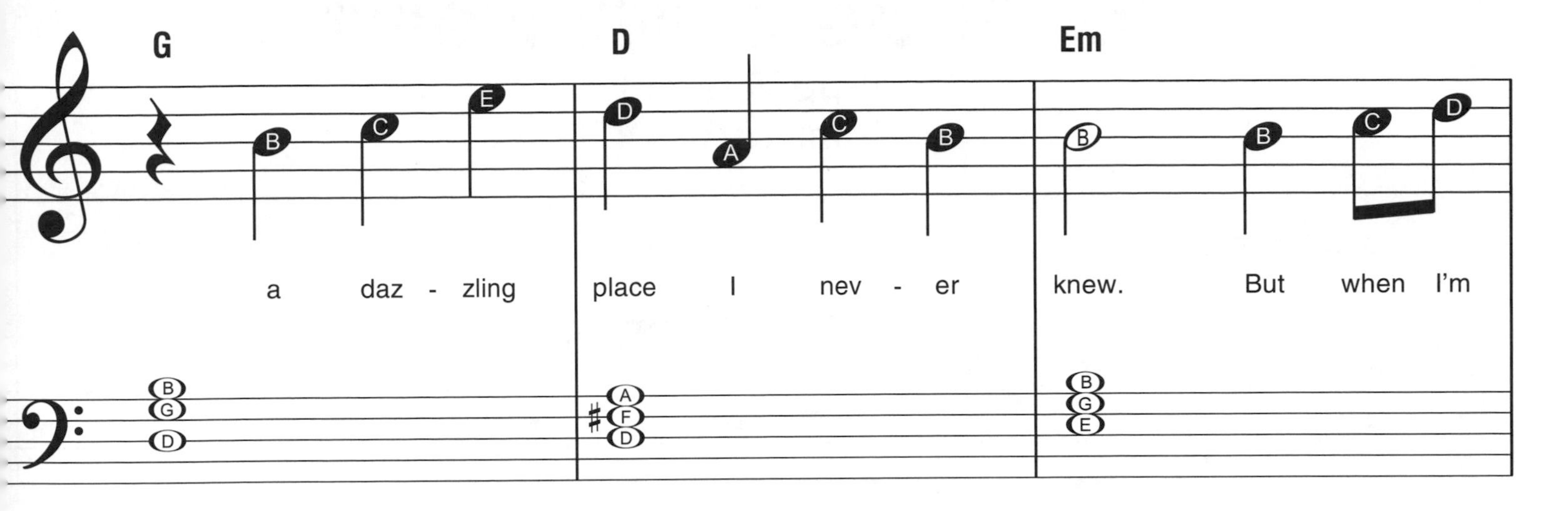
G
D
Em
a daz - zling
place I nev - er
knew. But when I'm

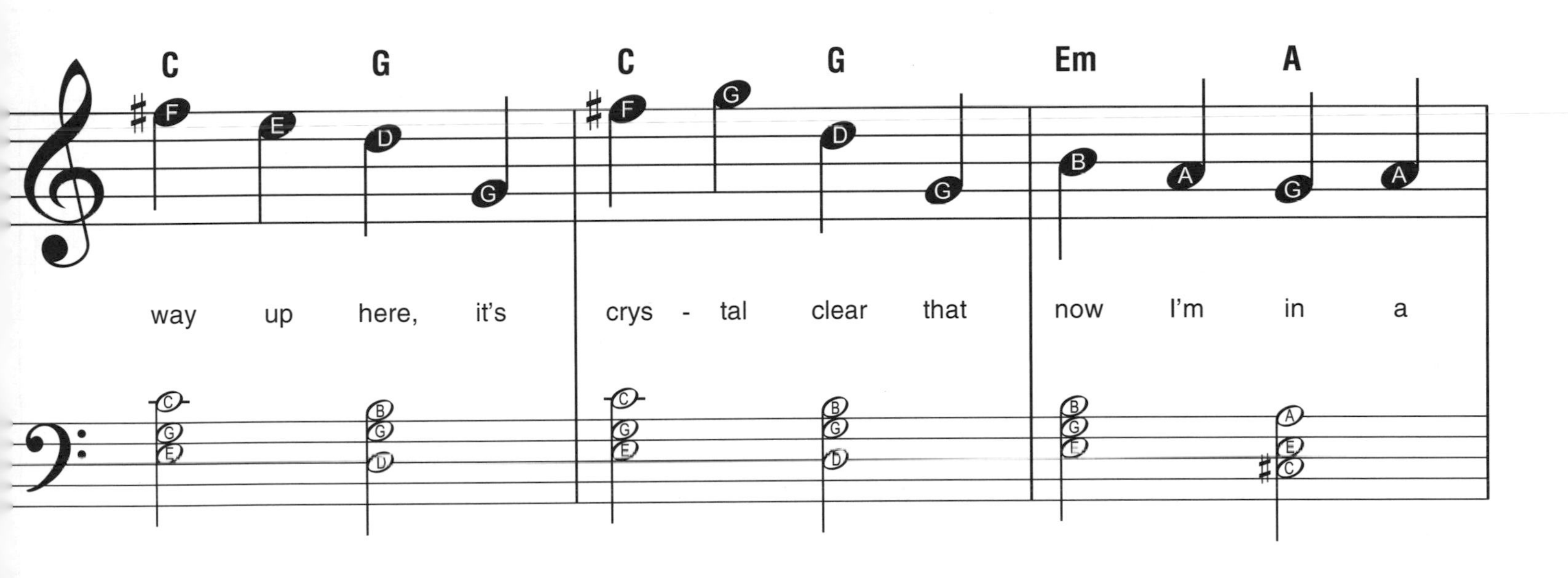
C
G
C
G
Em
A
way up here, it's
crys - tal clear that
now I'm in a

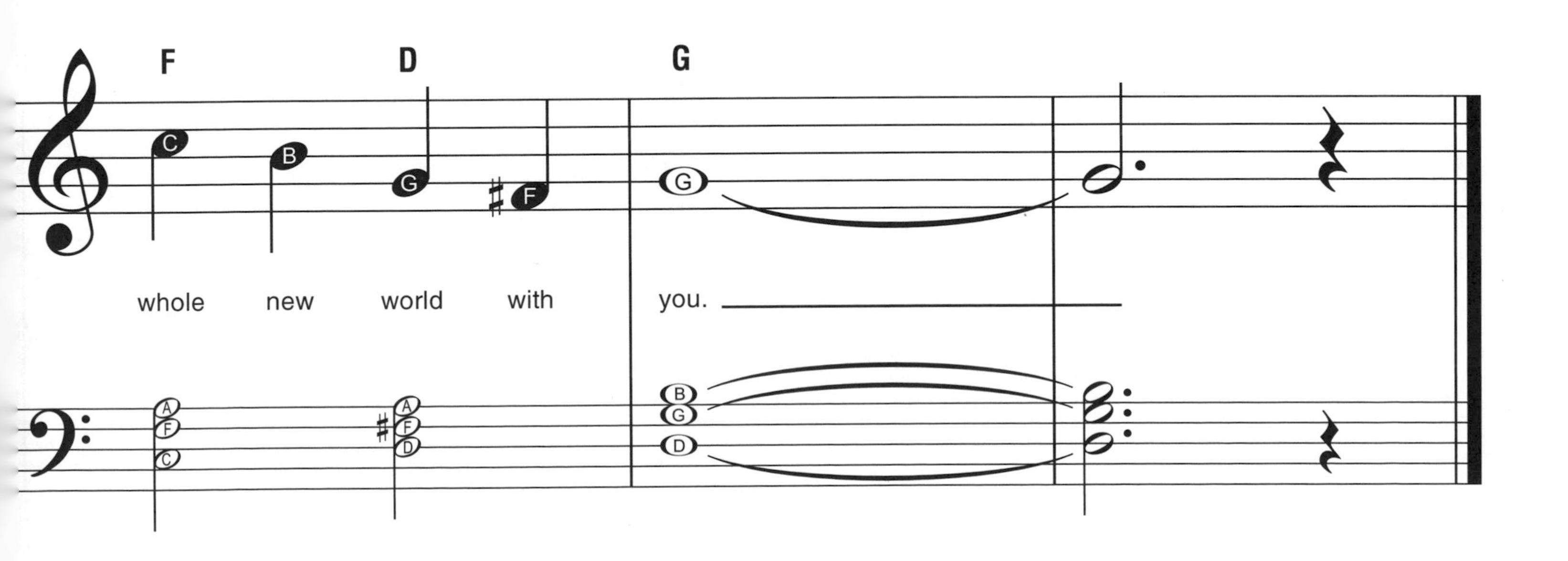
F
D
G
whole new world with
you.

You'll Be in My Heart
(Pop Version)
from TARZAN®

Words and Music by
Phil Collins

Moderately

F

Come, stop your cry - ing, it will be all right.

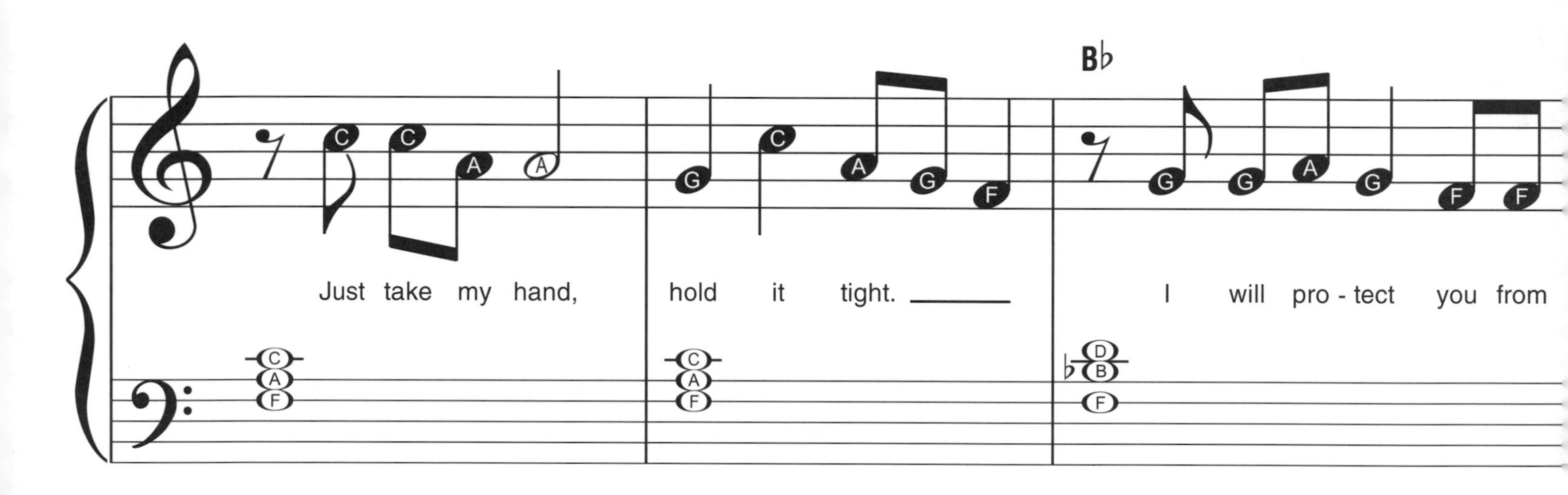

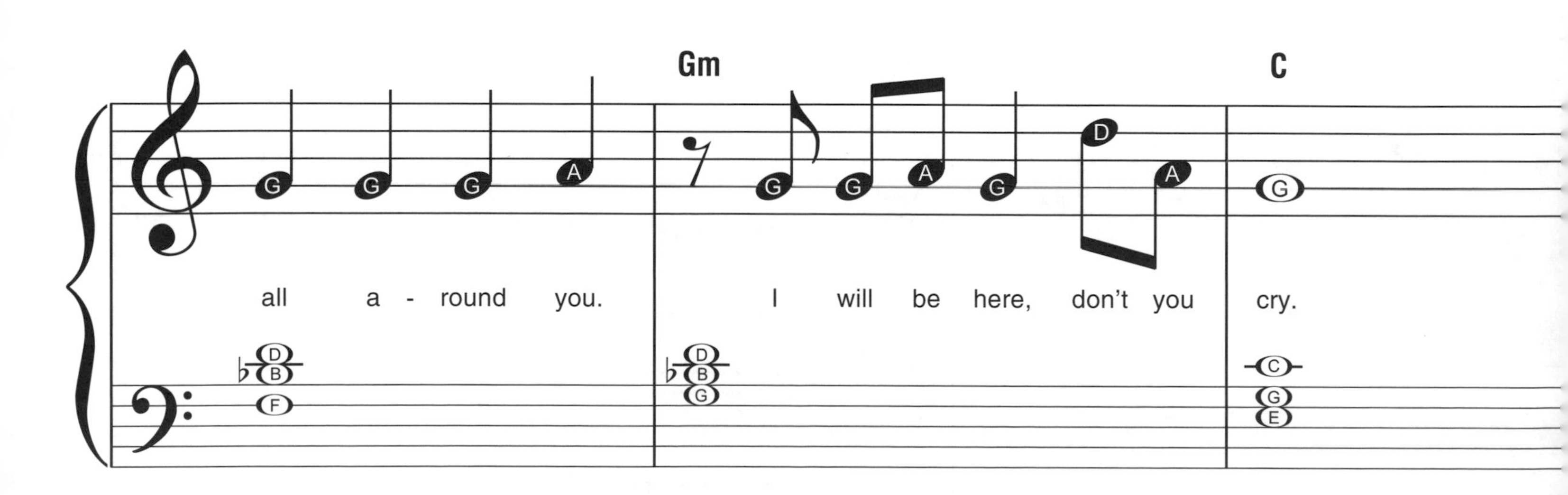

F
For one so small, you seem so strong. My arms will hold you, keep you
safe and warm. ______
B♭
This bond be - tween us can't be bro - ken.
Gm
I will be here; don't you
C A
cry. 'Cause
D
you'll be in my
G
heart, yes,
A
you'll be in my
F♯m
heart from

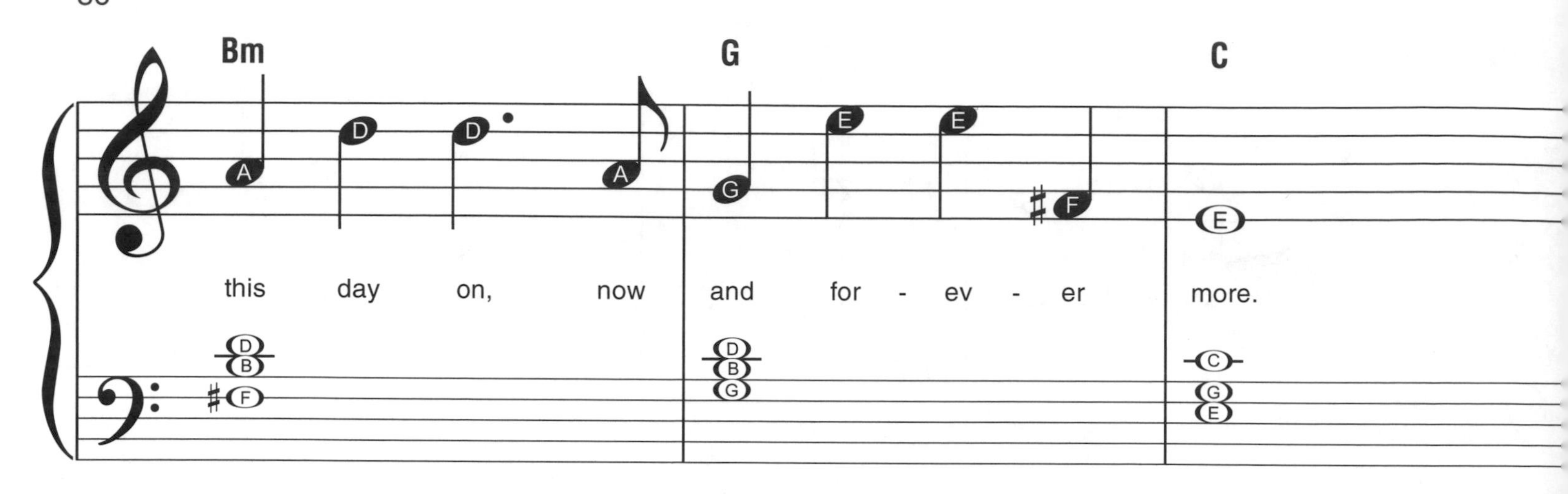
Bm
G
C
this day on, now and for - ev - er more.

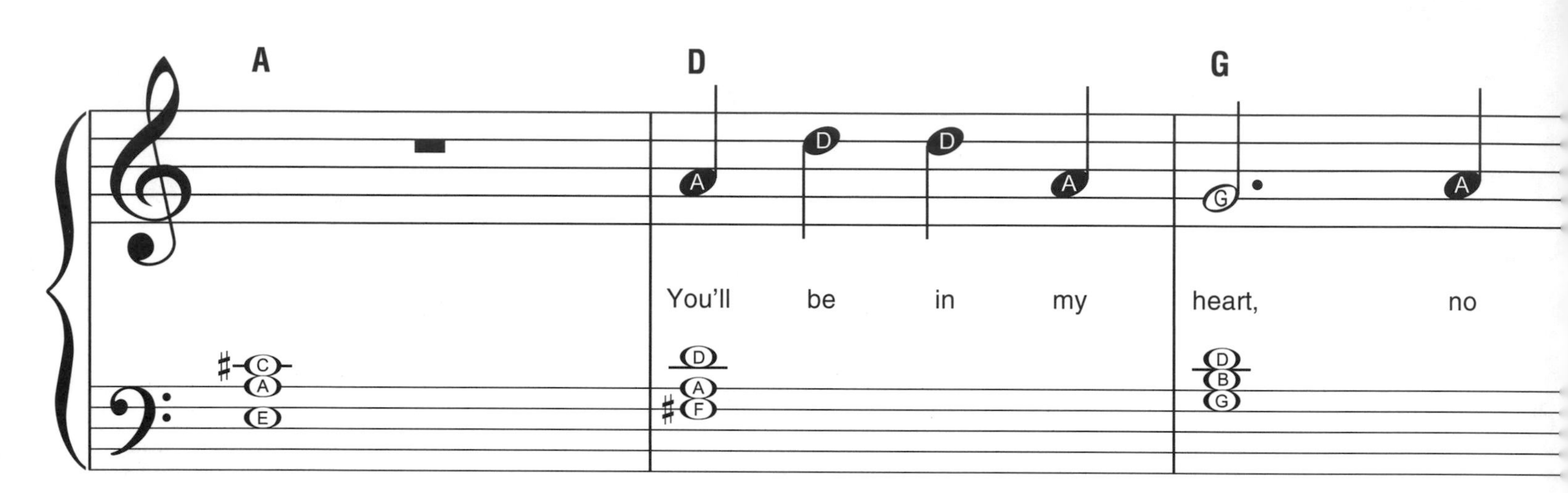
A
D
G
You'll be in my heart, no

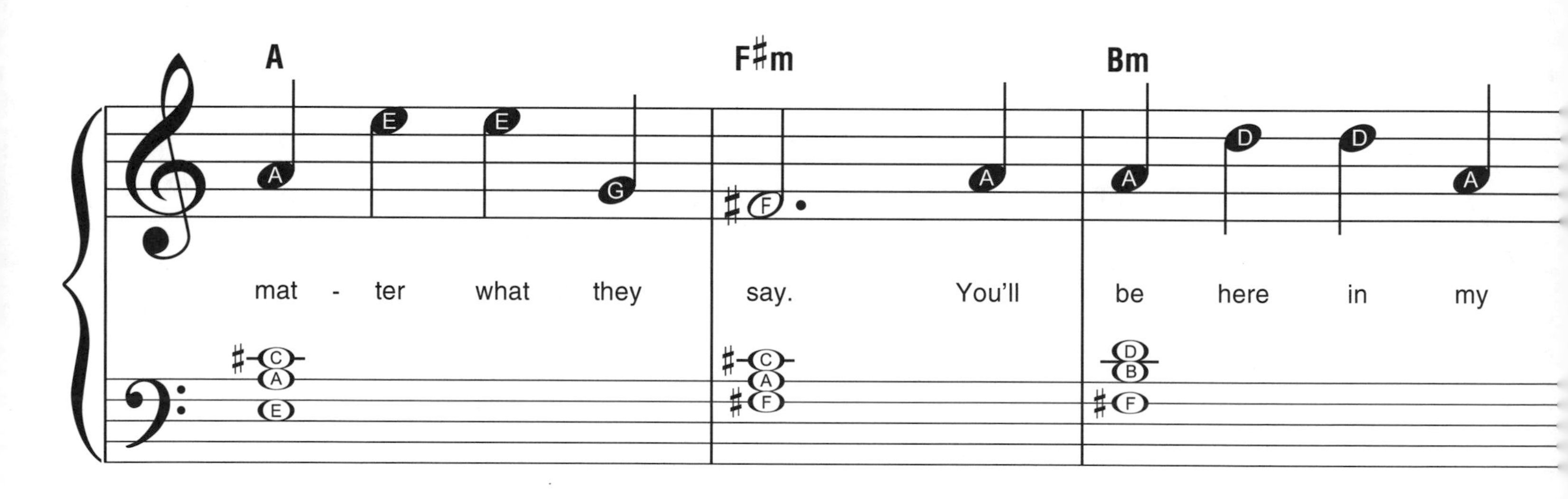
A
F♯m
Bm
mat - ter what they say. You'll be here in my

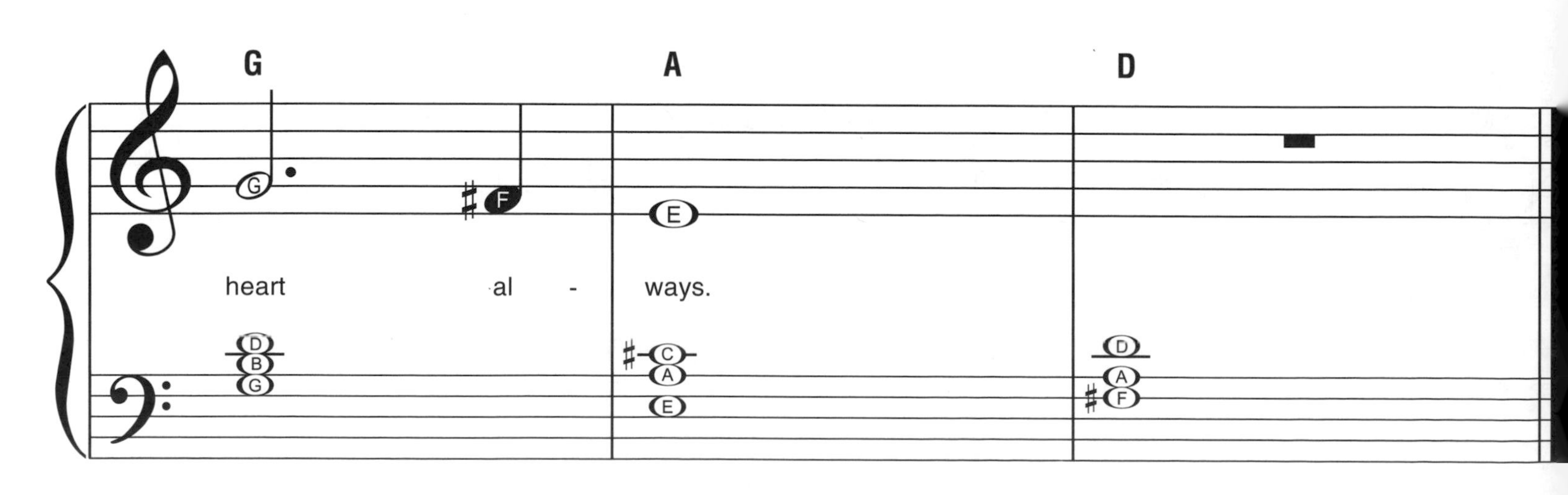
G
A
D
heart al - ways.

INSTANT Piano Songs

Audio Access Included

The ***Instant Piano Songs*** series will help you play your favorite songs quickly and easily — whether you use one hand or two! Start with the melody in your right hand, adding basic left-hand chords when you're ready. Letter names inside each note speed up the learning process, and optional rhythm patterns take your playing to the next level. Online backing tracks are also included. Stream or download the tracks using the unique code inside each book, then play along to build confidence and sound great!

THE BEATLES

All My Loving • Blackbird • Can't Buy Me Love • Eleanor Rigby • Get Back • Here, There and Everywhere • Hey Jude • I Will • Let It Be • Michelle • Nowhere Man • Ob-La-Di, Ob-La-Da • Penny Lane • When I'm Sixty-Four • With a Little Help from My Friends • Yesterday • and more.

00295926 Book/Online Audio $14.99

BROADWAY'S BEST

All I Ask of You • Bring Him Home • Defying Gravity • Don't Cry for Me Argentina • Edelweiss • Memory • The Music of the Night • On My Own • People • Seasons of Love • Send in the Clowns • She Used to Be Mine • Sunrise, Sunset • Tonight • Waving Through a Window • and more.

00323342 Book/Online Audio $14.99

CHRISTMAS CLASSICS

Angels We Have Heard on High • Away in a Manger • Deck the Hall • The First Noel • Good King Wenceslas • Hark! the Herald Angels Sing • Jingle Bells • Jolly Old St. Nicholas • Joy to the World • O Christmas Tree • Up on the Housetop • We Three Kings of Orient Are • We Wish You a Merry Christmas • What Child Is This? • and more.

00348326 Book/Online Audio $14.99

CHRISTMAS STANDARDS

All I Want for Christmas Is You • Christmas Time Is Here • Frosty the Snow Man • Grown-Up Christmas List • A Holly Jolly Christmas • I'll Be Home for Christmas • Jingle Bell Rock • The Little Drummer Boy • Mary, Did You Know? • Merry Christmas, Darling • Rudolph the Red-Nosed Reindeer • White Christmas • and more.

00294854 Book/Online Audio $14.99

CLASSICAL THEMES

Canon (Pachelbel) • Für Elise (Beethoven) • Jesu, Joy of Man's Desiring (Bach) • Jupiter (Holst) • Lullaby (Brahms) • Pomp and Circumstance (Elgar) • Spring (Vivaldi) • Symphony No. 9, Fourth Movement ("Ode to Joy") (Beethoven) • and more.

00283826 Book/Online Audio $14.99

DISNEY FAVORITES

Beauty and the Beast • Can You Feel the Love Tonight • Chim Chim Cher-ee • Colors of the Wind • A Dream Is a Wish Your Heart Makes • Friend Like Me • How Far I'll Go • It's a Small World • Kiss the Girl • Lava • Let It Go • Mickey Mouse March • Part of Your World • Reflection • Remember Me (Ernesto de la Cruz) • A Whole New World • You'll Be in My Heart (Pop Version) • and more.

00283720 Book/Online Audio $14.99

HITS OF 2010-2019

All About That Bass (Meghan Trainor) • All of Me (John Legend) • Can't Stop the Feeling (Justin Timberlake) • Happy (Pharrell Williams) • Hey, Soul Sister (Train) • Just the Way You Are (Bruno Mars) • Rolling in the Deep (Adele) • Shallow (Lady Gaga & Bradley Cooper) • Shake It Off (Taylor Swift) • Shape of You (Ed Sheeran) • and more.

00345364 Book/Online Audio $14.99

KIDS' POP SONGS

Adore You (Harry Styles) • Cool Kids (AJR) • Drivers License (Olivia Rodrigo) • How Far I'll Go (from Moana) • A Million Dreams (from The Greatest Showman) • Ocean Eyes (Billie Eilish) • Shake It Off (Taylor Swift) • What Makes You Beautiful (One Direction) • and more.

00371694 Book/Online Audio $14.99

MOVIE SONGS

As Time Goes By • City of Stars • Endless Love • Hallelujah • I Will Always Love You • Laura • Moon River • My Heart Will Go on (Love Theme from 'Titanic') • Over the Rainbow • Singin' in the Rain • Skyfall • Somewhere Out There • Stayin' Alive • Tears in Heaven • Unchained Melody • Up Where We Belong • The Way We Were • What a Wonderful World • and more.

00283718 Book/Online Audio $14.99

POP HITS

All of Me • Chasing Cars • Despacito • Feel It Still • Havana • Hey, Soul Sister • Ho Hey • I'm Yours • Just Give Me a Reason • Love Yourself • Million Reasons • Perfect • Riptide • Shake It Off • Stay with Me • Thinking Out Loud • Viva La Vida • What Makes You Beautiful • and more.

00283825 Book/Online Audio $15.99

SONGS FOR KIDS

Do-Re-Mi • Hakuna Matata • It's a Small World • On Top of Spaghetti • Puff the Magic Dragon • The Rainbow Connection • SpongeBob SquarePants Theme Song • Take Me Out to the Ball Game • Tomorrow • The Wheels on the Bus • Won't You Be My Neighbor? (It's a Beautiful Day in the Neighborhood) • You Are My Sunshine • and more.

00323352 Book/Online Audio $15.99

www.halleonard.com

0721
019